The Therapeutic Alliance In Brief Psychotherapy

The

Therapeutic

Alliance In Brief

Psychotherapy

Edited By
Jeremy D. Safran and
J. Christopher Muran

American Psychological Association
Washington, DC

Published by
American Psychological Association
750 First Street, NE
Washington, DC 20002

Copies may be ordered from
APA Order Department
P.O. Box 92984
Washington, DC 20090-2984

In the United Kingdom and Europe, copies may be ordered from
American Psychological Association
3 Henrietta Street
Covent Garden
London WC2E 8LU
England

Typeset in Meridien by Harlowe Typography, Inc., Cottage City, MD

Printer: Data Reproductions Corp., Auburn Hills, MI
Jacket designer: Design Concepts, San Diego, CA
Cover sculpture artist: Annette Hansen, awkndrm@juno.com
Technical/production editor: Marianne Maggini

Library of Congress Cataloging-in-Publication Data
The therapeutic alliance in brief psychotherapy / edited by Jeremy D. Safran
    and J. Christopher Muran.
        p.   cm.
    Includes bibliographical references and index.
    ISBN 1-55798-508-1 (casebound : alk. paper)
    1. Therapeutic alliance.   2. Brief psychotherapy.
3. Psychoanalysis.   4. Psychotherapist and patient. I. Safran,
Jeremy D. II. Muran, J. Christopher.
RC489.T66T47   1998
616.89' 14—dc21   98-16497
                                                        CIP

British Library Cataloguing-in-Publication Data
A CIP record is available from the British Library.

Printed in the United States of America
First edition

Contents

LIST OF CONTRIBUTORS *vii*
PREFACE *ix*

1

*Negotiating the Therapeutic Alliance in Brief
Psychotherapy: An Introduction* 3

J. Christopher Muran and Jeremy D. Safran

2

*The Therapeutic Alliance in Brief Psychoanalytic
Psychotherapy: A Drive–Conflict Perspective* 15

Harold Been and Arnold Winston

3

*The Therapeutic Alliance in the Relational Models of
Time-Limited Dynamic Psychotherapy* 39

Jeffrey L. Binder

4

*Functional Analytic Psychotherapy, the Therapeutic
Alliance, and Brief Psychotherapy* 63

Barbara S. Kohlenberg, Elizabeth A. Yeater, and
Robert J. Kohlenberg

5

*The Therapeutic Relationship and Alliance in Short-Term
Cognitive Therapy* 95

Cory F. Newman

6

The Therapeutic Alliance in Short-Term Humanistic and Experiential Therapies 123

Jeanne C. Watson and Leslie S. Greenberg

7

The Therapeutic Alliance in Brief Strategic Therapy 147

James C. Coyne and Carolyn M. Pepper

8

Perspectives on the Therapeutic Alliance in Brief Couples and Family Therapy 171

Douglas S. Rait

9

The Alliance in Time-Limited Group Psychotherapy 193

K. Roy MacKenzie

10

The Therapeutic Alliance in Brief Psychotherapy: General Principles 217

Jeremy D. Safran and J. Christopher Muran

INDEX   231

ABOUT THE EDITORS   237

Contributors

Harold Been, Beth Israel Medical Center and Albert Einstein College of Medicine, New York City

Jeffrey L. Binder, Georgia School of Professional Psychology, Atlanta, GA

James C. Coyne, University of Michigan Medical Center, Ann Arbor

Leslie S. Greenberg, York University, North York, Ontario, Canada

Barbara S. Kohlenberg, Reno Veterans Affairs Medical Center and University of Nevada School of Medicine, Reno

Robert J. Kohlenberg, University of Washington, Seattle

K. Roy MacKenzie, University of British Columbia, Vancouver, British Columbia, Canada

J. Christopher Muran, Beth Israel Medical Center and Albert Einstein College of Medicine, New York City

Cory F. Newman, University of Pennsylvania, Philadelphia

Carolyn M. Pepper, University of Michigan Medical Center, Ann Arbor

Douglas S. Rait, Palo Alto Veterans Affairs Medical Center and Stanford University School of Medicine, Palo Alto, CA

Jeremy D. Safran, New School for Social Research and Beth Israel Medical Center, New York City

Jeanne C. Watson, Ontario Institute for Studies in Education at the University of Toronto, Ontario, Canada

Arnold Winston, Beth Israel Medical Center and Albert Einstein College of Medicine, New York City

Elizabeth A. Yeater, University of Nevada, Reno

Preface

The objective of this book is to provide an in-depth examination of the way in which the therapeutic alliance is conceptualized and negotiated in the major contemporary approaches to brief psychotherapy. In recent years a variety of social, political, and economic factors have led to a tremendous surge of interest in the brief treatments. At the same time, there is a growing acceptance by all therapeutic orientations of the centrality of the therapeutic relationship to the change process. This acceptance has been influenced by the consistent empirical finding that the quality of the therapeutic alliance is the best predictor of outcome across a range of different approaches to therapy.

Much of the research demonstrating the importance of the therapeutic alliance has been conducted in the context of short-term therapy protocols. Ironically, however, there has been no systematic attempt to think about the alliance in a fashion that is specific to short-term therapy. Nor has there been a systematic attempt to clarify differences in the type of alliance necessary to conduct short- versus long-term therapy or the unique parameters bearing on the development and negotiation of the alliance in short-term therapy. Examples of such parameters are the need to maintain and establish a therapeutic focus early in treatment, the need to agree upon limited and circumscribed therapeutic goals, the need to take separation and termination issues into account throughout the treatment, the likelihood that the therapist will be more active than in many long-term approaches, and the absence of a long-term context in which to work through problems in the alliance or to promote treatment generalization.

Parameters of this type establish a context in which relationship issues between therapists and patients will be played out. For example, the need to establish a therapeutic focus early in treatment may on one hand facilitate the development of the alliance and on the other result in premature formulations. The imminence of treatment termination throughout the therapy brings to the forefront questions such as to what extent the patient can open up, trust, and depend on the therapist. The high level of therapist activity may be experienced by some patients as supportive and by others as intrusive. In this book, prominent representatives of the major brief therapy traditions have been asked to think about the ways such parameters influence the development of the therapeutic alliance in their approaches and to spell out the considerations relevant to developing and negotiating the alliance over the course of treatment.

Traditionally, there have been two general approaches toward the alliance in the psychoanalytic tradition. Practitioners of classical or drive–conflict theories, although very much interested in the alliance, have tended to view it as a necessary, but not sufficient, condition for change. Therapists who practice interpersonal and relational approaches have, on the other hand, tended to view the negotiation of the alliance as being at the heart of the change process.

Experiential and humanistic approaches blend more than one thread as well. On the one hand, there is the Rogerian influence, which specifies that therapist empathy, congruence, and unconditional positive regard are the core therapeutic ingredients. This places the therapeutic alliance, albeit a particular version of it, squarely in the middle of the change equation. These approaches are also influenced by Buber's I–Thou philosophy, a subtle and complex notion, which also places relational factors at the center of the therapeutic encounter. On the other hand, there are active interventions, such as those deriving from Gestalt therapy, which require a strong therapeutic alliance as a background and which place particular demands on the type of alliance that is negotiated.

Strategic, couples, and family therapies have traditionally been short term in nature. For the most part little has been written explicitly about the alliance in these approaches. Nevertheless, they are very much concerned with the skillful negotiation of the therapist–patient relationship in order to influence patients therapeutically. In couples and family therapies, the negotiation of the alliance is in some respects more complex than in individual treatment. It becomes necessary to think in both individual and systemic terms in that the therapist must negotiate a relationship to each individual within the system as well as with the system as a whole. The therapist also needs to understand the alliances between individual members of the system. Group therapy shares this level of complexity. An important difference, however, is that whereas the couples or family therapist becomes a member of an already existing system, the group therapist typically begins at the inception of the group. He or she thus has more potential opportunity to influence the development of the various alliances from the beginning.

Cognitive and behavioral approaches have traditionally placed less emphasis on the therapeutic relationship in general than either psychoanalytic or humanistic approaches. In their own ways, however, they are focused on dimensions relevant to the alliance. Examples include the articulation of clear therapeutic rationales, collaborative goal setting, and the skillful management of expectancy effects. In addition, more recent developments in both cognitive and behavioral approaches utilize the therapeutic relationship as an active ingredient of change.

We hope this brief preamble sets the stage for what is to come. We leave the more detailed exploration of the ways in which various short-term parameters intersect with the conceptualization and negotiation of the therapeutic alliance to the contributors. Our own interests in the intersection of these two themes are in some respects the mirror image of the implicit way in which the alliance is dealt with in some short-term approaches. The therapeutic alliance has been in the foreground of our theoretical and empirical work, while the short-term aspects of treatment have been background. Like many psychotherapy researchers, we have conducted most of our research using short-term protocols, not so much because we are intrinsically interested in brief treatment, but because it lends itself more easily to research. Over time, the short-term nature of our research treatments has inevitably shaped our thinking about the alliance, no doubt in ways of which we are not completely aware.

The inspiration for this book and for placing brief-term therapy at the center of our thinking emerged in dialogue with Peggy Schlegel of APA Books. When Peggy first approached us about writing something for APA, we had just guest-edited the first issue of the journal *In-Session: Psychotherapy in Practice* on the topic of ruptures in the therapeutic alliance, and were in the midst of working on a treatment manual for negotiating ruptures in the therapeutic alliance. We did not have the time to start on a new solo-authored book, nor the interest in duplicating or expanding the journal issue we had just edited. It was in this context that the idea of considering the alliance in brief psychotherapies emerged, and it seemed too intriguing to pass up. The project has proved to be a stimulating and rewarding one, and we thank Peggy for her encouragement and support. We also thank Judy Nemes at APA Books for her superb job as development editor and for her thoughtful review of the draft of the book that we initially submitted to APA. Thanks also to Adam Horvath, who took the time to go over each chapter in depth and to offer detailed and constructive criticisms. Finally, we thank the contributors to this book, who were cooperative with deadlines and responsive to our editorial comments, and who turned in chapters of such high quality that the task of editing was not an arduous one.

The

Therapeutic

Alliance In Brief

Psychotherapy

J. Christopher Muran and Jeremy D. Safran

Negotiating the Therapeutic Alliance in Brief Psychotherapy:

An Introduction

1

Like many aspects of the psychotherapeutic process, the importance of the therapeutic relationship was originally discussed by Freud in his early theoretical papers on transference. Although he first spoke of the importance of making a so-called collaborator of the patient in *Studies of Hysteria* (1885/1955), Freud (1912/1958) was primarily concerned with the transferential aspects of the relationship and the importance of transference analysis. For Freud, *transference* involved the displacement of affects from one object or person to another, traditionally the transference of attitudes formerly associated with a parent. He distinguished between positive and negative tranferences (i.e., the transference of positive vs. negative attitudes). Freud also spoke of the "unobjectionable positive transference"— the aspect of the transference that should not be analyzed because it provides the patient with the motivation necessary to collaborate effectively with the analyst. To a limited extent, he acknowledged the role of friendliness and affection as "the vehicle of success in psychoanalysis" (S. Freud, 1912/1958) and described the analyst and patient banding together against the patient's symptoms in a "pact" based on free exploration by the patient and competent understanding by the analyst (S. Freud, 1940/1964).

From Freud, one can trace the development of psychoanalytic perspectives on the therapeutic relationship to two emergent lines. The first develops through the influence of Ferenczi (see Aron & Harris, 1991). As analyst to Balint, Jones, Klein, and Rickman, he had great impact on British object relations. As analyst to Thompson, Roheim, and Rado, Ferenczi likewise influenced interpersonal and cultural psychoanalysis in America. Ferenczi (1932) was the first to suggest that it was essential for patients to not merely remember but to actually relive the problematic past in the therapeutic relationship. Thus he sowed ideas later cultivated by Balint (1968), Winnicott (1965), and Alexander (with his notion of the corrective emotional experience: Alexander & French, 1946). (Alexander was influenced by Ferenczi when both were associated with the Hungarian Psychoanalytic Society.) Ferenczi was also first to consider the role of the analyst's personality and experience in the treatment process. He highlighted the analyst as a real person and recognized the real impact of the analyst on the transference–countertransference enactment (Ferenczi, 1932). Thus he suggested ideas, such as participant observation, developed further by the interpersonalists (Thompson, 1944).

The second line can be identified as the ego-psychological tradition, which emphasized the reality-oriented adaptation of the ego to its environment (A. Freud, 1936; Hartmann, 1958). Largely in response to the exclusive view held particularly by Kleinians (e.g., Bion, 1970) that all meaningful reactions of the patient to the person of the analyst are transference manifestations and the only important interventions are transference interpretations, the ego psychologists refocused attention on the real aspects of the therapeutic relationship and developed the notion of the therapeutic alliance (Greenson, 1971). The concept of the therapeutic alliance was the ego-psychological attempt to bring the interaction between analyst and patient to the fore. In addition, it permitted modifications in the traditional analytic stance and the use of noninterpretive measures.

Sterba (1934, 1940) was the first to explicate the role of positive identification with the therapist in leading the patient to work toward the accomplishment of common therapeutic tasks. Specifically, he spoke about the importance of helping the patient to form a "therapeutic split in the ego" so that the reality-focused elements of the ego could become allied with the therapist in the task of self-observation. It was Zetzel (1956, 1966) who first introduced the therapeutic alliance as essential to the effectiveness of any therapeutic intervention. She argued that the alliance is dependent on the patient's fundamental capacity to form a stable trusting relationship, which in turn is rooted in his or her early developmental experiences. Zetzel believed that when this capacity does not exist at the outset, it is critical for the therapist to provide a supportive relationship which facilitates the development of an alliance, in the same way that a mother needs to provide the appropriate maternal environment to facilitate the development of a fundamental sense of trust.

Greenson (1967, 1971) extended this tradition with a seminal formulation of the therapeutic relationship. He described the relationship as consisting of a transference configuration and a real relationship (although he recognized that the boundary is somewhat artificial). The real relationship refers to the mutual human response of the patient and therapist to each other, including undistorted perceptions and authentic liking, trust, and respect for each other, which exist along with the inequalities inherent in the therapy situation. Greenson introduced the working alliance as the ability of the dyadic partners to work purposefully together in the treatment they have undertaken. Although the patient's transference reactions may support the working alliance, the essential core of the alliance is the real relationship. Thus, like Sterba (1934, 1940), Greenson emphasized the importance of rationality and objectivity in therapy with this concept.

Over the years, there has been much controversy in analytic circles over what is meant by the alliance concept (see Langs, 1976). In fact, there are those within the ego-psychological tradition, such as Brenner (1979), who find the distinction between alliance and transference neither meaningful nor useful, and still others, such as Meissner (1996), who find the distinction at least conceptually (if not practically) useful. Nevertheless, the ego psychologists have at least reminded many of the analytic community that it is meaningful to recognize that the psychotherapeutic process does involve a real and personal relationship (Lipton, 1983).

In contrast, among interpersonalists (e.g., Lionells, Fiscalini, Mann, & Stern, 1995), the alliance concept has not been the focus of much attention, given that their perspective is primarily one of interaction. The principle of participant observation fundamental to their field theory places the real relationship between patient and therapist prominently in the theoretical foreground and thereby has permitted greater technical flexibility. Recent developments in contemporary psychoanalytic theory toward a relational perspective (Mitchell, 1988) have extended the interpersonal emphasis on therapist participation and subjectivity. These include perspectives influenced by feminist theory, social constructivist discourse, and the notion of intersubjectivity (see Aron, 1996); these perspectives collectively oppose the rigid demarcation between subject and object, between observer and observed, with its emphasis on reason and rationality. What is real or unreal, true or untrue, is replaced by the recognition that there are multiple truths and that these truths are socially constructed. Thus, the therapeutic relationship can be understood as comprised of plural, perspectival, ever-changing truths co-created by patient and therapist.

The recognition that the psychotherapeutic process involves a real and personal relationship between patient and therapist is one not missed by other traditions. This is a perspective that has always been central to the humanistic–experiential tradition in which Rogers (1951) advocated for empathy, congruence, and unconditional positive regard as necessary and sufficient conditions for therapeutic change. It has also received increasing attention by behavioral therapists, who have come to recognize not only the value of therapist warmth and empathy but also the therapeutic relationship as a sample of behavior (e.g., Goldfried & Davison, 1976).

The psychotherapy research community represents another forum where the therapeutic alliance has been most topical. Interest in this concept among researchers can be partly attributed to the search for understanding change across treatments, given that no particular treatment has been shown to be consistently better than any other in effecting change (Smith, Glass, & Miller, 1980). It can also be attributed to Bordin (1979), who stirred the psychotherapy research community with his transtheoretical reformulation of the alliance concept. He suggested that a good alliance is a prerequisite for change in all forms of psychotherapy and defined the concept as consisting of three interdependent components: agreement on tasks, agreement on goals, and the bond. According to him, different types of therapy focus on different types of tasks and goals and thus require different types of bonds. The strength of the alliance is, therefore, a function of the degree of agreement between patient and therapist about the tasks and goals of psychotherapy and the quality of the affective bond between them. In other words, the quality of the bond mediates the extent to which the patient and therapist are able to negotiate an agreement about the tasks and goals of therapy, and the ability to negotiate an agreement about the tasks and goals in therapy in turn mediates the quality of the bond.

The tasks of therapy consist of the specific activities (either overt or covert) that the patient must engage in to benefit from the treatment. For example, classical psychoanalysis requires the patient to free associate by attempting to say whatever comes to mind without censoring it. An important task in cognitive therapy may consist of completing a behavioral assignment between sessions. The goals of therapy are the general objectives toward which the treatment is directed. For example, classical psychoanalysis assumes that the problems that bring people into therapy result from a maladaptive way of negotiating the conflict between instincts and defense, and the goal consists of developing a more adaptive way of negotiating that conflict. A behavior therapist, in contrast, may see as the goal of treatment the removal of a specific symptom. The bond component of the alliance consists of the affective quality of the relationship between patient and therapist (e.g., the extent to which the patient feels understood, valued, and so on). Bordin´s (1979) seminal contribution was a significant impetus to the proliferation of measures and research, which demonstrated that the most robust predictor of outcome in psychotherapy is the quality of the therapeutic alliance (Gaston, 1990; Hartley, 1985; Horvath & Symonds, 1991).

A Reconceptualization of the Therapeutic Alliance

Historically, the concept of the therapeutic alliance has played an important role in the evolution of the classical psychoanalytic tradition, insofar as it has provided a theoretical justification for greater technical flexibility. By highlighting the critical importance of the real, human aspects of the therapeutic relationship, it provided grounds for departing from the idealized therapist stance of abstinence and neutrality. An interpersonal or relational perspective does not adhere to classical notions of therapist abstinence and neutrality and provides considerably more scope for technical flexibility. Moreover, from such a perspective, the experience of a new, constructive interpersonal experience with the therapist is viewed as a critical component of change. In fact, one might say that the processes of developing and resolving problems in alliance are not simply prerequisite to change but rather the essence of the change process. The question thus arises as to whether the concept of the therapeutic alliance is still valuable or whether it is superfluous.

A broadened conceptualization of the therapeutic alliance along the lines that Bordin suggested still seems useful for several reasons (Safran & Muran, in press). First, it highlights the fact that at a fundamental level, the patient's ability to trust, hope, and have faith in the therapist's ability to help always plays a central role in the change process. Some aspects of this type of alliance may involve conscious, rational deliberation, but other aspects are unconscious and affectively based. This type of perspective on the alliance is closer in nature to Zetzel's conceptualization than it is to Sterba's or Greenson's. Second, Bordin's conceptualization of the alliance highlights the fact that different types of alliance are necessary depending on the relevant therapeutic tasks and goals. The type of alliance focused on by Greenson and Sterba, which emphasizes the patient's rational collaboration with the therapist in the task of self-observation, is only one such type. There is a wide range of other therapeutic tasks and goals both within psychoanalysis and within other forms of psychotherapy; for example, accessing painful feelings or reconstructing historical memories (psychoanalysis), monitoring and recording one's internal dialogue between sessions (cognitive therapy), and engaging in a dialogue between different parts of the self (Gestalt therapy). The process of relating to the therapist in an authentic and organismically grounded fashion (common to both existential and relational psychoanalytic approaches) can be thought of as another therapeutic task.

Each of these tasks places different demands on the patient and will tend to be experienced as more or less helpful depending upon the patients' capacities and characteristic ways of relating to themselves and others. A patient prone to self-criticism may experience the task of self-observation as difficult. Another patient may be easily susceptible to self-consciousness and shame before another and may find lying on a couch and sharing innermost thoughts easier than than facing the analyst. Of course, such experiences may shift from time to time within a given case; for example, a benign question in one moment can be a provocative one in another. This point has a number of important implications.

First, it highlights the interdependence of relational and technical factors in psychotherapy. It suggests that the meaning of any technical factor can only be understood in the interpersonal context in which it is applied. Any intervention may have a positive or negative impact on the quality of the bond between the patient and therapist depending on its idiosyncratic meaning to the patient, and conversely, any intevention may be experienced as more or less facilitative depending on the preexisting bond.

Second, our point provides a rational framework for guiding the therapist's interventions in a flexible fashion. Rather than basing one's approach on the basis of some inflexible and idealized criterion, such as therapeutic neutrality, one can be guided by an understanding of what a particular therapeutic task means to a particular patient in a given moment. For example, how is an exploratory question being experienced by a patient? Does it facilitate greater understanding of an issue? Does it close off an exploration because it feels intrusive to the patient or because it evokes too much anxiety to tolerate? And how is a given interpretation experienced? Does it communicate empathy by the therapist or is it experienced as criticism? Could it be that the therapist is using the interpretation to defend against the patient?

Third, as Stolorow and colleagues (Stolorow, Brandchaft, & Atwood, 1994) have highlighted, ruptures in the therapeutic alliance are the royal road to understanding the patient's representational world. As contemporary Kleinians such as Joseph (1989) point out, the therapist should continually attend to the way in which patients respond to their interventions. Exploring the factors underlying the patient's construal of an intervention as hindering can provide a rich understanding of the patient's idiosyncratic construal process and internal object relations.

Fourth, understanding patients (not to mention therapists) as diverse in capacity and variable in experiencing highlights the importance of the negotiation between patient and therapist about the tasks and goal of therapy. Conceptualizations of the alliance such as Sterba's and Greenson's assume that there is only one therapeutic task (i.e., rational collaboration with the therapist in the task of self-observation). Although they emphasize the importance of the therapist acting in a supportive fashion to facilitate the development of the alliance, ultimately, they assume that the patient will identify with the therapist and adapt to the therapist's conceptualization of the tasks and goals of therapy or accept the therapist's understanding of the tasks and goals of therapy. In contrast, Bordin's conceptualization of the alliance is more dynamic and mutual or reciprocal. It assumes that there will be an ongoing negotiation between therapist and patient at both the conscious and unconscious levels about the tasks and goals of therapy, and that this process of negotiation establishes the necessary conditions for change to take place and is an intrinsic part of the change process as well.

This conceptualization of the alliance as both dynamic and mutual is consistent with a view of the essence of therapy as entailing an ongoing negotiation between two subjectivities, between the patient and therapist (Mitchell, 1993). Pizer (1992) has described therapeutic action as constituted by the engagement of two persons in a process of negotiation. He suggests that therapists in their interventions and patients in their responses are recurrently saying to each other, "No, you can't make this of me. But you can make that of me" (p. 218). Pizer includes in this process all aspects of therapy, the agreement on fees, the arrangement about scheduling, and so forth. He summarizes that "the very substances and nature of truth and reality . . . are being negotiated toward consensus" (p. 218) in the therapeutic relationship. This view fits nicely with Bordin's emphasis on the negotiation of tasks and goals in his conceptualization of alliance.

The Therapeutic Alliance in Brief Psychotherapy

The history of short-term psychotherapy can likewise be traced back to Freud, whose clinical efforts were typically short term (Messer &

Warren, 1995). Other significant early contributions include Rank's (1929) setting of a specific time for termination to mobilize the patient's will and accentuate dependency and separation issues; Ferenczi's (Ferenczi & Rank, 1925) experiments with active, directive interventions to promote a more rapid and effective therapy; Deutsche's (Deutsche & Murphy, 1955) emphasis on focality and confining one's efforts to an exploration of a limited area in a patient's psychic world; and Alexander's (Alexander & French, 1946) focus on the need to formulate a comprehensive understanding of the patient in the first few interviews and to use that understanding to plan treatment. These contributions became central to the development of the short-term models that followed (see Flegenheimer, 1982; Messer & Warren, 1995).

Although therapeutic practice has a long-standing tradition of short-term treatment models fueled by both theory and research, the surge in interest in brief psychotherapies can be attributed to current changes in the social, political, and economic environment. Recent surveys indicate that short-term psychotherapy now constitutes a substantial component of the psychotherapy that is practiced (Messer & Warren, 1995), and it is likely that this trend will continue to increase as the shift toward managed care and greater accountability in the health care sector continues. When it comes to understanding the therapeutic alliance in short-term psychotherapy, there has been little in the way of a systematic attempt to explore the alliance concept specific to the short-term context (although most of the research demonstrating the importance of the alliance has been based on short-term psychotherapy).

A number of obvious factors need to be entered into the negotiation of the therapeutic alliance in short-term psychotherapy. To begin with, there is the establishment of the time limit. Short-term treatments also invariably involve a greater degree of focality and a high level of therapist activity, as the therapist intervenes constantly to maintain the focus in the given time frame, on a circumscribed area of difficulty. In addition, issues regarding separation and termination are much more salient throughout the treatment process because of the time limit. All these factors greatly shape the process toward agreement on tasks and goals, and they impact upon the affective experience between patient and therapist. How or when does the therapist intervene to limit the focus? How is this experienced by the patient? What effect does it have on their bond in a given moment?

This book is designed to acquaint the reader with how the therapeutic alliance is understood in short-term treatment from the perspective of various contemporary theoretical orientations and treatment modalities. Specifically, Harold Been and Arnold Winston present from a drive–structural model (influenced by Malan, Davanloo, and Sifneos); Jeffrey L. Binder presents from a relational perspective (including contributions by Luborsky, Horowitz, Weiss, and Sampson); Barbara S. Kohlenberg and colleagues present from a radical–behavioral perspective; Cory F. Newman presents from a cognitive therapy model; Jeanne C. Watson and Leslie S. Greenberg present from a humanistic–experiential perspective; James C. Coyne and Carolyn M. Pepper present from a strategic perspective; Douglas S. Rait presents from a structural family and couples therapy perspective; and K. Roy MacKenzie presents with respect to group psychotherapy.

To organize these chapters in a thematically consistent fashion, we have asked all the contributors to address the following questions in their chapters:

1. How do you conceptualize the therapeutic alliance? In other words, is there a specific conceptualization that you find particularly helpful in your work, or do you find some combination of conceptualizations (or some adaptation of a concept) to be useful?
2. In what way do the special demands of your short-term approach influence the way in which you conceptualize the alliance?
3. What implications do the specific demands of your short-term approach have for the initial establishment of the alliance?
4. What implications do the specific demands of your short-term approach have for the maintenance of the alliance?
5. What specific types of ruptures in the alliance are likely to be most common in short-term approach, and why?
6. What type of interventions are likely to be most useful for resolving ruptures in the alliance.

The therapeutic alliance has been described as the "quintessential integrative variable" because its importance does not seem to lie within one school of thought (Wolfe & Goldfried, 1988). We hope this volume will contribute to the dialogue necessary for diverse schools to see if there is common ground.

References

Alexander, F., & French, T. M. (1946). *Psychoanalytic therapy*. New York: Ronald Press.

Aron, L. (1996). *A meeting of minds: Mutuality in psychoanalysis.* Hillsdale, NJ: The Analytic Press.

Aron, L., & Harris, A. (Eds.). (1991). *The legacy of Sandor Ferenczi.* Hillsdale, NJ: The Analytic Press.

Balint, M. (1968). *The basic fault.* London: Tavistock.

Bion, W. (1970). *Attention and interpretation.* London: Heinemann.

Bordin, E. (1979). The generalizability of the psychoanalytic concept of the working alliance. *Psychotherapy, 16,* 252–260.

Brenner, C. (1979). Working alliance, therapeutic alliance, and transference. *Journal of the American Psychoanalytic Association, 27,* 137–158.

Deutsche, F., & Murphy, W. F. (1955). *The clinical interview.* New York: International Universities Press.

Ferenczi, S. (1932). *The clinical diary of Sandor Ferenczi.* Cambridge, MA: Harvard University Press.

Ferenczi, S., & Rank, O. (1925). *The development of psychoanalysis.* New York: Dover.

Flegenheimer, W. (1982). *Techniques of brief psychotherapy.* New York: Jason Aronson.

Freud, A. (1936). *The ego and mechanisms of defense.* New York: International Universities Press.

Freud, S. (1955). Studies in hysteria (with J. Breuer). In J. Strachey (Ed.), *The standard edition of the complete psychological works of Sigmund Freud* (Vol. 2). London: Hogarth. (Original work published 1885)

Freud, S. (1958). The dynamics of transference. In J. Strachey (Ed.), *The standard edition of the complete psychological works of Sigmund Freud* (Vol. 12). London: Hogarth. (Original work published 1912)

Freud, S. (1964). The technique of psychoanalysis. In J. Strachey (Ed.), *The standard edition of the complete psychological works of Sigmund Freud* (Vol. 23). London: Hogarth. (Original work published 1940)

Gaston, L. (1990). The concept of the alliance and its role in psychotherapy: Theoretical and empirical considerations. *Psychotherapy, 27,* 143–153.

Goldfried, M., & Davison, G. (1976). *Clinical behavior therapy.* New York: Holt, Rinehart & Winston.

Greenson, R. (1967). *The technique and practice of psychoanalysis.* New York: International Universities Press.

Greenson, R. (1971). The real relationship between the patient and the psychoanalyst. In M. Kanzer (Ed.), *The unconscious today* (pp. 213–232). New York: International Universities Press.

Hartley, D. E. (1985). Research on the therapeutic alliance in psychotherapy. In R. Hales & A. Frances (Eds.), *American Psychiatric*

Association annual review: Vol. 4. Psychiatry update (pp. 532–549). Washington, DC: American Psychiatric Association.

Hartmann, H. (1958). *Ego psychology and the problem of adaptation*. New York: International Universities Press.

Horvath, A. O., & Symonds, B. D. (1991). Relation between working alliance and outcome in psychotherapy: A meta-analysis. *Journal of Counseling Psychology, 38*, 139–149.

Joseph, B. (1989). *Psychic equilibrium and psychic change*. London: Routledge.

Langs, R. (1976). *The therapeutic interaction* (Vols. 1–2). Northvale, NJ: Aronson.

Lionells, M., Fiscalini, J., Mann, C. H., & Stern, D. B. (Eds.). (1995). *The handbook of interpersonal psychoanalysis*. Hillsdale, NJ: The Analytic Press.

Lipton, S. (1983). A critique of so-called standard technique. *Contemporary Psychoanalysis, 19*, 35–46.

Meissner, W. W. (1996). *The therapeutic alliance*. New Haven, CT: Yale University Press.

Messer, S., & Warren, C. S. (1995). *Models of brief psychodynamic therapy*. New York: Guilford Press.

Mitchell, S. A. (1988). *Relational concepts in psychoanalysis*. Cambridge, MA: Harvard University Press.

Mitchell, S. A. (1993). *Hope and dread in psychoanalysis*. New York: Basic Books.

Pizer, S. A. (1992). The negotiation of paradox in the analytic process. *Psychoanalytic Dialogues, 2*, 215–240.

Rank, O. (1929). *The trauma of birth*. New York: Harcourt, Brace.

Rogers, C. R. (1951). *Client-centered therapy*. Boston: Houghton Mifflin.

Safran, J. D., & Muran, J. C. (in press). *Negotiating the therapeutic alliance: A relational treatment manual*. New York: Guilford Press.

Smith, M. L., Glass, G. V., & Miller, M. I. (1980). *The benefits of psychotherapy*. Baltimore: Johns Hopkins University Press.

Sterba, R. (1934). The fate of the ego in analytic therapy. *International Journal of Psychoanalysis, 15*, 117–126.

Sterba, R. (1940). The dynamics of the dissolution of the transference resistance. *Psychoanalytic Quarterly, 9*, 363–379.

Stolorow, R., Brandchaft, B., & Atwood, G. (1994). *Psychoanalytic treatment: An intersubjective approach*. Hillsdale, NJ: The Analytic Press.

Thompson, C. (1944). Ferenczi's contribution to psychoanalysis. *Psychiatry, 7*, 245–252.

Winnicott, D. W. (1965). *The maturational process and the facilitating environment*. New York: International Universties Press.

Wolfe, B. E., & Goldfried, M. R. (1988). Research on psychotherapy integration: Recommendations and conclusions from an NIMH workshop. *Journal of Consulting and Clinical Psychology, 56*, 448–451.

Zetzel, E. (1956). Current concepts of transference. *International Journal of Psychoanalysis, 37,* 369–375.

Zetzel, E. (1966). The analytic situation. In R. E. Litman (Ed.), *Psychoanalysis in America* (pp. 86–106). New York: International Universities Press.

Harold Been and Arnold Winston

The Therapeutic Alliance in Brief Psychoanalytic Psychotherapy:
A Drive—Conflict Perspective

2

Our perspective on the therapeutic alliance is grounded in the ego-psychological tradition that can be traced from Freud (1912/1958, 1913) to Sterba (1934), Bibring (1937), Zetzel (1956), Stone (1961), and Greenson (1967). We consider the alliance as having a complex relationship to transference phenomena, although distinguishable from them (see chapter 1 in this volume for more on this perspective). Our perspective is also influenced by two transtheoretical formulations of the alliance. The first is by Bordin (1979), who operationalized the therapeutic alliance concept in terms of the degree of agreement between patient and therapist concerning the tasks and goals of psychotherapy and the quality of the bond between them. More recently, Gaston (1990) elaborated this concept further and identified four dimensions that defined the alliance: (a) the patient's affective bond to the therapist and commitment to therapy, (b) the patient's capacity to work purposefully in therapy, (c) the therapist's empathic understanding and involvement, and (d) the agreement of patient and therapist on the tasks and goals of therapy. In this chapter, we present our ideas about the role of the alliance in the type of brief psychoanalytically based psychotherapies that use a drive–conflict model approach.

Comparisons of Technique in the Drive–Conflict Models of Brief Psychotherapy With Technique in Standard Psychoanalysis

In classical psychoanalysis, the parameters of technique are governed by the central goal of optimizing the development and subsequent working through and resolution of the transference neurosis. In frequent sessions over many years using free association and the gradual, repetitive working through of derivative material, both analyst and patient increasingly focus on the transference–countertransference paradigms of the transference neurosis. Resistances are analyzed and worked through only when they become impediments to the process of free association or to the exploration of derivative material.

In brief psychoanalytically based psychotherapies, psychoanalytic principles are applied using more active, structured techniques. In the Sifneos model (Sifneos, 1972), the therapeutic strategy involves an incisive encounter with the core oedipal conflict underlying the circumscribed maladaptive behavior for which treatment is sought. In Malan's technique (Malan, 1976a, 1976b), the emphasis is placed on making repetitive linkages between conflicts involving current persons, past persons, and the therapist, most often focusing on issues of loss. In Davanloo's Short-Term Dynamic Psychotherapy (Davanloo, 1980), a multifocal psychoanalytic form of brief psychotherapy, the more ambitious goal of treatment is the restructuring of maladaptive compromises in order to undo the multifocal core neurotic conflicts in a relatively compressed period of time—less than one year. To accomplish these psychoanalytic goals, many technical parameters of the standard psychoanalytic approach need to be modified. All of these techniques profoundly affect and determine the nature of the working alliance.

In the Sifneos (1972) model of brief therapy, the therapeutic process is driven by a focused content-probing inquiry into the relationships with past figures, usually parents or siblings, that were found during the evaluation to be the significant core relationships underlying the current interpersonal difficulties. For instance, in a male patient with significant conflicts with his fiancée during the engagement period, the therapist might explore the patient's early remaining erotic attachment to his mother, highlighting this relationship pattern in some detail. Probing for details will frequently provoke a struggle with the therapist at some point. This ensuing struggle becomes the next focus of the treatment. The emergent details of this struggle with the therapist generally contain the remnants of the other arm of the oedipal conflict, such as, in the above case, the remaining competitive rivalry with the father. This past relationship is then further explored in detail.

In the Davanloo (1980) model, the strategic psychotherapeutic techniques used by the therapist are designed to prevent the development of a regressive transference neurosis as multiple characterological resistances are systematically explored. The techniques involve active focusing by the therapist, immediate interpretation of transference issues, and, similar to Malan (1976a, 1976b), the making of repetitive therapist–current-figure–past-figure (T–C–P) linkages. The focus shifts between clarifying and analyzing specific interpersonal relationships and clarifying, confronting, and interpreting defenses against the painful warded-off affects experienced in these relationships. In particular, the process of systematic active confrontation and concomitant analysis of the maladaptive defenses with the subsequent breakthroughs of painful affects most characterize the Davanloo process, particularly during the first phase (Laikin, Winston, & McCullough, 1991). These transference confrontations in the first few sessions heighten the immediate development of intense transference reactions, setting off the unfolding of transference–countertransference paradigms, which are often evident within the first few minutes.

Take for example, a 35-year-old professional man with relationship difficulties with his wife. In the first 15 min of the initial session, the therapist explored a recent conflict that the patient had with his wife in the preceding week. While exploring this conflict, the therapist asked the patient how he had experienced his anger toward his wife:

THERAPIST. How did you experience your anger toward your wife at that moment?

PATIENT. She was making me very angry.

THERAPIST. That does not tell me how you experienced your anger toward her.

PATIENT. I felt very angry at her.

THERAPIST. Can you describe how you experienced this anger toward your wife? . . . Do you notice that you are still not describing the experience of your anger?

PATIENT. I thought she was being very controlling!

THERAPIST. You are again answering with thoughts and not feelings. Are you aware that you avoid describing your feeling?

Perhaps you have difficulty with this. It is very important that we explore your feeling here. Let us try again.

PATIENT. This is very frustrating. You don't accept what I say and want me to answer the way you want.

THERAPIST. So now you experience me as controlling. Let's see how you experience your frustration here with me.

In the next 15 min, this question led to the exploration and further confrontation of the patient's feelings toward the therapist, until the patient was faced with his experience of heightened feelings of anger toward the therapist.

THERAPIST. So now you admit that you are angry at me for being controlling. Let us see how you experience this anger here with me.

PATIENT. Again, we are going to go through this nonsense! (Voice raised.)

THERAPIST. Are you aware that your voice is raised?

PATIENT. Of course I am. (Loud voice.) What do you expect? (Continuing loud voice.)

THERAPIST. During this experience of anger, are you aware of wanting to further lash out at me?

PATIENT. (Patient visibly anxious.)

This confrontation of the patient's anger toward the therapist then led to the anxiety-filled exploration of the patient's physically sadistic fantasies toward the therapist, which were highly conflictual and deeply connected to his ambivalent, painful relationship with his deceased father.

In such a heightened atmosphere, within the first one-half hour of an initial interview, therapists must monitor their own feelings and the patient's feelings, and simultaneously keep the therapy focused on the therapeutic task. The therapeutic alliance and the exploration of the patient's inner world unfold simultaneously. The therapeutic alliance in the above session was strengthened when the therapist reflected upon and summarized what had occurred during the above interchange.

THERAPIST. So we can now see why you initially had such difficulty in describing your anger toward your wife and then toward myself. Clearly, this is connected to highly conflictual, painful feelings toward your father. We need to both monitor our situation together when you want to distance from these feelings so we can quickly explore, understand, and move on. Otherwise you will continue to defeat yourself and then me. (Pause.) Do you agree?

PATIENT. It sure was difficult. I was never aware I had so much trouble expressing my angry feelings. (Patient smiles.)

Comparison of the Working Alliance in Standard Psychoanalysis and in the Drive–Conflict Models of Brief Psychotherapy

Greenson (1967) divided the analyst–patient relationship into three components: (a) the transference relationship, (b) the working alliance, and (c) the real relationship. He defined the *working alliance* as the primary therapeutic alliance between the patient and analyst that enabled the work of treatment to progress. The working alliance, according to Greenson, is formed by the identification of a patient's reasonable ego with the analyst's analyzing ego. This working alliance encompasses the patient's motivation, willingness, and capacity to cooperate with the analyst in both experiencing and observing the transference reactions. It is fostered gradually and usually flowers after a transference experience has been successfully understood and worked through with the analyst (around 6 months). Greenson emphasized that the maintenance of a good working alliance through the extended middle phase of treatment led to a successful therapeutic experience. He was not specific about the nature of the alliance between the patient and therapist during the first 6 months (a significant period in brief psychotherapy) before the full development of a working alliance. Specific techniques for maintaining a working alliance were also not offered by Greenson, although it was implicit that careful attention to the clarification, confrontation, and working through of transference reactions and the resistances to experiencing them, coupled with compassion and being human, were the core procedures. Greenson indicated that all three types of relationships (real, transference, and working alliance) were intertwined but could be readily separated to facilitate a discussion of the analytic process.

As in Greenson's definition of a working alliance in standard psychoanalysis, in both the Sifneos and Davanloo models the alliance encompasses the motivation, willingness, and capacity of the patient to experience and observe these transference reactions. In this process, the patient's reasonable ego must also identify with the analyst's analyzing ego. However, in the brief therapies, the monitoring of the working alliance by the therapist more explicitly pervades the treatment at all times. At any given moment of a session, the transference relationship may be the primary focus, but the focus on the working alliance will not be far behind in the same therapeutic hour. A greater burden falls on therapists to more actively structure the therapeutic field and enlist the patients to sustain the joint effort to face their neurotic conflicts. This type of working alliance must develop within the first session and be actively maintained. As in standard psychoanalysis, the working alliance rapidly expands as patients find they can face new painful experiences within the transference as they look at conflictual issues in their human relationships.

As a result of this intimate relationship between the working alliance and the transference relationship in the brief psychoanalytic psychotherapies, therapeutic misalliances and ruptures are frequent and problematic, particularly when a therapist is learning the technique. Therefore, it is necessary for the therapist to actively strive for a working alliance and then protect it from rupture by using the parameters built into the technique.

Parameters Affecting Working Alliance in Brief Psychoanalytic Psychotherapies

Various technical parameters have been developed to promote and protect the working therapeutic alliance in the intense interactional fields of the Davanloo, Malan, and Sifneos models. These parameters previously mentioned—the establishment of an active focus, the immediate interpretation of transference to avoid regression into a transference neurosis, and the repetitive current-figure–past-figure–transference-figure linkages—help to create the unfolding transference paradigms and are reciprocally influenced by them. These clinical processes will be illustrated in many of the following clinical vignettes in this chapter. Because the Davanloo model encompasses and extends the parameters of technique from the Sifneos and Malan models, most of the following clinical vignettes will reflect this model.

REPETITIVE CLARIFICATION AND REMINDERS OF THERAPEUTIC GOALS

The nature of patients' difficulties and their genesis are elicited in great detail in the initial evaluation after characterological resistances to emotional and cognitive communication are addressed. Patients are explicitly asked if they wish to pursue understanding their difficulties in collaboration with the therapist, in the manner they were pursued in the evaluation. The quality of the agreement is an indicator of the initial quality of the working alliance. As treatment progresses, the patient is frequently reminded of these goals and the previous wishes to pursue them. The patient is frequently again asked to rededicate himself or herself to these goals.

In the Sifneos model, the aforementioned patient who had entered treatment for problems with his fiancée again became very resistant when the therapist began to further explore the highly competitive relationship with his father. This was further highlighted when the patient during a midphase session described how he enjoyed strutting around bare chested in front of his mother and sister at age 18.

THERAPIST. How did your father feel?

PATIENT. I didn't do that for him.

THERAPIST. But clearly, he was also around the house.

PATIENT. (After pause.) I don't see why that's important.

THERAPIST. Now that's interesting. Haven't we already seen that you had a highly competitive relationship with him in your academic performance and in the way you worked on your car? (Pause.) Didn't you say earlier that you wanted to clarify your difficulties with your fiancée and then solve them? (Pause.) Haven't we already seen how competitive issues with other men have affected that relationship?

PATIENT. Well, yes.

THERAPIST. So, how can this issue about showing your physique be unimportant in relationship to your father?

The patient agreed and then went on to explore very conflictual adolescent competitive sexual fantasies.

Similarly, in the Davanloo model, the patient who had earlier explored his anger toward his wife would repeatedly develop further resistance in the early phase of treatment whenever anger toward close family members began to emerge. The therapist would then repeatedly remind the patient of his previously agreed upon goal— that in order to understand his pain in his marriage he had to understand, experience, and sort out the anger he experienced in many of his previous family relationships.

REPETITIVE FRAMING OF THE NEED FOR SPECIFIC COGNITIVE–EMOTIONAL EXPRESSION

In the Davanloo model the process parameters of the active, direct focusing and the challenging of the defenses obstructing meaningful, direct, affective–cognitive communication present the patient at all times with therapeutic tasks and immediate therapeutic goals. The active framing and structuring of these goals by the therapist become the model of the "therapist's analyzing ego" (Greenson, 1967) in this technique. As treatment unfolds, the patient identifies with these operating goals and begins to be able to internalize them as part of his "rational operating ego" (Greenson, 1967).

For example, a 25-year-old male patient had repeatedly experienced in the first three sessions distancing and anxiety linked with his avoidance of sad feelings in relationship to an older brother who died 5 years earlier in a tragic car accident. In the fourth session, the patient again was discussing his pleasant memories of his brother and the frequent hikes they would take in the neighborhood of their vacation home when he began to yawn and gradually to grow quiet.

THERAPIST. So it seems you have gotten very tired in the last few minutes.

PATIENT. Yes, I didn't sleep well last night.

THERAPIST. But I noticed that this happened here while you were relating some wonderful experiences that you had with Bob. Might that not also tell us something about your tiredness?

PATIENT. You mean that you think I am distancing again? Is that it?

THERAPIST. What do you think?

PATIENT. (Pause.) I don't know. I really am tired.

THERAPIST. I am not trying to say you are not tired. But we have seen repeatedly that you have distanced before when painful feelings were near the surface.

PATIENT. (Visibly anxious with a few tears.) I don't know. Perhaps.

THERAPIST. But look, just reminding you of your distancing has brought tears and you are trying to push them down. We have also seen that before.

PATIENT. (After a long tearful pause, the patient further describes in detail the last camping trip he took with his brother shortly before his accident.) . . . I guess you were right about my distancing.

THERAPIST. You guess?

PATIENT. (Smile.) I'm still trying to distance. But I know that isn't good for me . . .

In the above vignette the patient is showing his recognition that his defense of distancing is used to guard against the experience and expression of his painful affects. As early as the fourth session, the defense of distancing is becoming ego alien because of the repeated therapeutic challenge of this defense during the first three sessions.

REMINDER OF TIME CONSTRAINTS

As in any brief psychotherapy, the constraints of time heighten the separation–individuation issues for both therapist and patient. Mann (1973) has highlighted the importance of these time constraints in brief therapy in the heightening of the universal conflicts surrounding the repetitive separation crises experienced throughout life. "These universal conflict situations are (a) independence versus dependence, (b) activity versus passivity, (c) adequate self-esteem versus diminished or loss of self-esteem, and (d) universal or delayed grief"(Mann, 1973, p. 25). All of these four conflicts will be reflected in the patient's capacity to handle object loss. In the brief psychoanalytic treatments, the middle and termination phases are much more distinct as time periods, as contrasted with the therapeutic experience in an open-ended longer term treatment. Thus, patients' and therapists' anticipation of object losses surface in a more focused and charged manner during the course of treatment.

In the Davanloo model, this therapeutic parameter is frequently bought to the attention of the patient during periods of resistance when the patient uses mechanisms of defense such as passivity, avoidance, and procrastination. In the following vignette early in treatment, an obsessional male in his mid-30s was continuing to explore his tendency to frequently procrastinate in his professional life, which had often created major stress for himself and near panic episodes. While he was discussing this problem in relationship to his boss, the focus became his distress at his boss's pressuring of him.

THERAPIST. So, John is very demanding and the more he demands, the more you procrastinate doing your job.

PATIENT. Yes, I guess you could say that. But I think my procrastination is present no matter what the situation.

THERAPIST. So you want to deny that this is specific to particular situations like with John.

PATIENT. It's not denial. I just think it is a bigger issue.

THERAPIST. But you always try to avoid facing your conflicts head on by generalizing. We have already seen that in our previous discussions.

PATIENT. I'm not trying to avoid, but I don't agree that my reaction to John is specific to him.

THERAPIST. So again you want to evade how you run away from your feelings and move to intellectualization and generalization. And don't you think that you are avoiding facing these conflicts here with me?

PATIENT. There you go again making things specific to you and me.

THERAPIST. But it is specific. We have seen many times that you avoid conflict by procrastination and avoidance. With John, the more he asks, the longer you take to do the job, forcing him to push you more. (Brief pause.) Might that be going on here with me?

PATIENT. You think I am procrastinating with you?

THERAPIST. Well?

PATIENT. (With some hesitation.) I guess so.

THERAPIST. So now you "guess so," keeping things in limbo, and not committing to anything. Clearly, this is a problem in all of your life, and now particularly with John and with me. *Obviously, we only have a limited time together.* If you continue delaying in this way, what will happen here?

PATIENT. I see your point.

THERAPIST. So what can you do now about this avoidance and running away from facing yourself here?

Without using passivity in relationship to the therapist, the patient now proceeds to explore both his relationship with his boss and his use of defiant behavior. In this instance, the therapist is able to capitalize on the time limits of the treatment in order to heighten the patient's awareness of the nonadaptive qualities of his defensive procrastination and his use of avoidance with figures such as the boss, whom he has related to in a passive manner. In this instance, the therapist's active reminder to the patient of the time constraints and the patient's active, evolving awareness of time solidify the working alliance.

Therapists' sense of time, including the timing of the eventual termination, also makes them constantly sensitive to the progress of resolving core neurotic conflicts and achieving therapeutic goals. Therapists will often initiate assessment of the accomplishments of therapeutic work with the patient. Periodically, therapists will then remind patients about the remaining work to be accomplished and the remaining number of sessions available to further heighten patients' awareness of time, which intensifies the experience of the universal conflicts surrounding separation elaborated by Mann (1973, p. 25). Interestingly, patients in a good working alliance in the Davanloo and Sifneos models will often remind therapists of these very same issues.

MONITORING EFFECTS OF THE WORKING ALLIANCE

The technical requirement for the therapist to rapidly make current-figure–past-figure–therapist linkages, as emphasized by Malan (1976a, 1976b), is a major parameter of technique in the Davanloo model enabling the prevention of a regressive transference neurosis. This linking process also becomes part of the patient's working alliance as the patient rapidly learns to think in terms of linkages. An important feature of the repetitive current-figure–past-figure–therapist linkages is that it provides the therapist a means of monitoring the effectiveness of the working alliance. As treatment progresses, the therapist should be able to see evidence of actual changes in the patient's life between sessions that correspond to the transference work occurring in the sessions themselves, such as the restructuring of the defenses against the experience of painful affects or the reduction of the fear of closeness with the therapist. The process of linking this restructuring with other figures in the patient's past or current life during the sessions should become explicit in the patient's parallel changing interactions with significant people during the intersession period. Should these changes not occur, the therapist must look carefully at the nature of the current working alliance and at transference–countertransference issues.

For instance, in a series of sessions with a male patient that focused on his use of passivity to avoid competitive–aggressive feelings, the work involved frequent linkage of his use of defenses to avoid angry feelings with the therapist, to similar situations with his boss and other male colleagues. Paralleling the patient's decreased use of the defense of passivity and greater capacity to tolerate his aggressive feelings toward the therapist should be a simultaneous reported decrease in the use of the defense of passivity with the boss and his colleagues and a subsequent increase in assertiveness in his life.

Similarly, when a female patient, who is actively working with a male therapist in sessions on her use of distancing to avoid painful feelings of grief, uses less distancing as she realizes the genetic sources of this grief, a simultaneous decrease of the use of distancing should ensue in her relationship with her husband. An active inquiry by the therapist to check on this improvement is indicated. Should there be no improvement, the therapist must immediately reflect on hidden transference–countertransference issues which have not been explored or resolved. In the absence of the therapist's active inquiry, these unresolved issues would subsequently distort the working alliance and its time constraints.

MONITORING THERAPEUTIC OMNIPOTENCE AND PATIENT COMPLIANCE

As in any psychoanalytic process, the therapist must guard against therapeutic omnipotence as well as patient compliance. In the Davanloo (1980) model, these issues must immediately be addressed in order to prevent a regressive transference neurosis and to safeguard a working alliance based on time constraints. Patient compliance as a defense is particularly important to recognize in this conflict model because of the initial intensity of the process and the high activity level of the therapist. Many patients will immediately use passivity or compliance to ward off the inner experience of aggression toward the therapist and the experienced danger of the attachment to the therapist that arise from conflicts involving castration or separation anxiety. Sadomasochistic transference–countertransference paradigms can be readily activated. Therefore, one must repeatedly inquire and challenge the defense of compliance.

In the aforementioned case, the patient who had frequently procrastinated both at work and with the therapist had begun to vigorously cooperate with the therapist in exploring his use of procrastination as a defense to directly avoid experiencing competitive wishes to defeat authority figures. In the seventh session, an exploration of his conflictual relationship with his older brother Ned ensued:

> THERAPIST. So, Ned tended to try and dominate you when you played together.
>
> PATIENT. Yes, he would frequently set the rules for games we played, and I would follow his directions.
>
> THERAPIST. So you followed him—all the time?

PATIENT. Usually, but sometimes I would get cranky or tired, or I would let him win quicker to get it over with.

THERAPIST. So you had found early ways to genuinely delay finishing things when someone was in control of the situation.

PATIENT. Yep. I agree. (Pause.) It sure goes back a long time.

THERAPIST. Now, we have seen that procrastination and avoidance have occurred in your relationship to both your boss John and with me in earlier sessions. Do you remember?

PATIENT. Yes.

THERAPIST. Our recent talks in the past few sessions have been very direct with no evidence of procrastination. This looks good on the surface, and I believe it is a real change for you and me. But, it is very important to see if you agree. Because, it is very important to make sure that there aren't any ways that you still feel the need to defeat me. This can occur by compliance with me—which isn't a genuine working together . . . just as in your use of defiance—like you did during your play with your brother. What do you think?

PATIENT. You know . . . (Pause.) I also feel we are moving along easier. I feel we are playing this game differently than Ned and I did. You always ask for my input.

THERAPIST. So you would agree with me that we are working well together at this time.

In this instance, although the therapist felt the therapeutic relationship to be in good alliance, he felt it necessary to make this belief explicit and explore any potential destructive patient compliance.

ACTIVE MONITORING OF THE PATIENT'S POTENTIAL TO DEFEAT TREATMENT

The need for self-sabotage, fear of closeness, and fear of separation found in various degrees in all patients in psychoanalytic psychotherapy need continuous monitoring and intervention in the brief form of psychoanalytic psychotherapy. This active monitoring illustrates the profound and continuous linkage of the transference relationship with the therapeutic working alliance, particularly in the Davanloo (1980) model. The origin and nature of human neurosis provides the patient with inner security and equilibrium. The underpinning of psychoanalytic practice is embedded in the understanding that the development of character structure affords a person a stable sense of self, (i.e., boundary regulation, affect regulation, narcissistic equilibrium, and the capacity for object relations). This character structure provides a set of potential interactional schemas to regulate emotional distance in human relationships, thus preserving a patient's sense of self-security. Freud showed how early superego development defended against guilty and shameful affects in relationships to significant others. He also demonstrated the inner needs for remaining attached to significant early figures. During development, these needs become embedded in the character structure and exert powerful influences against change. The high level of therapist activity alerts the patient unconsciously to the potential disruption of this internal equilibrium. Although there may be considerable pain for the patient stemming from their neuroses, the patient will always try to defeat the therapist's attempt to intrude into their neurotic structure by self-sabotage, distancing, and regression. Though this is true in standard psychoanalytic work, in the Davanloo model these transference tendencies unfold together from the very first moments of the therapeutic engagement owing to the rapid therapeutic challenge of the characterological resistances. The working alliance is thus constantly in flux.

As previously mentioned, the therapist's rapid intrusion into the patient's inner life as a result of the therapist's high activity level and the accompanying challenge of the defenses against direct emotional expression immediately produce strong resistances that emerge early in the evaluation and treatment process (Been & Sklar, 1985). Simultaneously, the therapist also explicitly highlights these same forces as direct threats to the ongoing and future working alliance because of their potential to defeat both the therapist and patient in reaching the agreed upon goals of the initial evaluation. Both the self-defeating nature of the patient's defenses and his or her concomitant avoidance of closeness are repetitively commented upon and explored by the therapist in order to enable a strong therapeutic working alliance to continue to develop. The male patient described earlier who had relationship difficulties with his wife clearly demonstrated an example of the potential need stemming from superego factors for self-defeat and defeat of the therapist.

In another example, a 35-year-old obsessional man was seen for evaluation for the Davanloo technique. After 45 min into the interview, his defenses against the experience of his underlying painful affects (i.e., anger, sadness) significantly weakened as indicated by an increase in manifest anxiety. However, it then became apparent that the major operational defense was the patient's distancing in order to avoid further closeness with the therapist. The therapist at this point challenged this resistance using techniques that explicitly addressed the therapeutic alliance.

THERAPIST. So, we can now see that you want to remain distant with me.

PATIENT. (Softly.) What do you mean?

THERAPIST. Clearly, you are not letting me close to your feeling life. This creates a massive barrier of distance between us.

PATIENT. (Nods in agreement.)

THERAPIST. We are both in agreement with this. But the question remains. What can you do about this distancing? Because if you maintain this wall between us, what will happen?

PATIENT. (After reflection.) Nothing.

THERAPIST. Absolutely! Just like in the other important relationships of your life which have failed. Obviously, you are terrified about closeness with me and all that might mean to you.

PATIENT. (Glances at therapist with misty eyes.)

THERAPIST. This brings tears to your eyes. What brought the tears?

PATIENT. (Silent.)

THERAPIST. But you are trying to hold the tears back— again maintaining distance. Closeness must be terrifying for many reasons we don't yet understand. But this wall can only lead to defeat for both of us and, clearly, who loses the most?

PATIENT. (Misty eyed and looking at therapist, he begins to relate in a tearful way memories of a close relationship with a teenage friend who suddenly moved away because his parents divorced.)

In this situation, the appeal to the patient's use of distancing by simultaneously addressing the potential failure of the therapeutic alliance and also its transferential meaning provided impetus for forward movement in the therapeutic process.

In the termination phase, particularly with patients with more complex characterological pathology, the resistance to separation from early attachments becomes more intense. This occurs as the patient more actively senses the emergence of depressive affects associated with the exploration of his maladaptive early attachments, the need to give up behaviors perpetuating these attachments, and the ultimate need to face the loss implicit in giving up the maladaptive aspects of these early attachments.

For instance, a 32-year-old male was in the midphase of treatment in the Davanloo model, working on the pathological mourning surrounding the death of his father when the patient was 8 years old. He entered treatment with symptoms of a moderate inhibition of assertiveness at work and difficulty with intimacy in his marriage. During the first 20 sessions, the relationship with his father was deeply explored—both the oedipal components and the profound sense of loss compounded with the patient's oedipal guilt. It became explicitly clear in the 20th session that the patient was ready to emotionally bury his father in a meaningful manner (which would also imply finishing the treatment and leaving the therapist). The following vignette occurred in the 22nd session after the first 15 min during which time the patient was complaining of his inability to put together the final pieces of a project at work which was clearly within his capacity to finish efficiently.

> PATIENT. I just can't concentrate on it. All it would take would be an hour of work—just reorganizing the report.
>
> THERAPIST. Don't you think that it is strange that you should be having trouble at work at this time?
>
> PATIENT. Why do you say that?
>
> THERAPIST. Work hasn't been a problem for 2 months. Might this just be a distraction from a more difficult issue?
>
> PATIENT. (Silent and thoughtful.)
>
> THERAPIST. What happened to all the thoughts and feelings of needing to bury your father and to leave treatment that you told me about in our last two sessions?
>
> PATIENT. (Brief pause.) You know, I had a dream with my father in a coffin.

The patient then related the dream and began to sob as he envisioned the funeral of his father which he had actually never attended. In the last 10 min of the session, the therapist and patient reflected together about the patient's need to avoid the finality of separation.

> THERAPIST. It's obvious that you have wanted to avoid all this pain you are feeling now—isn't it? You have always handled this by keeping alive the wish that you and your father were still in an intense relationship—you as the dependent child and he as the all powerful Dad. Haven't we seen before in our work together, how your hanging onto childlike ways—like your unneeded dependency and fear of asserting yourself—has hurt your relationship with your wife and has also inhibited your work?
>
> PATIENT. (Nodding in agreement.) It's terrible to really say "goodbye" to him. (Tears again emerge.)
>
> THERAPIST. Now, you also said you have to say "goodbye" to someone else, didn't you?

PATIENT. (Looking directly at therapist.) I can't face that.

THERAPIST. But that is now our job together in the next few sessions. Hanging onto me as a little boy is another way of hanging onto the fantasy of your powerful father. How would that help you resolve your problems?

The therapist in this vignette is now helping the patient focus his attention on the final transference paradigm of this treatment. The therapist's active clarification and confrontation of this issue is necessary to solidify the therapeutic alliance in the termination phase and to avoid entering into a regressive transference development which would prolong the treatment.

In summary, the establishment and maintenance of the working alliance is a constant active endeavor of both the patient and the therapist in the drive–conflict models of brief psychotherapy. Again, this alliance is always strongly challenged by the intense transference reactions, particularly during the initial phase. During this beginning phase, the working alliance is challenged because of the breakthrough of painful affects and attendant feelings of guilt and shame; whereas, during the middle and final phases, the working alliance is primarily challenged by the patient's resistance to the dislodging of important internal objects with the accompanying emergent depressive affects.

Therapeutic Misalliances and Ruptures in Brief Psychoanalytic Psychotherapies

The sources of misalliance in the brief psychoanalytic psychotherapies can be arbitrarily divided for discussion into (a) those caused by errors in technique and (b) those caused by countertransference issues, although these issues often work together. The technical parameters of the drive–conflict models of brief psychotherapy are demanding for the therapist. Particularly difficult to learn are the Davanloo techniques, which are used to apply pressure to the defenses while the therapist works to free the underlying affects. The timing, sequencing, and structuring of the therapeutic interventions are not natural to most beginning therapists, and frequent errors are the rule. The therapist either brings too much pressure or, more often, too little pressure to bear on the patient's conflicts and defenses, usually leaving the patient burdened with unexpressed conscious, preconscious, or unconscious negative feelings. These feelings may heighten despair, depression, distancing, and the use of regressive and obsessional defenses, which then cause a rupture in the working alliance. This process can rapidly lead to premature termination of treatment by the patient. Similarly, the therapist may also experience conscious, pre-conscious, or unconscious feelings related to frustration with the patient, him- or herself, and the technique.

Frequently, the patient will attempt to address this issue in an indirect or direct way. The therapist or supervisor must be alert to any communication from the patient that the therapist has made a real error as opposed to hearing the patient's communication as only a fantasy about the therapist. It is only in this way that the working alliance can be reestablished.

For example, in a very early session with a male graduate student with an obsessive character structure, a male trainee (who was already an experienced therapist) tried to apply the techniques of confronting the patient's defenses of passivity and intellectualization that were used against the emergence of painful feelings. The therapist was not able to initially break through these defenses and kept up a continuing, highly aggressive challenge in the face of the patient's distancing and passivity. While concentrating on applying the techniques, the therapist remained unaware of the intensity of his own frustration and anger with the patient's seeming uncooperation. He was vaguely aware of his own inner humiliation at his failure to apply the technique. The therapist's conscious perception between sessions was that he was struggling with the patient's characterological resistances against experiencing inner frustration, rage, and competitive anxieties and that he, the therapist, would need to continue to confront these defenses.

In the next session, the patient initially related the events of a recent meeting with his current thesis advisor, during which time he felt ignored because of his professor's preoccupation with a long phone call. The therapist heard this communication as an invitation to again explore the patient's underlying anger at the professor and/or therapist, and he proceeded again to apply vigorously the challenge to the patient's defenses against his underlying feelings toward male authority figures. As the session proceeded, the patient showed increasing distancing and passivity, while the therapist experienced exhaustion and despair. The therapist remained unaware that the patient's communication reflected a realistic perception that the therapist, like the professor, was not responsive to his needs.

In the following supervisory hour, the supervisor was able to help the therapist explore his own frustration and anger with the patient, himself, and the technique, and to also explore his embarrassment for appearing as a failure to the supervisor. The therapist and supervisor then further explored how the patient was realistically commenting to the therapist about the therapist's unconscious self-preoccupation while he applied the technique. The therapist's realization that the patient was accurately commenting on his behavior subsequently allowed the therapist to be attuned to the full transference–countertransference paradigm of the moment. This understanding then enabled the therapist to work quickly on mending the misalliance by allowing himself to ask the patient whether he had felt understood by the therapist. An active exploration into the patient's sadness at having been neglected by the therapist prevented a premature termination and promoted an active working alliance.

Two issues that often occur in both the Sifneos and Davanloo models are the rapid switch of transference paradigms during the sessions and the significant internal work accomplished by the patient between sessions. Therapists are often still lingering over material from a previous session when patients have significantly moved on during the week between sessions. This process is often heightened when therapists watch an audiovisually recorded tape of the previous session during the intervening week both during supervision or alone for self-monitoring. Special attention has to be focused on the first 5 to 10 min of each session to grasp the nature of the patient's inner conflicts in his or her overt verbal communication and behavior. The therapist must learn to accommodate quickly to the patient's communication about his or her inner psychological state and rapidly assimilate this to his or her own conception of the patient. This is a very demanding task, as there are significant time pressures impinging on the therapist to actively assist the patient with the unfolding of the dynamic process. Failure of this assimilation or accommodation process in the session causes a rupture in the therapeutic working alliance, which again can lead either to termination or a significant lengthening of treatment.

For example, a male therapist trainee had worked successfully in a previous session with a female patient in exploring her very competitive, negative feelings toward her mother. This session had been emotionally taxing for the patient because of her experience of intense anger and grief. In the week interval between sessions, the therapist reviewed the audiovisually recorded session 3 days before the next session, and again with his supervisor 1 day before the next session. The therapist looked forward to seeing the patient in order to further explore this material.

In this session, and after several minutes of expressing her discomfort experienced on a crowded subway ride to the session and then apologizing for being a few minutes late, the patient reported having been very embarrassed about a homosexual dream that occurred two nights earlier. The therapist was eager to explore this dream, which seemed to him like a natural development of the previous session. The patient eagerly followed the therapist's not-so-subtle clues to discuss further her relationship with her mother. After 35 min of dialogue, the therapist realized that the session was noticeably less emotionally moving than the previous session, but he was unable to decide on a direction to take.

In the following supervisory hour, the therapist and supervisor watched the first 15 min of the tape after the therapist related his frustration with the session. The supervisor was able to point out to the therapist the patient's communication about her discomfort on the crowded subway and her lateness to the session. A discussion then followed about how the patient might have felt toward the therapist at the end of the previously emotionally charged session. It then became clear to the therapist that the patient's communications, including the dream, indicated that the patient probably was experiencing very tender feelings toward the therapist for having helped her explore and accept some very painful feelings and that she was terrified of the closeness she was subsequently experiencing toward the therapist. This had been somewhat disguised in the dream. The shift from the focus on anger experienced toward a past figure (mother) in the intervening week between sessions to the conflictual experience of tenderness toward the therapist requires the therapist to be alert and psychodynamically sophisticated and agile. Failure to perceive thematic shifts can cause a therapeutic stalemate and transference regression. Unless this situation is quickly monitored and attended to, a rupture in the therapeutic alliance or a significant prolongation of treatment will ensue.

As seen earlier, patients and therapists experience many sources of alliance ruptures secondary to the emergence of countertransference issues. One common group of countertransference reactions occurs because of the application of the technique itself. The Sifneos and Davanloo models require the therapist to be active, assertive, and intrusive into the therapeutic field. Therapists who have difficulties with assertion, taking an active role, or being confrontative may misuse the technique by the underutilization or by the compensatory overutilization of any of the parameters of technique, thereby creating a misalliance. In the previous example of the trainee who was working with the obsessional graduate student, aspects of the trainee's own competitive issues and difficulties dealing with anger had to be repeatedly explored as he continued to effectively struggle to learn the technique.

A second group of countertransference issues arises subsequently to the experience of the intense affects of aggression and mourning stimulated by the technique in a relatively short period of time, particularly in the Davanloo model. Therapists who have unresolved mourning or who have suffered recent losses are particularly vulnerable to colluding with patients to ward off the experience of intense grief. This type of countertransference problem is difficult to handle because of the compressed nature of the treatment. Therefore, therapists need to be very aware of their countertransference vulnerabilities when they treat patients in this treatment.

A third type of countertransference reaction arises when therapists have been previously trained in standard psychoanalytic technique. Besides the usual above-mentioned countertransference issues, these therapists frequently encounter an inner conflict over their loyalty to another model of technique (which has been supported by powerful identifications formed during their training, in their personal psychoanalyses, and in their clinical practices).

All of these countertransference issues need careful monitoring by the therapist and in the supervisory process in order to avoid major breaks in the therapeutic working alliance. During the training period, it is incumbent upon the therapist to vigorously watch the tapes and prepare an overview for the supervisor. The supervisor must be sensitive not only to the microscopic technical moment-to-moment therapeutic process, but also to the psychodynamic overview. The supervisor must keep these two perspectives in the therapist's consciousness as well. Only in this way can breaks in the therapeutic working alliance be avoided. Even well-trained therapists using brief psychotherapeutic techniques find it useful and necessary to work in ongoing group supervisory sessions with their peers because of the pressures engendered by the technical parameters and time constraints of the brief psychotherapy drive–conflict models.

Summary

Clinical work in the brief psychoanalytic psychotherapies, as illustrated in the Davanloo and Sifneos models, further elaborates and highlights the intertwining of the therapeutic alliance with transference–countertransference reactions. Particularly in the supervisory situation, it is helpful to distinguish between these two factors to help therapists realize the impact of the techniques they are using with patients.

High levels of therapist activity are by their nature very intrusive. This activity level has a real impact on both the therapist and patient in the experience of their work with each other partially independent of the transference–countertransference paradigms of the moment. Both of these issues need constant attention during an ongoing therapy, with or without supervision, in order to maintain a successful therapeutic working alliance.

The impact of the parameters of technique of brief psychoanalytic psychotherapy on the therapeutic alliance suggests that more attention be paid to the impact of the parameters of psychoanalytic technique on the therapeutic alliance in standard psychoanalysis. Often these techniques, such as the nature of the analytic listening process itself, are accepted as axioms instead of being seen as arbitrary technical parameters that shape the therapeutic alliance. The importance of this understanding for elucidating and understanding the therapeutic process and the subsequent derived metapsychology is critical. The therapists' and patients' capacities for mutual influence and the nature of the interpersonal–intrapsychic matrix can only be understood by critically evaluating the reciprocal interaction of all the process variables in the therapeutic field. The relationship of the therapeutic alliance and transference–countertransference paradigms in the conflict–drive model of brief psychotherapy offers one exciting avenue of approach to study these interactions.

References

Been, H., & Sklar, I. (1985). Transference in short-term dynamic psychotherapy. In A. Winston (Ed.), *Short-term dynamic psychotherapy* (pp. 1–18). Washington, DC: American Psychiatric Press.

Bibring, E. (1937). Therapeutic results of psychoanalysis. *International Journal of Psychoanalysis, 18*, 170–189.

Bordin, E. S. (1979). The generalizability of the psychoanalytic concept of the working alliance. *Psychotherapy, 16*, 252–260.

Davanloo, H. (1980). *Short-term dynamic psychotherapy.* New York: Jason Aronson.

Freud, S. (1913). On beginning the treatment. In J. Strachey (Ed.), *Standard edition of the complete psychological works of Sigmund Freud* (Vol. 12, pp. 121–144). London: Hogarth Press.

Freud, S. (1958). The dynamics of transference. In J. Strachey (Ed.), *The standard edition of the complete psychological works of Sigmund Freud* (Vol. 12, pp. 97–108). London: Hogarth Press. (Original work published 1912)

Gaston, L. (1990). The concept of the alliance and its role in psychotherapy: Theoretical and empirical considerations. *Psychotherapy, 27*, 143–153.

Greenson, R. (1967). *The technique and practice of psychoanalysis* (Vol. 1). New York: International Universities Press.

Laikin, M., Winston, A., & McCullough, L. (1991). Intensive short-term psychotherapy. In P. Crits-Christoph & J. P. Barber (Eds.), *Handbook of short-term dynamic psychotherapy* (pp. 80–109). New York: Basic Books.

Malan, D. H. (1976a). *The frontier of brief psychotherapy.* New York: Plenum.

Malan, D. H. (1976b). *Towards the validation of dynamic psychotherapy.* New York: Plenum.

Mann, J. (1973). *Time-limited psychotherapy.* Cambridge, MA: Harvard University Press.

Sifneos, P. E. (1972). *Short-term psychotherapy and emotional crisis.* Cambridge, MA: Harvard University Press.

Sterba, R. (1934). The fate of the ego in analytic therapy. *International Journal of Psychoanalysis, 15,* 117–125.

Stone, L. (1961). *The psychoanalytic situation.* New York: International Universities Press.

Zetzel, E. (1956). Current concepts of transference. *International Journal of Psychoanalysis, 37,* 369–376.

Jeffrey L. Binder

The Therapeutic Alliance in the Relational Models of Time-Limited Dynamic Psychotherapy

3

When characterizing models of psychotherapy, the term *relational* refers to those models in which the foundation is psychoanalytic theory, but the superstructure is comprised of the synthesis of interpersonal and object relations theories, as well as attachment theory, concepts and principles from the cognitive sciences, and observations from object relational infant research (Messer & Warren, 1995). In their book on brief psychodynamic therapies, Messer and Warren identified four relational models and masterfully explicated their commonalities and differences. These models are supportive–expressive psychoanalytic treatment (S–E dynamic therapy) developed by Lester Luborsky and studied by the University Of Pennsylvania research group (Luborsky, 1984; Luborsky & Crits-Christoph, 1990); time-limited psychodynamic treatment of stress response syndromes (SRS brief therapy), developed by Mardi Horowitz and the research group at the Center for the Study of Neuroses (Horowitz, 1986; Horowitz et al., 1984); and the plan formulation method (PFM therapy) developed by Joseph Weiss (1993) and studied by Weiss, Sampson, and the Mount Zion Hospital Research Group (1986). The fourth model is time-limited dynamic psychotherapy (TLDP), which was developed by Hans Strupp and myself, along with other members of the Vanderbilt Center for Psychotherapy Research (Binder & Strupp, 1991; Strupp & Binder, 1984).

I use the relational models identified by Messer and Warren (1995) to discuss how this form of psychodynamic psychotherapy deals with the therapeutic alliance. My own approach, TLDP, will receive the most attention. I should note that my discussion of the other relational models is based on the published writings of the developers, although my comments about TLDP are based on what both Strupp and I have previously written, as well as my current—and, perhaps idiosyncratic—evolving thoughts about the model.

The relational treatment models share certain theoretical perspectives. Internal self-representations, object representations, and patterned interactions between these representations (sometimes referred to as *working models* or *structured role relationships*) are viewed as the core of personality structure. The cardinal human motive is to attain a form of connectedness with others that evokes a sense of well-being associated with feelings of safety and security. Psychotherapists view dynamic conflict in terms of incompatible internal relational configurations. *Psychopathology* is conceived of as recurrent patterns of maladaptive interpersonal behavior that reflects incompatible and conflict-ridden internal working models or structured role relationships. The persistence of psychopathology is explained by emphasizing the reinforcing properties of cyclical interpersonal patterns (Messer & Warren, 1995). A major assumption characterizing the relational view of therapeutic change processes is that if psychopathology originates with the internalization of conflictual childhood interpersonal experiences and the resultant creation of self-perpetuating maladaptive interpersonal patterns, then to some extent corrective interpersonal experiences in the therapeutic relationship can catalyze healthy changes in internal self–object configurations and patterns of interpersonal behavior.

While sharing commonalities that categorize them as relational models, each treatment approach has distinguishing characteristics. S–E dynamic therapy is the most reliant on standard psychoanalytic intrapsychic principles. Psychological conflict originates in the opposition of hidden wishes and expected negative consequences. This conflict is manifested interpersonally in the form of transference. The therapist's role is to remain as neutral as possible in the face of transference pressures and to interpret the influence of transference on the patient's relationships, particularly the therapeutic relationship. The therapist's technical strategies are determined by the patient's capacity to tolerate the discomfort and work associated with dynamic therapy; if this capacity is strong, then expressive techniques are emphasized, and if this capacity is weak, then supportive techniques are used (Luborsky, 1984). The unique contribution of S–E dynamic therapy is the precise, research-informed conception of transference—the core conflictual relationship theme (CCRT)—which serves as a focal problem formulation and guides the content of the therapist's interventions. The aim of this treatment model is to modify the CCRT in the direction of healthier interpersonal adaptation, particularly by reducing the negative expectations associated with acting on one's desires (Luborsky & Crits-Christoph, 1990).

SRS brief therapy has a 12-session time limit and focuses on traumatic life events. It combines certain standard psychoanalytic principles regarding therapeutic process and technique with more crisis-oriented techniques and with a conception of personality functioning that relies heavily on schema theory adapted from cognitive psychology. A working assumption is that stressful events become overwhelming when they are associated with unresolved conflicts or predisposing personality factors. The principal therapeutic strategy is similar to the S–E dynamic therapy model in that therapists tailor their approaches to the patients' state of mind, which in the case of SRS brief therapy is typically characterized as either overwhelmed or overly controlled in reaction to some external trauma. The therapist's role is to remain neutral and to interpret transference minimally, usually around termination issues. Interventions are guided by a precise formulation model that refers to internal structured role relationships and their interpersonal manifestations. The aim of this treatment approach is to modify existing internal "working models" of self and the world to accommodate changes associated with the experienced trauma. This usually involves discovering the uniquely personal meanings of the trauma in the context of the patient's life (Horowitz, 1986). This model has been adapted for dealing with emotionally uncomfortable states of mind associated with various personality problems (Horowitz et al., 1984).

Although categorized as a relational model because of its conception of the therapeutic process, PFM therapy relies heavily on certain ego-psychological concepts, particularly the notion of complex unconscious ego processing (problem solving) and the persistent striving to master anachronistic emotional problems. The source of current psychopathology is conceived of as a patient's unconscious so-called pathogenic beliefs about the harmful consequences should he or she attain certain essentially healthy desires or aspirations. These beliefs inhibit attempts to attain healthy life goals. Although the language is cognitive, these pathogenic beliefs refer to anticipated negative interpersonal scenarios and are, therefore, relationally oriented (Messer & Warren, 1995).

The patient enters therapy with an unconscious plan to "test" his or her beliefs in the hope that the therapist will disconfirm them. This plan is automatically put into operation through various transference enactments. The role of the therapist is to pass these tests, presumably by not engaging in countertransferential reactions. The therapist also interprets evidence of the patient's tests. These interventions do not have to refer to transference enactments in order to have maximum impact. This treatment model posits that the relevance to the patient's unconscious plan of the content of an intervention is the crucial factor in producing therapeutic change. Interventions are guided by a precise formulation that includes a description of unconscious pathogenic beliefs and goals. The aim of this model is to disconfirm the patient's pathogenic beliefs and, thus, remove the obstacles to his or her attaining cherished personal goals (Weiss, 1993).

Of the four relational models, TLDP is the most reliant on interpersonal theory, principles, and technical strategies. *Psychopathology* here refers to rigid and anachronistic internal working models or structured role relationships that are enacted interpersonally in the form of maladaptive patterns of interacting. These maladaptive interpersonal patterns are defined as transference, which is inextricably linked to the reactions (countertransference) evoked in the therapist by the patient's transference enactments. Transference and countertransference are part of a seamless interpersonal scenario in which patient and therapist jointly participate, although ideally not to the same extent. The therapist cannot avoid recurrently becoming snared in these maladaptive interpersonal patterns, so his or her role is to minimize the time spent unreflectively participating in them. At the same time, the therapist is helping the patient to learn to identify and control these maladaptive patterns in all areas of the patient's life. The therapist's interventions are guided by a precise problem formulation called the *cyclical maladaptive pattern* (CMP), which is very similar to (if not identical with) the CCRT. The aim of TLDP is to facilitate modification of maladaptive internal relational configurations and their interpersonal correlates (Binder & Strupp, 1991; Strupp & Binder, 1984).

All four of the relational treatment models were developed by psychotherapy research teams whose primary interest was (and remains) the investigation of the psychotherapy process and outcome. The models' brevity was an afterthought, although time-limited treatments have always been logistically easier to investigate than time-unlimited treatment. However, as Budman and Gurman (1988) point out, there are crucial differences between brief therapy by *design* and brief therapy by *default*. In some respects the relational models were brief by default; that is to say, they were not developed primarily to capitalize on any presumed curative effects of time limits. On the other hand, no empirically proven effects of this sort have been discovered.

In any event, my own current set of working assumptions is that competently conducted psychotherapy by its nature will be effective and efficient. In a well-conducted therapy, time is always thought of as a precious commodity from which the maximum benefit should be extracted. This attitude is associated with a disciplined approach to treatment that Strupp and I discussed in our manual (Strupp & Binder, 1984) and that Budman and Gurman (1988) referred to in their descriptions of brief treatment technique as "time effective" or "time sensitive" rather than time limited. All four of the relational treatment models discussed subscribe to the notion that certain characteristics define well-conducted psychotherapy. These characteristics include the following:

1. An interpersonal diagnostic assessment that addresses personality characteristics and environmental circumstances most relevant to potential therapeutic change,
2. Formulations of a specific problem focus that will guide treatment interventions,
3. A theory-guided view of the therapeutic process and therapeutic change from which a coherent set of technical strategies and tactics are derived, and
4. The establishment and maintenance of a therapeutic alliance.

It is to this last characteristic that I now turn my attention.

Conceptualizations of the Therapeutic Alliance

The relational models represent various conceptions of the therapeutic alliance, all of which are to some extent congruent with Bordin's (1994) pantheoretical definition of the alliance as composed of three interacting components:

1. A respectful and friendly bond between patient and therapist,
2. An agreement on therapeutic goals, and
3. An agreement on therapeutic tasks designed to achieve these goals.

There appears to be a tendency for these relational models to emphasize the collaborative task or working components of the alliance. Only in S–E dynamic therapy are the bond and task components explicitly distinguished and referred to as two types of "helping alliance."

To the extent that the relational models share a basic psychodynamic perspective of the therapeutic process, they reflect similar views about the role of the therapeutic alliance in that broader process. S–E dynamic therapy, SRS brief therapy, and the original TLDP model all conceived of two facets to the therapeutic relationship: the irrational, anachronistic part (transference) and the rational, adaptive part (the real relationship). The therapeutic alliance is located in this latter portion of the therapeutic relationship, although it can be undermined by transference. Therapists presume that this event typically occurs early in therapy, and if treatment progresses successfully, it is less likely to happen. PFM therapy also appears to view the alliance as part of the rational relationship between patient and therapist, but this is not as clearly articulated.

Even in our original discussions of the alliance, Strupp and I (Strupp & Binder, 1984) adumbrated a radically modified view when we alluded to the alliance as "ambivalent" (p. 155). By this we meant that the distinction between real and transference relationships was artificial because we understood transference experiences as being determined by misinterpretations of the therapist's actual behavior, which, in turn, was partly determined by the patient's evocative transference actions (countertransference). In other words, we envisioned the therapist and patient influencing each other's experiences and actions in a complementary fashion, so that the patient's transference experiences were always to some extent reactive to the therapist's actions. Consequently, the distinction between rational and irrational perceptions becomes blurred.

These notions were explicitly articulated by Henry and Strupp (1994), who eradicated the conceptual boundaries among the real relationship, transference relationships, and the therapeutic alliance. They stated that the therapeutic process is always an admixture of rational, transferential, and alliance elements, and the particular proportion of each element is continually changing from interaction to interaction. The practical implication is evident: A therapist cannot rest on the laurels of an established alliance, because the climate can change instantaneously.

My own view of the alliance is midway between this more interpersonally fluid conception and the more traditional conception (represented by the other relational models) of the alliance as very slow to change. I concur with Henry and Strupp in their view of the alliance as a facet of a seamless interpersonal process. However, I presume that its mutability is more consistent with a malleable solid than with a fluid. Furthermore, I presume that significant declines in the alliance are in fact "ruptures" produced by transference–countertransference enactments that have reached a critical threshold of influence. The alliance is restored to effective influence after resolution of these "alliance ruptures" (Safran, Crocker, McMain, & Murray, 1990; Safran, Muran, & Samstag, 1994). A cardinal implication for brief therapy in this perspective of a fluctuating alliance is that to make the most of the time available, the therapist must be scrupulously attuned to decreases in the alliance and react quickly to rectify such ruptures, because when the alliance is in poor shape, therapeutic work is impossible. On the other hand, if the alliance is malleable, then it is conceivable that an initially poor alliance can be improved in the delimited time available in brief therapy (Foreman & Marmar, 1985).

In addition to commonalities, there are differences in the role played by the alliance within broader conceptions of the therapeutic process when these conceptions vary across treatment models. S–E dynamic therapy and SRS brief therapy represent a more traditional, intrapsychic psychoanalytic conception of the contribution made by the therapeutic alliance to patient change. The alliance provides a relationship context that fosters the patient's receptivity to the therapist's technical interventions. It creates a so-called powerbase, a source of the therapist's influence without which the therapist would have little impact on the patient (Freud, 1953). Technical interventions are presumed to be the direct agent of therapeutic change. PFM therapy and the original TLDP model (the latter representing a more purely relational viewpoint) conceive of therapeutic change as resulting directly from two parallel sources: cognitive insight associated with technical interventions, and the internalization of a corrective interpersonal experience associated with a strong therapeutic alliance.

My current view of the role of the alliance in promoting therapeutic change is based on a more elaborate conception of therapeutic change agents than we had articulated when Strupp and I originally codified TLDP. I postulate four agents of therapeutic change, which will vary in relative influence across patient–therapist dyads and across time in any given dyad. These four change agents are the following:

1. Cognitive insight about maladaptive internal working models and their associated interpersonal patterns. These insights can be achieved in the examination of any interpersonal interaction or relationship. Although conceptually appealing, the presumption that insights about interpersonal patterns have more impact when derived from examining the therapeutic relationship has yet to be proven.
2. Cognitive learning of certain generic skills that are required in order to capitalize on the aforementioned change agent of identifying and managing maladaptive interpersonal patterns. These skills include pattern recognition, self-reflection,

and self-monitoring. Although people may vary in their natural capacities for learning these skills, I assume the skills can be enhanced with appropriate techniques and by encouraging practice.

3. Internalization of corrective interpersonal experiences encountered in the therapeutic relationship. It is this process through which the therapeutic alliance functions as a direct agent of change.

4. The creation of new corrective interpersonal experiences outside of therapy, as the patient practices what he or she has learned in the therapy sessions.

The therapist's general role in promoting a strong therapeutic alliance also varies across treatment models as a function of each model's broader view of the therapeutic process. Once again S–E dynamic therapy and SRS brief therapy represent the more traditional psychoanalytic view, in which the problem resides primarily in and around the patient. Consequently, the therapist should maintain a stance that is removed from the interpersonal manifestations of the patient's problems. In more familiar psychoanalytic terms, the therapist should avoid countertransference reactions to the patient's transference.

PFM therapy takes a similar perspective but articulates it within the cognitive–dynamic language of unconscious plans and tests. The therapist should avoid failing the patient's tests of his or her pathogenic beliefs. Reflecting a more interpersonal conception of psychopathology, TLDP has always maintained that it is inevitable that the therapist will be recruited into roles within the maladaptive interpersonal scenarios enacted by patients. Consequently, the therapist's role in encouraging an alliance involves *minimizing* the time spent unreflectively participating in these transference–countertransference scenarios.

The Impact of Brevity on Conceptions of the Alliance

I have stated before that the relational models were not developed with an eye toward time as a change agent. All the same, the developers of these models were interested in maximizing the efficient use of time, and the conceptions of the therapeutic alliance that are associated with these models do have implications for conducting brief treatment. There is accumulating evidence that the patient's capacity for contributing to alliance development is determined by the maturity of his or her level of interpersonal relating (Hoglend, Sorlie, Heyerdahl, Sorbye, & Amlo, 1993; Piper et al., 1991). Those brief treatment models that view the alliance as a contribution made primarily by the patient have stringent selection criteria in order to ensure the presence of a strong alliance. These models share a no-nonsense approach that can be quite emotionally taxing, and at the same time, they expect that with properly selected patients, the alliance should be operating reliably in the background and not require servicing (e.g., Davanloo, 1980; Malan, 1976; Sifneos, 1979).

To varying degrees, the relational models view the therapeutic alliance as an interactive concept. Patient and therapist contribute jointly to the quality of the therapeutic relationship and, consequently, by their attitudes and actions therapists can influence the establishment and maintenance of an alliance. As a result, selection criteria can be more lenient. In all of the relational therapies, the therapist is advised to convey respect for and a warm interest in the patient and to treat the patient as a co-equal collaborator in their work. This demeanor serves to encourage the rapid development of an alliance where time is at a premium. In addition, technical strategies directly address the aim of encouraging a strong alliance. In S–E dynamic therapy, either supportive or expressive techniques are emphasized depending on the degree of self-exploration the patient can tolerate. Similarly, in SRS brief therapy, either supportive or expressive techniques are used depending on the cycle of affective–cognitive regulation (i.e., overwhelmed or overcontrolled) evidenced by the patient. In PFM therapy, the therapist's alertness to passing the patient's tests of his or her pathogenic beliefs serves the purpose of maintaining a strong alliance.

In TLDP the conceptions of the alliance and of the problem focus for brief intervention have always been inextricably entwined. This treatment model was originally developed specifically to deal with patients who have difficulty establishing and maintaining positive therapeutic alliances. Strupp and I (Strupp & Binder, 1984) assumed that the interpersonal manifestation of the patient's problems would always affect the therapeutic relationship. Consequently, in the original TLDP model, the superordinate technical strategy was to identify and interpret the ways in which the patient's interpersonal problems undermined the therapeutic alliance. A corollary assumption was that by focusing on examination of transference–countertransference patterns, both cognitive insight and corrective interpersonal experiences would be maximized. Consequently, the maximum therapeutic gain would be whatever the time constraints placed on the treatment.

As I have said before, my current thinking is that a strong alliance is crucial for efficient use of time. A strong alliance indirectly contributes to therapeutic change by creating a collaborative working climate, and it directly contributes to change through internalization of healthy relationship experiences. However, the alliance need only be examined when undermined by enactments of the patient's interpersonal problems that have reached a critical threshold of influence. My current postulation is that efficient use of time is maximized in brief therapy when the problem focus is addressed in that area of the patient's life in which the problem is most accessible to therapeutic influence. At times, this area will be the therapeutic relationship—that is, the alliance.

Establishing an Alliance

How critical is the initial quality of the therapeutic alliance for the eventual outcome of treatment? Although a significant correlation exists between early alliance ratings and treatment outcome (Gaston, 1990; Horvath & Greenberg, 1994; Luborsky, 1994), many studies also indicate that the quality of the alliance can be influenced by therapist interventions during the course of treatment (Foreman & Marmar, 1985; Klee, Abeles, & Muller, 1990; Joyce, Duncan, & Piper, 1995; Lansford, 1986; Piper et al., 1991; Piper, Boroto, Joyce, McCallum, & Azim, 1995; Safran & Muran, 1996). Evidently, the briefer a treatment or the less a treatment model emphasizes addressing alliance problems, the greater the reliance will be on selecting patients who demonstrate relatively high levels of interpersonal relating.

All of the relational models are time sensitive by virtue of the importance placed upon establishing a strong therapeutic alliance as rapidly as possible. All of the models maintain the view that the therapist must encourage the patient to feel safe in their relationship as soon as possible. In S–E dynamic therapy, the patient is provided a sense of security by the therapist's attitude of sympathetic understanding and by a decision early in treatment about whether the alliance must be directly fostered through a supportive approach. In SRS brief therapy and PFM therapy, practitioners anticipate that the patient will test the therapist's ability to provide a safe relationship. In the former model, the tests typically are limited to the early phase of therapy, during which the therapist passes the tests by choosing the technical strategy appropriate for the patient's initial phase of regulatory affect–cognitive control (i.e., overwhelmed vs. overcontrolled). In PFM therapy, the tests are assumed to occur much further into treatment and involve the therapist's ability to respond in a manner that disconfirms the patient's pathogenic beliefs.

The three aforementioned models share a common assumption that the therapist fosters an alliance by avoiding countertransferential entrapments. The tacit theory is that in brief therapy the therapist must be even more immune to the patient's transference than in time-unlimited treatment, otherwise valuable time will be lost in unproductive interactions associated with a poor alliance. An opposite view is represented by a model of pure interpersonal therapy advocated by Kiesler (1996). In this model, for the initial development of an alliance, it is essential that the therapist be "hooked" into participating in transference–countertransference scenarios, otherwise the relationship will not be experienced as familiar enough for the patient to feel safe. Of course, the therapist must eventually become "unhooked" in order to maintain the alliance. This model of alliance formation received support from one study (Kiesler & Watkins, 1989).

TLDP has a conception of initial alliance formation that is located midway between the two aforementioned theoretical positions. Through a process we (Strupp & Binder, 1984) termed *interpersonal empathy*, the therapist inevitably will be recruited into countertransferential roles associated with the patient's salient maladaptive interpersonal patterns (transference–countertransference). However, being hooked in this fashion is not required for alliance formation. In fact, in the TLDP conception of the therapeutic process, becoming hooked into the patient's maladaptive interpersonal patterns is the embodiment of an alliance rupture. In order to promote the establishment of an alliance, the therapist must *minimize* the time spent participating in transference–countertransference scenarios, and then, engage the patient in examining the nature of these occurrences. The view that transference–countertransference enactments early in treatment are detrimental to outcome—and by implication detrimental to alliance formation—was strongly supported in two studies (Henry, Schacht, & Strupp, 1986, 1990). In the original TLDP model, practitioners assume that the therapist's first priority is to examine these transference–countertransference enactments. Consistent with what I have said before, my current thinking is that there are patients who possess a strong capacity for contributing to the formation of a positive alliance with a particular therapist. In such circumstances, from the inception of treatment, the therapist can concentrate on manifestations of the patient's problems in other relationships, while remaining alert to future problems for the alliance.

Maintaining an Alliance

As a general observation, researchers can say that the relational models share a common strategy about what is required to maintain a therapeutic alliance once established, namely, to keep doing what worked initially. In both SRS brief therapy and PFM therapy, practitioners assume that patients will continue testing their therapists, and the latter must continue passing these tests. In PFM therapy, therapists continue to pass tests when they avoid countertransference responses and when the contents of their interventions are relevant to the problem focus. S–E dynamic therapy emphasizes systematic interpretation of the problem focus in the form of the core conflictual relationship theme (CCRT) as a primary means of maintaining a positive alliance (Crits-Christoph, Barber, & Kurcias, 1993). TLDP advocates the same strategy, the only difference being the specific form of the problem focus. This tracking of a problem focus throughout the course of therapy as an important strategy for maintaining a positive alliance is particularly germane to brief treatments. Approaching the issue from another direction, the practitioners of SRS brief therapy shortened their model from 20 to 12 sessions because of a tendency for the focus to become diffused and the alliance to falter around Session 10—indirect evidence for the association between tracking a focus and maintaining an alliance.

As I have said before about TLDP, in this model practitioners expect that the alliance will be maintained to the degree that the therapist is able to minimize (as opposed to avoid) transference–countertransference enactments. The tone of the therapeutic relationship is less adversarial. The therapist does not have to be vigilant for signs of a test being sprung by the patient (the patient is devious in this regard even if he or she is secretly pulling for the therapist). TLDP emphasizes being alert to signs of *disguised allusions*, that is, problems in the therapeutic relationship that are symbolized in references to other relationships or are embodied in nonverbal qualities of the interaction between patient and therapist. When these problems arise, as they are expected to, the therapist treats them as the joint responsibility of both participants and invites the patient to collaborate on figuring out what happened. Although the original TLDP model is characterized by the assumption that such metacommunication about the patient–therapist relationship must occur for treatment to be maximally successful, I now believe that it only needs to take place if the alliance is ruptured (minor strains may not require attention).

TLDP includes the notion that in important respects the alliance is maintained by therapist's flexibility in response to changing patient needs and general circumstances. This notion is more or less shared by other brief treatment approaches. In conducting any sort of psychotherapy, and brief therapies in particular, much of what the therapist does constitutes improvising in indeterminate problem contexts (Schon, 1983). The idea that the ability to improvise effectively is the hallmark of a competent therapist has not been appreciated in the psychodynamic therapy literature. As the noted relational theorist, Jay Greenberg (1995) has observed, the psychoanalytic therapy literature has been cursed by having "idealized our method" (p. 193); that is to say, the quality of psychodynamic therapies has tended to be evaluated by their purity of method, rather than by their therapeutic efficacy. This philosophy stifles flexibility, creativity, and improvisation, which, I think, are necessary for the practice of good therapy and, particularly, for good brief therapy.

Ruptures in the Therapeutic Alliance

A *strain* or *rupture* in the therapeutic alliance refers to some degree of breakdown in the positive feelings between patient and therapist and some aspect of their working collaboration (Safran et al., 1990). Safran and colleagues have identified at least two types of rupture, which often occur in some combination: (a) confrontation ruptures during which the patient directly complains to the therapist about some aspect of their relationship; and (b) withdrawal ruptures during which patient or therapist disengage from each other. They also view the rupture of an alliance as the direct product of enactment of a patient's maladaptive interpersonal pattern in which the therapist has been snared and which neither of them has recognized (Safran & Muran, 1996; Safran et al., 1994).

I have not encountered any explicit references to alliance ruptures in the published writing about the relational models. However, the relational models do tacitly recognize these breakdowns in patient–therapist collaboration, although they appear to vary in their anticipation of the frequency and intensity of alliance fluctuations over the course of treatment. S–E dynamic therapy and SRS brief therapy recommend that the therapist be alert to recurrent "transference provocations" that reflect enactments of structured internal role relationships in the form of specific interpersonal patterns. Although not stated in so many words, practitioners can infer that such provocations will detrimentally influence the alliance if the therapist does not adequately attend to them. At the same time, these two models appear to view the fate of the alliance as being established early in therapy and not easily changed thereafter.

While the PFM therapy model does not explicitly refer to alliance ruptures, its concept of the therapeutic process provides a tacit albeit precise definition of such an occurrence. An alliance rupture is operating when the patient unconsciously presents the therapist with a test in order to try to disconfirm a pathogenic belief, and the therapist fails the test. The patient is expected to unconsciously provide these tests repeatedly over the course of treatment. If the therapist fails several minor tests, he or she can recoup by passing more and bigger tests. Failure of too many tests may irreparably damage the treatment, indicated typically by the patient dramatically increasing self-defeating behavior. This concept could be translated into the language of alliance ruptures, if not for one major discrepancy. It does not appear that the PFM therapy model acknowledges the inevitability of alliance ruptures (i.e., failed tests). On the contrary, it strongly implies that a competent therapist conceivably could pass most, if not all, tests, and thereby avoid any alliance ruptures. This point is also markedly discrepant from the TLDP concept of the therapeutic process.

The theory of alliance ruptures appears to be most congruent with the TLDP conception of therapeutic process. The inevitable recruitment of the therapist into the enactment of countertransference roles that are complementary to the patient's transference roles, in an inextricably entwined maladaptive interpersonal scenario, is conceptually synonymous with an alliance rupture (Safran & Muran, 1996). In TLDP these transference–countertransference scenarios are considered to be recurrent, inevitable, and when identified and effectively managed by the therapist, opportunities for major therapeutic change through the processes of cognitive insight and the internalization of corrective interpersonal experiences. Safran and Muran have translated this conception of therapeutic process into the language of alliance theory, have operationalized central concepts, and have developed a program of research to specify how occurrences of these maladaptive scenarios are either resolved or persist.

Technical Strategies for Managing Therapeutic Alliance Ruptures

The technical strategies and tactics employed by each of the relational models to deal with alliance ruptures are congruent with each of their conceptions of therapeutic process. There are, however, three common themes that characterize all of the models and that are relevant to maximizing the efficiency—and therefore the brevity—of treatment:

1. Each model recommends the formulation of a precise problem focus and the consistent tracking of that focus throughout the course of treatment.
2. Each model recommends that the therapist engage in active efforts to ensure that the patient experiences the therapeutic relationship as supportive.
3. Properly employed technical strategies and tactics are considered as essential for maintaining a positive therapeutic alliance and for rectifying alliance strains and ruptures when they occur.

Before discussing more specific similarities and differences in technical strategies and tactics among the relational models, I describe the circumstances of a hypothetical patient and then use this material to illustrate my points:

> Susan is a 40-year-old, Caucasian woman who has been divorced for several years after a 10-year marriage. During her marriage, she had one child and resumed her career after a several-year hiatus while her child was very young. She was advancing rapidly in her career when her husband announced that he was seeking a divorce because he did not want a wife who divided her time between home and a career. Although her husband had occasionally voiced mild complaints about her career, Susan was surprised at his precipitous decision and felt that she had somehow failed her husband and child. As a single mother, she continued to be successful in her career and involved in parenting her child. Over the past few years she had several failed romantic relationships, the typical pattern being that she felt misunderstood or unsupported by the man in her attempts to pursue a career and simultaneously be involved in an intimate relationship. Susan's parents had divorced when she was 5 years old. Her father had quickly remarried and, although he always met his financial responsibilities in providing for her, he was more emotionally involved with his second family. Her mother never remarried. She worked to support herself, had a network of friends, and occasionally dated, but Susan was her only intimate relationship. When Susan married and had a child, her mother was noticeably upset over having less of Susan's time available to her. Her mother died after a short illness approximately 1 year prior to Susan seeking psychotherapy. Susan decided to seek help because of a series of disturbing nightmares in which her mother was drowning and Susan was unable to rescue her. In addition, memories of various activities with her mother while she was growing up had been intruding on her mind, accompanied by intense sadness and the fear that she would always be alone.

S–E dynamic therapy and SRS brief therapy share similar relatively traditional views of the therapist's role in the therapeutic process and, consequently, these models share certain similarities in their technical strategies. Both models define two broad intervention strategies, and the therapist must choose the one most appropriate for the patient at hand in order to foster the establishment of a therapeutic alliance. In S–E dynamic therapy, the two choices are the more exploratory and confrontive expressive strategy, appropriate for patients who can readily join in an alliance, or the supportive strategy that requires more straightforward encouragement, for those patients who are relatively less open and trusting. In the case of Susan, the therapist might choose a supportive strategy because of her general avoidance of intimate relationships and because of her history of painful rejections and abandonments starting with her father.

In SRS brief therapy, there are two alternative technical strategies relevant for the early period of treatment. These strategies are differentially responsive to the phase in the regulatory affective–cognitive control cycle that is currently operating to cope with a recent or reactivated traumatic stress. If the patient is in the phase of "denial-numbing," then the appropriate choice is a more interpretive strategy. In the case of Susan, the active phase is repetitive–intrusive, associated with the anniversary of her mother's death, as evidenced by her nightmares, unbidden memories, and intense painful feelings. Consequently, a more supportive technical strategy is called for, perhaps including psychoeducation about anniversary grief reactions, to help in alleviating anxiety and sleeplessness, and possible evaluation for medication.

In PFM therapy, the therapist's superordinate technical strategy is to sufficiently understand the patient's unconscious plan in order to be able to adopt an interpersonal stance that is congruent with passing the patient's unconscious tests. In the case of Susan, the PFM therapist might formulate her unconscious plan as to pursue the satisfactions associated with success in her career while simultaneously establishing a gratifying intimate relationship with a man. However, in order to achieve this goal, she must overcome the pathogenic belief that anyone with whom she desires an intimate relationship will abandon her if she perseveres with her career ambitions. Consequently, Susan may unconsciously test this pathogenic belief by making it difficult for her therapist to schedule a regular appointment time because of her busy business schedule. The therapist can pass this test by at least initially demonstrating flexibility in the scheduling of therapy appointments and, thereby, maintain a positive alliance. If the therapist fails the test, then an alliance rupture will ensue. This conception shares with the aforementioned two models the relatively traditional psychodynamic notion that the therapeutic alliance will be fostered

only if the therapist avoids technical mistakes and countertranferen-
tial responses.

TLDP represents a relatively more interpersonal model of therapeutic process, as reflected in the characteristic technical strategy and
role of the therapist. The therapist is expected to be a "participant
observer" in the enactments of the patient's maladaptive interpersonal
patterns, and the therapist's role is to minimize the time spent unreflectively participating in these patterns (as opposed to being expected
to avoid the occurrence of such participation). To paraphrase the noted
interpersonal psychoanalyst Edgar Levenson (1972), the therapist's
strategy is to become immersed in the interpersonal world of the
patient and then to work his or her way out. Likewise, practitioners
of this model expect that the alliance may repeatedly undergo strain
and rupture, which provides the therapist and the patient the opportunity to examine the interpersonal patterns enacted between them
that created the rupture.

In the case of Susan, she talks to her therapist about how much
she confides in her daughter and another close female friend. The
therapist observes that perhaps Susan is having a difficult time trusting and confiding in her therapist. Susan responds by becoming quiet
and then mournfully relating how guilty she feels about not have
spent more time with her mother before her death. The therapist realizes that Susan may have experienced the therapist's comments about
her difficulty trusting the therapist as critical and complaining, symbolizing in Susan's mind a repetition of her mother's upset over
Susan's independence from her. The therapist begins to explore with
Susan whether she indeed had felt criticized and blamed.

A technical strategy is implemented through specific interventions. All four of the relational models, tracing their lineage from psychoanalytic treatment principles, use interpretations of various kinds
as the primary technique for ameliorating psychopathology, and by
association, for directly or indirectly dealing with alliance ruptures.
Three of the four models rely on transference interpretations as the
premier type of interpretation. PFM therapy takes the position that the
relevance of the content of the interpretation with regard to the
patient's unconscious plan is crucial for fostering a continuing therapeutic alliance, rather than the type of interpretation offered. This
assertion has been supported by empirical studies of the PFM treatment process (Silberschatz, Fretter, & Curtis, 1986). An example of a
"pro-plan" interpretation for Susan might go something like this: "You
are afraid that your involvement in your career precludes your ever
being able to satisfy the emotional needs of a man and, therefore, you
will always be alone." Another pro-plan transference interpretation
might be the following: "You were afraid that in response to your

request for some flexibility in your appointment times in order to accommodate your work schedule, I would probably tell you that we could not work together."

In the early phase of treatment when the aftereffects of trauma in the form of regulatory overcontrol or undercontrol of affects and cognitions are the primary target of intervention, SRS brief therapy uses a large array of interventions. Later in treatment when the focus shifts to the personal meanings attributed by the patient to the trauma, and particularly in the termination phase when the impending end of the relationship tends to be understood in terms of these personal themes, SRS brief therapy advocates transference interpretations as the most effective intervention. Writings about this model do not specify whether transference interpretations focus on here-and-now patient–therapist interactions or on links between current transference and its origin in patterns of childhood interpersonal experiences. Apparently, with regard to fostering a positive therapeutic alliance, the emphasis in this model is on appropriate interventions to deal with the aftereffects of trauma early in treatment and appropriate transference interpretations about termination late in treatment. In the case of Susan, an example of the former intervention would be to explain her nightmares about her mother as a product of unresolved grieving. An example of the latter type of intervention would be the following transference interpretation toward the end of treatment: "You still can't shake the fear I am following through on our plan to complete therapy in two more sessions because I don't like it that you continue to devote a substantial amount of time to your career."

Although not stated explicitly in so many words, S–E dynamic therapy and TLDP share the view that the therapeutic alliance will be repeatedly strained and ruptured by the enactment in the form of transference of the patient's maladaptive interpersonal patterns. The models differ with regard to the therapist's role in these enactments, as I have discussed previously. This difference has implications for technique. S–E dynamic therapy advocates dealing with transference enactments and the associated alliance ruptures through the use of here-and-now transference interpretations, the content of which closely corresponds to the content of the problem focus of the CCRT which the therapist originally formulated. Empirical evidence has been adduced that in S–E dynamic therapy, the practice of consistently adhering to the CCRT in the content of interventions is correlated with a positive alliance and a good treatment outcome (Crits-Christoph et al., 1993; Crits-Christoph, Cooper, & Luborsky, 1988). These studies have not supported the postulate that transference interpretations serve to maintain a positive alliance, but this fact has not influenced reliance on this type of intervention. An example of a here-and-now transference interpretation with a CCRT focus with Susan would be the following: "You would like to request from me some continued flexibility in scheduling your appointments in order to accommodate your business schedule, but you are afraid that I will be offended that you don't take our work seriously enough and will decide that we cannot work together. Consequently you hold back from making this request."

In TLDP, the therapist expects that enactments of the patient's maladaptive interpersonal patterns will be in the form of transference–countertransference scenarios involving complementary patient–therapist participation. In reaction to this interactive view of the therapist's role in the process, original advocacy for here-and-now transference interpretations, which is primarily a psychodynamic technique, has shifted to advocacy for metacommunication, which is more closely aligned with interpersonal treatment models. *Metacommunication* is a concept that can include transference interpretations but is more inclusive. It emphasizes examination of immediate patient–therapist interactions, although links to identified patterns in other relationships are encouraged when such links serve to elaborate the significance and meanings of a transferential pattern. However, metacommunication also refers to greater emphasis than is typical of psychodynamic therapy on the immediate experiences and contributions of the therapist to transference–countertransference enactments. Judicious self-disclosure (e.g., acknowledging one's contribution to an alliance rupture or sharing something about one's personal life that could put into relief a misinterpretation by the patient about the therapist's attitude toward him or her) is an accepted part of metacommunication, in contrast to standard psychoanalytic technical guidelines that view it as unacceptable.

An example of metacommunication in TLDP would be a situation in which Susan repeatedly requests changes in appointment times in order to accommodate her business schedule. The therapist finally becomes exasperated with all of the changes and, in an impatient tone of voice, requests that Susan try to stabilize her business schedule so that she can attend regular appointments, because it is becoming increasingly difficult to adjust the schedule. In response to the therapist's request, Susan's communications begin to focus on all of the failed romantic relationships that she felt have been ruined by her devotion to her career. The therapist in retrospect recognizes his or her impatient tone of voice and also recognizes the implications of threatened rejection in the patient's communications. Consequently, the therapist suggests that perhaps Susan is experiencing the therapist's request about her schedule as a warning that their relationship is being placed in jeopardy by her work. The therapist invites her to examine what has been transpiring between them that would lead her to this conclusion. In response to Susan admitting that she feels chastised by her therapist, the therapist acknowledges having sounded impatient. The therapist adds, however, that Susan appears to have drawn certain fearful conclusions about the meaning of the therapist's reaction, perhaps based on past experiences, and they should jointly examine these conclusions.

The original TLDP model advocated primary reliance on the kind of metacommunicative strategy that I have just illustrated. There is some empirical support for this technical strategy (Foreman & Marmar, 1985; Kolden, 1996). Some convincing evidence suggests, however, that use of transference interventions is risky, raising the possibility of either strong positive or strong negative effects on the therapeutic alliance and on treatment outcome (Gabbard et al., 1994; Joyce & Piper, 1996; Lansford, 1986). These empirical findings, as well as my continuing clinical experiences, have resulted in my current position that metacommunication should be used only when the therapist judges it to be necessary for dealing with alliance ruptures, rather than assuming that this technique must be used to the maximum in order to enhance the therapeutic alliance and treatment outcome.

Concluding Comments About the Therapeutic Alliance

Certain general comments about the role of the therapeutic alliance in brief therapies bear repeating. First, the shorter the therapy, the more important it is that the prospective patient have personality traits that are conducive to rapid establishment of the type of therapeutic alliance characteristic of the treatment. Second, alliance strains and ruptures will be of greater detriment to a brief therapy than to a time-unlimited treatment, so the abilities to quickly identify and efficiently rectify such ruptures are particularly important for the brief therapist. Finally, the pressures created by an explicit or implicit time limit—and the associated meanings of separation, loss, rejection, and abandonment—will probably create strains on the alliance throughout the treatment. A rapidly approaching planned termination could particularly undermine the therapeutic alliance. On the other hand, the sparse research available about the termination phase of brief therapies indicates that it is likely to proceed smoothly if the treatment as a whole has been successful (Quintana, 1993; Quintana & Holahan, 1992).

I have alluded before to Messer and Warren's (1995) observation that the relational therapies do not specifically address any postulated curative influences in time limits per se. In fact, only SRS brief therapy has a specific time limit arranged, and the developers of this model did not claim any curative effects for this arrangement. These models, however, do have features that exert a powerful influence on the efficiency with which treatment can be conducted, which of course is relevant to time limits:

1. The precision with which a problem focus can be formulated in each of these treatment models facilitates consistent tracking of a focus over the course of the therapy.
2. Each model specifies technical strategies and tactics that are relevant to the particular problems, characteristics, and needs of the patient at any point in the treatment.
3. Each model encourages the therapist through his or her manner of relating to actively foster the patient experiencing the therapeutic relationship as safe and supportive.
4. Each model encourages the therapist to be flexible and to improvise in order to constructively respond to any circumstance that arises during the course of treatment.

All of these features serve to facilitate the rapid development of a therapeutic alliance and the efficient resolution of alliance ruptures if they arise.

References

Binder, J. L., & Strupp, H. H. (1991). The Vanderbilt approach to time-limited dynamic psychotherapy. In P. Crits-Christoph & J. P. Barber (Eds.), *Handbook of short-term dynamic psychotherapy* (pp. 137–165). New York: Basic Books.

Bordin, E. S. (1994). Theory and research on the therapeutic working alliance: New direction. In A. O. Horvath & L. S. Greenberg (Eds.), *The working alliance. Theory, research, and practice* (pp. 13–37). New York: Wiley.

Budman, S. H., & Gurman, A. S. (1988). *Theory and practice of brief therapy.* New York: Guilford Press.

Crits-Christoph, P., Barber, J. P., & Kurcias, J. S. (1993). The accuracy of therapists' interpretations and the development of the therapeutic alliance. *Psychotherapy Research, 3,* 25–35.

Crits-Christoph, P., Cooper, A., & Luborsky, L. (1988). The accuracy of therapists' interpretations and the outcome of dynamic psychotherapy. *Journal of Consulting and Clinical Psychology, 56,* 490–495.

Davanloo, H. (Ed.). (1980). *Short-term dynamic psychotherapy*. New York: Jason Aronson.

Foreman, S. A., & Marmar, C. R. (1985). Therapist actions that address initially poor therapeutic alliances in psychotherapy. *Amercian Journal of Psychiatry, 142,* 922–926.

Freud, S. (1953). The dynamics of transference. In J. Strachey (Ed.), *The standard edition of the complete works of Sigmund Freud* (Vol. 12). London: Hogarth.

Gabbard, G. O., Horwitz, L., Allen, J. G., Frieswyk, S., Newsom, G., Colson, D. B., & Coyne, L. (1994). Transference interpretation in the psychotherapy of borderline patients: A high-risk, high-gain phenomenon. *Harvard Review of Psychiatry, 2,* 59–69.

Gaston, L. (1990). The role of the alliance in psychotherapy: Theoretical and empirical considerations. *Psychotherapy, 27,* 143–153.

Greenberg, J. (1995). Self-disclosure: Is it psychoanalytic? *Contemporary Psychoanalysis, 31,* 193–205.

Henry, W. P., Schacht, T. E., & Strupp, H. H. (1986). Structural analysis of social behavior: Application to a study of interpersonal process in differential psychotherapeutic outcome. *Journal of Consulting and Clinical Psychology, 54,* 27–31.

Henry, W. P., Schacht, T. E., & Strupp, H. H. (1990). Patient and therapist introject, interpersonal process, and differential psychotherapy outcome. *Journal of Consulting and Clinical Psychology, 58,* 768–774.

Henry, W. P., & Strupp, H. H. (1994). The therapeutic alliance as interpersonal process. In A. O. Horvath & L. S. Greenberg (Eds.), *The working alliance. Theory, research, and practice* (pp. 51–84). New York: Wiley.

Hoglend, P., Sorlie, T., Heyerdahl, O., Sorbye, O., & Amlo, S. (1993). Brief dynamic psychotherapy: Patient suitability, treatment length, and outcome. *Journal of Psychotherapy Practice and Research, 2,* 230–241.

Horowitz, M. J. (1986). *Stress response syndromes* (2nd ed.). Northvale, NJ: Jason Aronson.

Horowitz, M. J., Marmar, C., Krupnick, J., Wilner, N., Kaltreider, N., & Wallerstein, R. (1984). *Personality styles and brief psychotherapy*. New York: Basic Books.

Horvath, A. O., & Greenberg, L. S. (1994). Introduction. In A. O. Horvath & L. S. Greenberg (Eds.), *The working alliance. Theory, research, and practice* (pp. 1–9). New York: Wiley.

Joyce, A. S., Duncan, S. C., & Piper, W. E. (1995). Task analysis of "working" responses to dynamic interpretation in short-term individual psychotherapy. *Psychotherapy Research, 5,* 49–62.

Joyce, A. S., & Piper, W. E. (1996). Interpretive work in short-term individual psychotherapy: An analysis using hierarchical linear modeling. *Journal of Consulting and Clinical Psychology, 64,* 505–512.

Kiesler, D. J. (1996). *Contemporary interpersonal theory and research. Personality, psychopathology, and psychotherapy.* New York: Wiley.

Kiesler, D. J., & Watkins, L. M. (1989). Interpersonal complimentarity and the therapeutic alliance: A study of relationship in psychotherapy. *Psychotherapy, 26,* 183–194.

Klee, M. R., Abeles, N., & Muller, R. T. (1990). Therapeutic alliance: Early indicators, course, and outcome. *Psychotherapy, 27,* 166–174.

Kolden, G. G. (1996). Change in early sessions of dynamic therapy: Universal processes and the generic model of psychotherapy. *Journal of Consulting and Clinical Psychology, 64,* 489–496.

Lansford, E. (1986). Weakenings and repairs of the working alliance in short-term psychotherapy. *Professional Psychology: Research and Practice, 17,* 364–366.

Levenson, E. A. (1972). *The fallacy of understanding: An inquiry into the changing structure of psychoanalysis.* New York: Basic Books.

Luborsky, L. (1984). *Principles of psychoanalytic psychotherapy: A manual for supportive-expressive treatment.* New York: Basic Books.

Luborsky, L. (1994). Therapeutic alliances as predictors of psychotherapy outcomes: Factors explaining the predictive success. In A. O. Horvath & L. S. Greenberg (Eds.), *The working alliance. Theory, research, and practice* (pp. 38–50). New York: Wiley.

Luborsky, L., & Crits-Christoph, P. (1990). *Understanding transference: The CCRT method.* New York: Basic Books.

Malan, D. H. (1976). *The frontier of brief psychotherapy.* New York: Plenum Press.

Messer, S. B., & Warren, C. S. (1995). *Models of brief psychodynamic therapy. A comparative approach.* New York: Guilford Press.

Piper, W. E., Azim, H. F. A., Joyce, A. S., McCallum, M., Nixon, G. W. H., & Segal, P. S. (1991). Quality of object relations versus interpersonal functioning as predictors of therapeutic alliance and psychotherapy outcome. *Journal of Nervous and Mental Disease, 179,* 432–438.

Piper, W. E., Boroto, D. R., Joyce, A. S., McCallum, M., & Azim, H. F. A. (1995). Pattern of alliance and outcome in short-term individual psychotherapy. *Psychotherapy, 32,* 639–647.

Quintana, S. M. (1993). Toward an expanded and updated conceptualization of termination: Implications for short-term, individual psychotherapy. *Professional Psychology: Research and Practice, 24,* 426–432.

Quintana, S. M., & Holahan, W. (1992). Termination in short-term counseling: Comparison of successful and unsuccessful cases. *Journal of Counseling Psychology, 39,* 299–305.

Safran, J. D., Crocker, P., McMain, S., & Murray, P. (1990). Therapeutic alliance rupture as a therapy event for empirical investigation. *Psychotherapy, 27,* 154–165.

Safran, J. D., & Muran, J. C. (1996). The resolution of ruptures in the therapeutic alliance. *Journal of Consulting and Clinical Psychology, 64,* 447–458.

Safran, J. D., Muran, J. C., & Samstag, L. (1994). Resolving therapeutic alliance ruptures: A task analytic investigation. In A. O. Horvath & L. S. Greenberg (Eds.), *The working alliance. Theory, research, and practice* (pp. 225–255). New York: Wiley.

Schon, D. A. (1983). *The reflective practitioner.* New York: Basic Books.

Sifneos, P. E. (1979). *Short-term dynamic psychotherapy: Evaluation and technique.* New York: Plenum Press.

Silberschatz, G., Fretter, P. B., & Curtis, J. T. (1986). How do interpretations influence the process of psychotherapy? *Journal of Consulting and Clinical Psychology, 54,* 646–652.

Strupp, H. H., & Binder, J. L. (1984). *Psychotherapy in a new key: A guide to time-limited dynamic psychotherapy.* New York: Basic Books.

Weiss, J. (1993). *How psychotherapy works. Process and technique.* New York: Guilford Press.

Weiss, J., Sampson, J., & the Mount Zion Psychotherapy Research Group. (1986). *The psychoanalytic process: Theory, clinical observations, and empirical research.* New York: Guilford Press.

Barbara S. Kohlenberg, Elizabeth A. Yeater, and Robert J. Kohlenberg

Functional Analytic Psychotherapy, the Therapeutic Alliance, and Brief Psychotherapy

4

The mechanisms by which the therapeutic relationship facilitates change have long been of interest to scientists and practitioners alike. Although the majority of therapists would contend that the quality of the therapeutic relationship undoubtedly affects the outcome of psychotherapy, those who adhere to different theoretical conceptualizations of human behavior have traditionally arrived at disparate analyses regarding the importance of the relationship, the mechanisms by which the relationship affects change, and the specific exemplars that define a "good therapeutic relationship" (Horvath, 1995).

Efforts to delineate the critical aspects of the psychotherapy relationship have occurred both on conceptual and on evidence-based fronts. Historically, theorists and practitioners have been active in developing and distinguishing between such aspects of the therapy relationship as transference (positive and negative), countertransference, real relationship, alliance, and working relationship (e.g., Adler, 1980; Greenson, 1965; Klee, Abeles, & Muller, 1990; Zetzel, 1956). Contemporary theorists and practitioners have been committed to the study of the alliance and its relationship to positive therapeutic outcome, the ebb and flow of the alliance within a therapeutic relationship, the requirements needed (both in-session interactional requirements, client characteristics, and therapist characteristics) for the alliance to occur, and the role of alliance ruptures in therapy (e.g., Blatt, Stanislow, Zuroff, & Pilkonis, 1996; Horvath & Luborsky, 1993; Meissner, 1996; Omer, 1995; Safran & Muran, 1995,

1996; Watson, 1996). To date, behavioral theorists and therapists have generally been quiet on these issues, remaining on the sidelines, offering interpretive analyses of traditional psychodynamic therapies (F. Alexander, 1963; Ferster, 1972; Greenspoon & Brownstein, 1967; Hobbs, 1962; Mowrer, 1939; Rosenfarb, 1992, Shaffer, 1947; Shaw, 1946; Shoben, 1949; Skinner, 1957) or critical analyses (Salter, 1963; Wolpe, 1958, 1981). Regarding developing a unique position or extending an existing analysis that considers the complexity of the therapy relationship, behavioral theorists have traditionally remained silent (at best) or condemnatory (at worst).

Accordingly, behavioral scientists have not analyzed finer distinctions such as the therapeutic alliance. This lack of emphasis is in stark contrast to other empirically based scientists who recognize that the therapist–client relationship is an important—although complex—variable in the conduct of psychotherapy, and that the stronger the therapeutic alliance, the better the outcome (Horvath & Symonds, 1991; Howard & Orlinsky, 1972, Orlinsky & Howard, 1986; Strupp, 1996). The therapeutic relationship has been viewed most often by behavioral therapists as ancillary to technique (O'Donohue, 1995; Rimm & Masters, 1979; Wilson & O'Leary, 1980; Wolpe, 1958) or as instrumental in terms of potentiating the use of other behavioral techniques—which are the actual active ingredient in promoting client change (DeVoge & Beck, 1978; Turkat & Brantley, 1981; Wilson & Evans, 1977).

Of late, the position of behavioral theorists and practitioners on the importance of the therapeutic relationship has evolved significantly. In fact, some behavioral approaches to therapy now articulate the viewpoint that the interactions between the therapist and the client, or the therapeutic relationship, is the *most effective variable* in producing change in psychotherapy (Kohlenberg & Tsai, 1991). Other behavioral approaches are taking seriously the notion of relationship, although they do not argue that it is the most effective variable (S. C. Hayes, 1987; S. C. Hayes, Streusal, & Wilson, in press; Linehan, 1993a). Although the many nuances of the therapeutic relationship have traditionally been within the theoretical purview of psychodynamically oriented researchers and clinicians, those who adhere to a more contextual or radical behavioral understanding of human behavior have also begun to investigate the mechanisms by which the therapeutic relationship becomes a sufficient (and perhaps necessary) condition for client behavioral change (e.g., Callaghan, Naugle, & Follette, 1996; Follette, Naugle, & Callaghan, 1996; Kohlenberg & Tsai, 1991, 1994b; Kohlenberg, Tsai, & Kohlenberg, 1996).

Investigations of the therapeutic relationship, both past and present, and across theoretical orientations, have sought to increase both conceptual and practical understanding of the factors that lead to successful outcome in psychotherapy. In today's era of managed care and the emphasis on the provision of cost-effective treatments, the study of the therapeutic relationship becomes valuable for pragmatic reasons. It is possible that the study of the therapeutic relationship can lead to a more precise understanding of the operative variables in psychotherapy, thereby allowing for the development of more efficient, efficacious treatments. Similarly, increasing our understanding of the operative variables in psychotherapy can lead to the enhancement or support of existing treatments. Although the study of the therapeutic relationship will, we hope, serve to delineate scientific standards that will inform the guidelines set by managed care organizations, it is also important to carefully consider the effects of these guidelines as they exist today. Some important aspects of brief psychotherapies, such as agreeing on specified treatment goals and maintaining focus in therapy, are important areas for scientific study.

The purpose of this chapter is to describe and expand upon functional analytic psychotherapy (FAP), an approach to treatment developed by Kohlenberg and Tsai (1991). This behavioral approach to psychotherapy recognizes that the relationship between the client and the therapist can be curative for specific reasons centered on clinically relevant behaviors (CRBs) and behavioral exchanges between the therapist and the client in the session. We offer a perspective on the specific concept of the therapeutic alliance, which we hope will complement or even extend existing literature in this area, and may offer a more parsimonious and useful way of conceptualizing some of the more confusing aspects of existing alliance analyses and research. Finally, an FAP perspective on short-term or time-limited psychotherapy is offered.

Functional Analytic Psychotherapy (FAP)

WHAT IS FAP?

FAP is an approach to therapy that embraces the notion that intensive, in-depth, emotional, involved, and authentic experiences during therapy provide special opportunities for producing clinically significant change. Although FAP can be used as an "add in" to complement and enhance almost any type of treatment (Kohlenberg & Tsai, 1994a, 1994b; Kohlenberg, Tsai, & Dougher, 1993), in this chapter we focus on FAP as a stand-alone approach. In some cases, the intensive experiences that are the focus of FAP are what some clients seek therapy for and may be necessary in order to produce change. FAP offers specific guidelines based on behavioral principles that lead the therapist to create and work within an emotionally intense therapeutic relationship. In short, FAP is an approach to therapy that is relationship-focused, emotion-based, and guided by behavioral principles.

At this point, the average reader might be somewhat confused. How could a therapy be relationship-focused, emotion-based, and also guided by behavioral principles? Are not behavioral therapies generally characterized by the absence or at least the minimization of relationship focus and emotional intensity? We agree that many forms of behavior therapy have absolutely neglected to place emphasis on the therapeutic relationship, as traditionally conceived. Mainstream behavior therapy and cognitive-behavior therapy with outpatient adults typically rely on the report of behavior occurring outside of the session, and thus do not attend specifically to relationship factors within sessions.

FAP, conversely, focuses on any and all behavior (including emotions, bodily sensations, thoughts, talk, and physical behavior) that occur in session between the client and the therapist. FAP is based on a Skinnerian, or radical behavioral, philosophical position. Radical behaviorism is a minority position, and not well understood, even among those identifying themselves as behaviorists. In fact, the majority of behaviorists would best be described as *methodological behaviorists* (for elaborations on the distinctions between radical and methodological behaviorists, see Day, 1969; S. C. Hayes, 1987; Moore, 1981).

We preface our discussion of therapy issues with a cursory introduction to radical behaviorism. The principles offered of radical behaviorism here are philosophically more consistent with some psychodynamic ways of conceptualizing complex issues than with contemporary methodological behavior or cognitive–behavioral analytic positions. Specifically, radical behaviorism and some psychoanalytic analyses converge philosophically. First, both approaches embrace a coherence, rather than a correspondence, notion of truth and, accordingly, a constructivist epistemology (e.g., Day, 1983; Dougher, 1993; Hanly, 1992; S. C. Hayes, Hayes, & Reese, 1988; Sandler & Sandler, 1984).

RADICAL BEHAVIORISM IN RELATION TO FAP

The three most essential aspects of radical behaviorism, which serve to distinguish it from methodological behaviorism, are as follows. First, radical behaviorism considers all of human experience as being legitimate subject matter for scientific inquiry. Inner experiences such as consciousness, thoughts, and emotions (private events) are just as real and legitimate to study scientifically as overt physical behavior. Radical behaviorism is not limited by the positivistic notion of public agreement (as are methodological behaviorists), which would exclude the direct study of consciousness, feelings, and thinking. Extending a radical behavioral position to the therapy interaction entails allowing full and complete consideration of anything and everything that can be seen or felt and even the absence of such things (as in latent content or unconscious material).

Second, radical behavioral theory is essentially a contextualistic theory (e.g., S. C. Hayes, 1987; S. C. Hayes et al., 1988; Pepper, 1957; Skinner, 1945). There is no objective "truth." Nothing can be considered or defined independent of its context. Accordingly, a complete account of an observed event must include a full and complete account of the events surrounding the observer who is observing that event. Thus, a therapist ascribing certain meaning to a client statement is as amenable to analysis as is the client statement. This essentially invites attending to the "process" as well as to the "content" of psychotherapy. It further recognizes that the therapist is not a technical instrument who is objective in any way. The thoughts and feelings of the therapist become a critical source of data as to the meaning of the clients' statements, and also invite considerations of what is generally called *countertransference*.

Finally, radical behaviorism embraces the practice of functional analysis. A *functional analysis* is an analysis that specifies the "external variables of which behavior is a function" (Skinner, 1953, p. 35). For the purposes of psychotherapy, the critical aspects of performing a functional analysis are as follows. First, any and all behavior that occur in the session—ranging from overt motor behavior to the content of verbal behavior to feelings and emotional states that occur in the session—must be understood by focusing on the interactions between the client and the therapist. Utilizing the concept of functional analysis focuses the analysis on the in-session behavior between the client and the therapist.

Consider a client who presents in therapy and describes herself as "freezing up" or becoming "tongue tied" from time to time in relationships. Consider that this very behavior occurs in session, with the therapist. A functional analysis would entail noting the kinds of behaviors that occurred between the therapist and the client surrounding the client's experience of her problem. Say, for example, that the client began freezing up when she realized she forgot her checkbook and would need to delay payment until the next session. This might occasion a belief that she is irresponsible and thus will be rejected or discounted by the therapist. Perhaps she had a history of being rejected or discounted by a parent for such forgetfulness. The point is that the behavior of freezing up will be best understood by understanding the conditions in the session that gave rise to the behavior, which then leads to further exploration and to the development of new repertoires of behavior when confronted with other functionally similar circumstances.

THE BASIC RULES OF FAP

Psychotherapy involves two people sitting in an office talking. Clients come to therapy because of problems in their daily lives. They attend therapy generally once per week, and they pay for the session. The therapists do not intervene in their clients' daily lives—interventions occur strictly in the context of the therapy hour. How is it that in this short slice of time, conditions are created which favorably affect the daily lives of clients?

Functional analytic psychotherapy essentially rests upon the principles of discrimination, consequential responding, and the development of the ability to make interpretations about the relationship between behavior (including thoughts and feelings), the conditions that give rise to behavior, and the consequences occasioned by the behavior. In less behavioral language, the therapist must (a) notice instances of problematic client behavior (often centering on emotional avoidance, e.g., the client changing the subject when an emotionally difficult topic is introduced); (b) be aware of occasioning these behaviors (e.g., by asking the client what the client is feeling about the therapist or a statement made by the therapist); and (c) be able to contingently respond to instances of improvement (being more attentive to the client when the client engages rather than avoids a traditionally troublesome topic). In summary, to be an FAP therapist, one must develop the repertoire to notice instances of problem behavior (clinically relevant behavior), notice instances of improvement in the clinically relevant behavior, respond in a contingent manner to these improvements, and verbalize the relationship between behavior and the events that surround it.

FAP divides therapy into two general categories: the three most relevant client behaviors that occur during the therapy session, and the five rules that constitute the therapeutic technique. A description of these aspects of the therapeutic interaction follows (for elaboration on these categories, see Kohlenberg & Tsai, 1991).

Three Clinically Relevant Client Behaviors

CRB1: Client Problems That Occur in the Session

Client problems that occur in the session consist of actual, in-session demonstrations of clinically relevant behaviors. They are typically related to the presenting problems of the client and consist mostly of (but not exclusively) behaviors that serve to help the client avoid experiencing difficult material. For example, the client who states that she always feels distant and disconnected from people and who in session changes topics frequently when emotional subject matter comes up, gets angry about being misunderstood, and cuts a session short after making an intimate disclosure, would be demonstrating clinically relevant behaviors in session.

CRB2: Client Improvements That Occur in Session

Client improvements that occur in session are typically not observed in the earliest stages of therapy. A woman whose emotional needs were rarely attended to as a child, who thus learned to get positive attention through being theatrical, who in therapy states she has no idea who she is or what she wants, might over the course of therapy gradually begin to focus less on entertaining the therapist and more on revealing her inner wants and desires. Her increasing ability to experience and directly express her feelings to the therapist would be examples of client improvements that occur in session.

CRB3: Client Interpretations of Behavior

Client interpretations of behavior involve the clients observing and then describing their own behavior in terms of causes. *Causes*, in a radical behavioral sense, refer to statements of contingent, functional relationships that occur between behavior and the events that surround it. During the course of therapy, clients will learn to generate statements that are descriptive or interpretive of their own behavior. This skill requires that the clients also have developed the ability to "observe" their own behavior. An example of an instance of this interpretive skill might involve a client stating to the therapist:

> When I saw you glance at your watch, I felt hurt, and I started to go into my shell. I am aware that this is an old pattern of mine, which always ends up with me distancing from people, so I am doing what we have been working on, which is to let you know directly how I feel so that we can talk about it—because in the

past I have felt closer to you when I make myself be revealing rather than hide.

The acquisition of interpretive repertoires helps clients become more aware of the variables that contribute to and maintain their behaviors, thus engendering the possibility that they can develop more satisfying relationships both in and out of therapy.

The Five Rules of FAP Therapeutic Technique

The techniques of FAP are provided in the form of five basic rules, which are not mandatory for the therapist, but are better described as governing principles, intended to inform or guide therapeutic technique, not therapists' behavior.

Rule 1: Watch for CRBs

This is the primary rule in conducting FAP. Kohlenberg and Tsai (1991) suggest that following this rule will lead to better therapeutic outcome and increased emotional experiences between the therapist and the client during psychotherapy. The theoretical assumptions of FAP dictate that the more skilled the therapist at noticing occurrences of problematic client behavior, the more positive the therapy outcome.

During psychotherapy, client behavior is ultimately affected by the therapist's reactions. If the therapist fails to notice behavior as it occurs, responses that occur during the therapy hour will not be functionally related to client behavior. Without an accurate conceptualization of CRBs, reinforcement of client improvements may not occur in a strong enough manner to effect change during the process of psychotherapy. Although accurately identifying clinically relevant behaviors will not ensure a positive therapeutic outcome, it will assist in decreasing the occurrence of inappropriate or iatrogenic therapist responses. For example, consider a client who has great fears of being abandoned and thus is overly compliant and has difficulty expressing anger. Imagine that the therapist announces that the therapy fees are going to be raised shortly. Consider further that the client responds in a compliant, agreeable way but in fact is very inconvenienced and angry about this new financial requirement. Therapy will be greatly enhanced if the therapist is able to notice that a clinically relevant behavior has occurred (the avoidance of expressing anger) and works with the client on this issue. If the therapist simply accepts the client's compliant behavior and moves to the next issue, a precious therapeutic opportunity is lost. Within an FAP paradigm, Rule 1 cannot be overstated. The philosophical assumptions of FAP dictate that a successful therapeutic outcome is possible if the therapist does nothing but follow Rule 1. In short, the therapist, who is facile at noticing occurrences of clinically relevant behaviors in session and who then responds contingently (i.e., naturally) to these behaviors, will ultimately help the client work on those behaviors that brought him or her into therapy in the first place.

Rule 2: Evoke CRBs

Kohlenberg and Tsai (1991) suggest that a good therapeutic relationship is one that evokes clinically relevant behavior and provides those therapeutic, interactional opportunities that allow for the development of client improvements in specific clinically relevant behavior (CRB2). Although the intensity and duration of problems people bring to therapy vary, many people enter therapy because of problems related to intimate relationships. Therapy, presumably, can help them acquire skills that will help them be more successful in these relationships. If the therapeutic relationship evokes clinically relevant behavior (CRB1), then it is likely that the relationship is providing opportunities for intimacy that are both difficult and potentially helpful for the client. For example, the client who avoids expressing anger and who states that her relationships feel constricted and flat and who also denies feeling angry toward her therapist when the therapist insists on charging for a session canceled 23 hr in advance (not the 24-hr rule specified by the therapist) is demonstrating clinically relevant behavior. Similarly, a client who feels that she is being "set up" and becomes suspicious when complimented might also feel this if the therapist compliments her. Essentially, if a client has difficulty with intimacy, and the therapeutic relationship begins to feel intimate, clinically relevant behavior will be evoked.

The use of Rule 2 of FAP requires some sophistication on the part of the therapist. Although it is imperative that the therapist evoke clinically relevant behavior during the session, he or she must be able to accomplish this in a manner that is natural and uncontrived. The intimacy of the therapeutic relationship must be real, genuine intimacy if clinically relevant behavior that is functionally the same as what occurs in relationships outside of therapy is to occur in session. Although contrived responding on the part of the therapist might lead to intense therapeutic interactions, it is much more likely that the client might recognize the contrived nature of these responses, and consequently fail to emit further clinically relevant behavior when the therapist responds in a similar manner. For example, if the therapist complimented a client for whom compliments generated feelings of being "set up" to be exploited, and if the therapist offered the compliment merely to evoke clinically relevant behavior and not because the therapist actually meant the compliment, the client might become aware of this insincerity, and his or her beliefs about compliments would have been confirmed. In short, it would be iatrogenic to both the therapeutic relationship and to therapy outcome if the therapist feigned private responses to elicit clinically relevant behavior during the course of therapy.

Rule 3: Reinforce Improvements in CRB2s

Kohlenberg and Tsai (1991) comment that it is often difficult to adhere to this rule when conducting FAP. Because the therapist only has access to what goes on in the therapeutic interaction, all reinforcers must be found and provided within this setting. Thus, the reactions that the therapist has to the client's behavior are what will have consequences for, and thus affect, the behavior of the client. The problem is that the more the therapist *tries* to be reinforcing, the more the risk that the reinforcement will be arbitrary in nature, which can be detrimental to shaping more useful responses on the part of the client. In short, therapists must strive to deliver natural reinforcers in the context of psychotherapy if their goal is to help clients change and develop more useful behaviors.

The distinction between natural and arbitrary reinforcement is a critical one and is elaborated upon by Ferster (1972) and Kohlenberg and Tsai (1991). The essential aspect of this distinction is that *arbitrary reinforcement* is reinforcement that would not be found in the natural environment for the particular behavior of interest. Rewarding eye contact with candy, or rewarding a child for learning to say "apple" by giving him a token, would be examples of arbitrary reinforcement. Natural reinforcement, conversely, specifies reinforcers that are typically found in the natural environment. Good eye contact would be rewarded with the increased interest of the therapist; a baby learning to say "apple" would be rewarded by being given an apple. The therapist who reinforces a client's difficult self-disclosure by stating enthusiastically "that was good sharing" might in fact be rendering the client's attempt as insincere and might in effect punish that behavior. A more natural response to the client's attempt to self-disclose would be increased interest, increased attention, emotional behavior on the part of the therapist, and so on.

For many clients, arbitrary reinforcement would be iatrogenic for several reasons. First, it would create difficulties in the area of generalization. Behavior reinforced by way of arbitrary reinforcers would not be expected to generalize to the natural environment, where different classes of reinforcers are available. Self-disclosing so that the therapist will praise you is actually a different behavior than self-disclosing that results in increased intimacy and respect. Second, many clients have had extensive aversive experience with arbitrary reinforcement, in that arbitrary reinforcement generally exists for the benefit of the person doing the reinforcing, not for the person being reinforced. People with abuse histories or who had very self-absorbed, inattentive, or abusive parents generally have had aversive experience with arbitrary reinforcement. The use of arbitrary reinforcement for people with such histories would probably work in that new behavior could be generated, but this new behavior would reflect changes that the therapist wanted, not necessarily helping the client learn to engage in relationships in which their own wants and needs are carefully considered.

Kohlenberg and Tsai (1991) provide many guidelines to strengthen the use of natural reinforcement, including being aware that the therapeutic relationship exists for the benefit of the client, not for the benefit of the therapist. Therapists are encouraged to seek supervision (directly and through reviewing tapes of sessions), do good deeds that benefit others in general, and select clients for whom FAP would be appropriate in that CRBs are likely to occur. In addition clients with whom the therapist would have the requisite repertoire for developing a curative relationship should be selected for FAP.

Rule 4: Observe the Potentially Reinforcing Effects of Therapist Behavior in Relation to Client CRBs

This rule illustrates a very important behavioral emphasis, which is that all behavior, even therapist behavior, must be evaluated in the context in which it is applied. In other words, in FAP therapist behavior is effective when it "works" to impact client behavior in a favorable manner, not when it sounds good by being theoretically consistent, or when a therapist is praised for his or her behavior by colleagues. This rule emphasizes the importance of "the effects of the consequences of behavior on the future probabilities of that behavior" (Kohlenberg & Tsai, 1991, p. 36). In short, behavior that is reinforced or punished by the therapist will alter the rate of responding by the client on future occasions. If therapists are able to notice and respond to the reinforcing effects of their own behaviors upon their clients during the session, they increase the likelihood of being effective therapists.

Rule 5: Give Interpretations of Variables That Affect Client Behavior

This rule is intended to help clients increase their understanding of the types of variables that influence their behaviors. The therapist essentially models statements that identify antecedents and consequences of behavior. Ultimately, clients learn to be aware of how their own reactions and behavior are related to environmental events. Awareness of this kind can help clients obtain more positive reinforcement in their daily lives. According to this rule, the therapist's task is to reinterpret the client's behavior "in terms of functional relationships, a learning history, and behavior" (Kohlenberg & Tsai, 1991, p. 40). This strategy is helpful to the therapeutic process in that it assists the client in attending to the external variables of which their feelings and behavior are a function. A therapist might comment:

> I notice that you became very quiet after I forgot the name of
> your husband—I wonder if my error made you feel that I am not
> interested in you, which resulted in you withdrawing. I realize
> that in the past you have been very hurt by your mother's lack
> of interest in you, and you felt that you had no power with her.

Interpretations, or statements, such as that illustrated above, model for clients ways to describe their own behavior and the variables that contribute to its occurrence.

Adhering to the principles noted above will increase the emotional intensity of the therapeutic relationship and will also maximize the potential for behavior change on the part of the client. If the problems that the client struggles with manifest themselves in the session, and the therapist is aware of these in vivo demonstrations of client problematic behavior, the therapist will then be able to naturally reinforce client improvements. These procedures during therapy will result in behavior change, which will be strengthened if the clients can also learn to generate statements regarding the relationship of their feelings, thoughts, and overt behaviors to actual events that occur within the relationship.

Traditional Accounts of the Therapeutic Alliance: Problems in the Use of the Term

An FAP consideration of the operative variables in the therapeutic relationship begins with intensive study of actual in-session behavior demonstrated by both therapist and client. No a priori theoretical model exists in FAP that instructs the therapist to be watchful of one particular form of behavior over another. In short, from an FAP perspective, any type of behavior may be conceptualized as clinically relevant. It is our opinion that traditional attempts to delineate relevant aspects of the therapeutic relationship have yielded distinctions that are confusing in part because they are tied to theoretical constructs and to the topography (or content), rather than the function, of actual in-session behavior. An FAP conceptualization of in-session behavior focuses on how a particular behavior functions for the therapist on a private level, not whether the behavior "looked" like transference or alliance-type behavior.

In the following section, we discuss some of the more traditional conceptualizations of the therapeutic relationship. It is our hope that this discussion will show that there exists transtheoretical consistency with regard to identifying behaviors that are indicative of client progress, while at the same time showing that there also exists conceptual confusion about how to verbalize the process of identifying these behaviors. The radical behavioral view of conceptualizing critical behaviors capitalizes on those elements that unite most therapists, despite theoretical orientations.

Fine-grained analyses of the general notion of the therapeutic relationship have resulted in the generation of more specific terms, such as the *therapeutic alliance*, the *working alliance*, *transference* and *countertransference*, and the so-called *real relationship* (e.g., Brenner, 1980; Greenson, 1965; Klee et al., 1990). These terms presumably have been defined to help practitioners and theoreticians attend to and be able to describe clinically relevant aspects of the therapeutic relationship. We have found, however, that definitional problems exist in the literature that may both reflect and induce problems at the level of practice.

DEFINITIONAL PROBLEMS

Although one might expect that the delineation of terms such as *therapeutic alliance*, *working alliance*, and *real relationship* would foster a more thorough and comprehensive understanding of the therapeutic relationship, a significant amount of controversy currently exists in the field over the meaning and utility of such delineations. Although some theorists posit that the provision of such aspects of the relationship leads to further conceptual clarification and progress, others dictate that further elucidation and measurement development are needed before these concepts can progress to a stage of pragmatic and theoretical fruition (e.g., Gelso & Carter, 1994; Greenberg, 1994). For us, the very confusion in the field over the delineation of these concepts is demonstrative of what happens when concepts are compared with concepts rather than with actual behavior and how this behavior functions in the context of the therapeutic relationship. For example, Alder (1980) noted that what appears topographically to be alliance in session often functions as compliance, which is merely an example of transference. The "good feeling" in the session due to client compliance may contribute to client progress or may be an in vivo example of client problematic behavior; the therapist who is adept at making these distinctions between the topography and function of behavior at an idiographic level will be a more effective therapist. In short, clarification of these concepts occurs when the discussion is brought to the level of actual behavior and how it functions, rather than to distinctions that are largely semantic in nature.

CONTEMPORARY ALLIANCE CONSIDERATIONS

In recent years, researchers have also contributed various concepts pertaining to the therapeutic relationship, such as alliance ruptures, alliance rupture resolutions, and corrective emotional experiences (e.g., Greenberg & Safran, 1987; Safran & Muran, 1995; Watson & Greenberg, 1995). Contemporary investigations of the term *therapeutic alliance* generally ignore the distinctions considered in the above sections. Some researchers ignore these distinctions generally because of inconsistent uses of the terms (Safran & Muran, 1995). Investigators have focused instead on the measurement of alliance (e.g., L. B. Alexander & Luborsky, 1987; Hartley & Strupp, 1983; Horvath & Symonds, 1991) and on doing careful analyses of the relationship between alliance and therapy outcome (e.g., Horvath & Symonds, 1991; Safran, Crocker, McMain, & Murray, 1990). Much of this work is being driven by the empirical evidence that the therapeutic alliance is perhaps the best transtheoretical predictor of therapeutic success and thus warrants careful analysis and consideration (Safran & Muran, 1996). For much of the empirical work on alliance that attempts to examine the predictive validity of the alliance transtheoretically, *alliance* is defined as both the strength of the relationship between the client and the therapist and as a measure of the degree of collaboration on agreed upon goals (Bordin, 1979).

An important area of interest in the area of therapeutic alliance is found in the study of alliance ruptures and their resolution. An *alliance rupture* is a description of an interactional sequence between therapist and client characterized by a deterioration in their relationship. This deterioration is thought to be an opportunity for furthering the therapeutic process (e.g., Newirth, 1995; Omer, 1995; Safran & Muran, 1995, 1996; Watson & Greenberg, 1995). Safran and Muran (1995) assert that their research in the area of alliance has led them to focus on the interaction between the client and the therapist, with the alliance rupture and subsequent resolution as the central focus of therapy. One exciting feature of this work is the emphasis on the intensive study of actual therapy transcripts and observations of therapist and client behaviors. Essentially, Safran and Muran are interested in underlying change processes, enacted through the present, observable behaviors that occur between client and therapist.

Much of the empirical work regarding alliance rupture and repair contends that this interactional sequence is a very important, if not the most important, critical element in effective psychotherapy. The resolution interaction is regarded as important in that it can "provide patients with opportunities to acknowledge disowned parts of themselves and to learn to negotiate the dialectically opposed needs for self-agency and relatedness in a constructive fashion" (Safran & Muran, 1996, p. 448). We support the empirical work occurring in this area. When clinical scientists study raw data (the transcripts of therapy sessions) and draw conclusions based upon these data, the possibility of increased understanding of the complexity of the interaction is enhanced. Although the interpretation of the observed interactional sequences is naturally theory driven, there is great promise in increasing our understanding of complex human interactions when the raw data are given a prominent place along with one's theoretical model of choice.

FAP Analysis of the Therapeutic Alliance

An FAP analysis of the therapeutic alliance both deviates and converges with psychoanalytic discussions of alliance and shares much in common with Safran and Muran's (1995, 1996) analyses of alliance and alliance ruptures. We first consider our divergence and convergence from analytic discussions.

THE PURPOSE OF AN FAP ANALYSIS OF ALLIANCE

Strupp (1996) reminded us that "there is one fundamental question in psychotherapy practice and research: What are the basic ingredients of therapeutic change and how can therapeutic change be brought about?" (p. 135). In accordance with this question, an FAP analysis is primarily a pragmatic one that attempts to produce useful, parsimonious, and effective ways to discuss the therapeutic relationship and how the process of change occurs during psychotherapy. Toward this end, practitioners of FAP do not find it useful to divide the therapeutic relationship into constructs such as alliance, transference, working relationship, and so forth. These attempts at fine-grained distinctions are cumbersome and tend to collapse because of lack of conceptual specificity. In addition, these terms focus primarily on the topography rather than the function of in-session behavior. This lack of behavioral specificity inherent in more psychodynamic concepts does not assist the clinician to identify, in behaviorally specific ways, the "active ingredients" of the therapeutic relationship that will ultimately facilitate change on the part of the client. It makes the terms *transference, real relationship, alliance,* and so forth essentially meaningless. The identification of in-session behavior between the client and therapist in terms of client problems that occur in the session, client improvements that occur in session, and client interpretations of in-session behavior (CRB1s, CRB2s, and CRB3s) leads to greater conceptual clarity and a more parsimonious and useful treatment plan for the course of psychotherapy.

METAPHORICAL (TRANSFERENTIAL) VERSUS REAL (RATIONAL) BEHAVIOR IN THERAPY

The issue of metaphorical, illusory, or distorted (transferential) versus real (rational) responding on the part of the client is not a meaningful distinction in a radical behavioral sense. From a behavioral point of view, behavior is always controlled by both remote and immediate contingencies. Interactions that occur in the present are considered to be the end product of one's entire history (L. Hayes, 1992, 1993). If a client is angry at a therapist, it does not really matter if that anger is controlled mostly by that therapist's preceding comment, the fact that the client is always angry at authority figures, or the fact that the client had an argument with his or her spouse immediately before the session. What matters most is that the anger emitted by the client will have a particular function, or impact, in the context of the therapy relationship, and will also have a particular function with respect to that client's entire history with regard to anger. Both are true; it is not an either/or situation. In short, we believe that the transference versus real relationship dichotomy is a false one. Both relationships are always factors. Behaviors serve to "work well," or enhance a relationship, or they work "less well." There are times when being aware of one's history with regard to a particular moment in therapy can serve to greatly enhance intimacy. Paying the therapist at the end of the session, a rather "real" behavior, can be very intimacy enhancing if clients write their checks while emoting about instances of not feeling valued for who they are inside, *and* while recognizing that the therapists seeking payment (which formally resembles past painful situations) presently means something very different than functionally similar situations in the past. It is not relevant to ask whether the memory described is "true"; rather, the verbal material is evaluated based upon current effects.

IMPORTANCE OF THE ALLIANCE IN PSYCHOTHERAPY

The significance and importance of the therapeutic relationship is not lost on radical behaviorists (e.g., Callaghan et al., 1996; Follette et al., 1996; Kohlenberg & Tsai, 1991). This fact is most evident in FAP, which dictates that the therapy relationship provides a *sufficient* condition for change to occur. Although FAP's intensive focus on the therapeutic relationship is similar to both psychoanalysis and other forms of psychotherapy, FAP may offer a theoretical framework that makes the concept of alliance more comprehensible and useful to the practicing clinician and researcher.

Kohlenberg and Tsai (1991) noted that there are similarities between FAP and psychoanalysis, specifically, the focus on the therapy relationship. This is no accident given that FAP was informed by the sensitivities to the therapy relationship and the analysis of verbal exchanges that are integral to psychoanalytic practice and theory. In addition, radical behaviorism and some forms of contemporary psychoanalysis share similar philosophical foundations, such as embracing a coherence versus a correspondence theory of truth (Hanly, 1992; L. Hayes, 1993; Schafer, 1982), interest in constructivist theories of knowledge that manifest themselves in interest in hermeneutics (Dougher, 1993; Schafer, 1982), and sensitivities to interpretation rather than strict experimental method (Hanly, 1982; Skinner, 1945, 1957). Kohlenberg and Tsai (1991) further commented that these similarities, both philosophically and in technique, are important in that they may point to "universal variables" (p. 169) that are inherent in all forms of psychotherapy and that may ultimately provide the basis by which change occurs. Furthermore, the long-standing behavioral emphasis on empirical validation may enhance the work going on in traditions in which empiricism has been valued differently.

As mentioned previously, an FAP perspective makes distinctions between transference, alliance, and other related concepts unnecessary and tenuous at best. However, we would not claim that the "strength," so to speak, of the therapeutic relationship is unimportant. We realize that for the FAP therapist to effectively provide clients with specific, contingent feedback on the function of their behavior during session, there must exist a sense of respect and caring by the therapist for the clients, and vice versa. An FAP perspective allows us to explain and predict how this "alliance" would originate in the relationship. The notion of alliance, as discussed by more traditional psychodynamic therapists, comes about as the result of more general contingent reinforcement by the therapist at the beginning of therapy. For example, the FAP therapist may reinforce the client at the beginning of treatment for simply coming to session or continuing to work on a problem that seems to have no solution. This type of reinforcement would provide a foundation (i.e., alliance) upon which the client would be able to tolerate and come to accept the contingent feedback by the therapist about the function of the client's more problematic behaviors that occur during session. Without this more general, less specific reinforcement at the beginning of therapy, the therapist might not be able to accomplish the goals of FAP (Callaghan et al., 1996). This analysis of the development of the "strength" of the therapeutic relationship provides the clinician with a behaviorally specific way in which to accomplish such a goal.

According to Kohlenberg and Tsai (1991), the concept of *transference* is important because it refers to client behavior that occurs within the session and thus focuses attention on the therapy relationship. Within an FAP framework, those behaviors that have traditionally been called transference are conceptualized as clinically relevant behaviors occurring in the session (CRB1s). Essentially, these are the clinically relevant behaviors that cause the client to experience difficulties in other interpersonal contexts as well. Although psychoanalysis has traditionally viewed the behaviors conceptually identified as "transference" as directly related to how the client has experienced important persons from the past and not the current therapist, an FAP perspective would posit that these behaviors are the direct result of the process known as *stimulus generalization*. This behavioral principle dictates that behavior emitted within session is directly related to behavior that has occurred in other relationships (Kohlenberg & Tsai, 1991). Problematic behavior is then elicited in session because of the functional similarities between the therapist and other significant individuals in the client's life. In short, our behavior toward other people is ultimately based on our learning history either with that person or with other individuals (Kohlenberg & Tsai, 1991). As a consequence, all behavior that occurs during session is learned behavior that is the result of the functional similarities between what the therapist does and past relationship history, as well as the learning history that is constructed between the therapeist and the client during the therapeutic relationship (Kohlenberg & Tsai, 1991). The FAP assumption is that new and more useful behavior can be shaped during the process of psychotherapy by the contingent responding of the therapist to client problems that occur in session and to improvements in those behaviors (CRB1s and CRB2s).

It is important to emphasize that the analysis of client behavior in FAP is an idiographic rather than a nomothetic one. FAP postulates that problematic behavior will be specific (i.e., idiographic) to the individual and directly related to that individual's unique learning history. A nomothetic assumption regarding client behavior may generate a rule for the therapist that may prevent him or her from noticing and responding to other CRBs that are of more importance in case conceptualization and treatment planning. An idiographic analysis allows the therapist to avoid heuristic errors and other confirmatory biases during the assessment process by requiring the therapist to generate hypotheses regarding client behavior and search for confirmatory and disconfirmatory evidence.

One could assume that anger exhibited by the client is a sign of negative therapeutic process (i.e., a nomothetic rule generated for all clients by the assumptions of the therapy), the theoretical assumptions of FAP dictate that this behavior may be either a problem behavior or an improvement (CRB1 or CRB2, respectively). Because one of the premises of FAP is to watch for and evoke CRBs occurring in session that are either problematic or intimacy enhancing to the therapeutic relationship, this may indicate that the therapist has been successful at eliciting the client's clinically relevant behavior. This is beneficial to the therapeutic process because the behavior that the client struggles with outside therapy is now occurring in therapy with the therapist. This, in turn, allows the therapist either to reinforce improvements (CRB2) or to punish or ignore in-session demonstrations of problem behavior (CRB1). Contingent responding and feedback on the part of the therapist will ultimately shape more useful behavioral repertoires on the part of the client, which will eventually generalize to other interpersonal contexts.

Imagine for a moment a client who is raised in a home where demonstrating any type of negative or angry affect is continually punished. The only way that the client is able to adapt to this environment is to keep angry feelings inside and maintain distance from relationships that become too close (possibly provoking angry feelings). As therapists, we realize that this situation is problematic because becoming angry with each other at times is often the normal course of an intimate relationship, and we recognize that sometimes we need to become angry in order to defend and protect ourselves from others. This client then grows up unable to rightfully become angry in close intimate relationships. The client maintains distance from other people, out of fear of abandonment following an angry outburst. This client presents for therapy as lonely, depressed, and unhappy.

An FAP therapist would posit that angry behavior emitted by the client in this context is a CRB2 and is an indication of negative process. Angry behavior that occurs in session is reinforced by the therapist in order to shape a behavioral repertoire that allows the client to communicate these feelings to others within various interpersonal contexts. To punish this behavior or to conceptualize it as being detrimental to the therapeutic relationship would be to behave as others had in the past and to ultimately inhibit the client's developing repertoire for dealing with such feelings.

FAP and psychoanalytic theory and practice converge, for the most part, with regard to their positions on countertransference. FAP's theoretical assumptions dictate that without countertransference reactions, the therapist would be unable to do FAP. Because client change in FAP is essentially viewed as a result of contingent responding on the part of the therapist, countertransference, or the private behavioral responses of the therapist, are essential to psychotherapy. This is not to suggest that all reactions on the part of the therapist are therapeutic. Ultimately, therapists struggle with their own discrimination and repertoire issues that make it difficult to respond to their clients in a way that will facilitate positive emotional change. The task for the FAP therapist (and potentially for all therapists) is to discriminate between private emotional responses due to their own idiosyncratic history and those that are representative of most individuals in the same situation. The manner in which FAP therapists improve upon their ability to discriminate and respond accurately and usefully with clients may vary. It is conceivable that the therapist could receive this type of training from FAP supervision, which attempts to establish those stimulus conditions that will elicit problematic behavior on the part of the therapist. The task of the FAP supervisor then parallels that of a therapist with a client. It also seems reasonable to assume that FAP therapists could refine their own repertoires by engaging in personal therapy. It is almost axiomatic that therapists will identify their repertoire limitations when training to become FAP therapists. The FAP therapist ultimately wants to be able to respond to the client in a manner that is not contrived, yet is essentially equivalent to those responses that would be emitted by most persons in the general population.

FAP, Alliance, and Empirically Based Treatments

The alliance between the therapist and client may be more or less important depending upon the presenting problem of the client. In short, some presenting problems suggest that the relationship itself may, at times, be ancillary to the treatment. Examples of this might include specific phobias, panic disorder, or panic disorder with agoraphobia. Although we do not suggest that the relationship is unimportant in these cases, we do, however, posit that the relationship may not be curative in and of itself. Ultimately, no form of treatment can be delivered successfully without some type of reasonable and respectful relationship between client and therapist.

Various questions arise for the clinician who believes in conducting psychotherapy that is driven by either data or empirically validated principles. One of the most important of these is whether we refuse to treat the client who presents for psychotherapy with multiple or diffuse problems for which there exist no manualized or empirically validated treatment. What then becomes the more ethical and accountable response? If we choose to treat, what principles should we use to guide our treatment? In cases of specific forms of psychopathology, for example, specific phobias, panic disorder, and panic disorder with agoraphobia suggest that therapists use empirically validated treatments, especially when clients have met the inclusion criteria for these disorders.

There are two situations, however, in which difficulty arises in the use of empirically validated treatments. The first is when the client fails to improve, a frequent occurrence when empirically validated treatments are applied. For example, only about 50% of the depressed clients who received an empirically validated treatment were not depressed at follow-up (Jacobson et al., 1996; Shea et al., 1992). The second and more frequently occurring situation occurs when the client does not match the inclusion criteria often incorporated within various psychotherapy outcome studies, and there is no applicable empirically validated treatment. We must then wonder if the results of these studies generalize to the clients who present for therapy with complex and idiosyncratic problems. For example, what type of treatment would we suggest for the client who presents for psychotherapy declaring, "I just don't know who I am or what I need," or who claims that "relationships just don't work for me. All my life I have found that people just don't like me. I'm really unhappy, doc." If we attempted to find a manualized treatment for clients who presented with such complaints, we would be unsuccessful.

We believe that FAP solves some of the difficulties that are inherently problematic for the practicing clinician attempting to make difficult treatment decisions. Although there exists little psychotherapy outcome data at present to substantiate our basic premises, FAP is based on behavioral principles that have been shown to be valid time and again in the laboratory. The types of client characteristics that suggest FAP as the treatment of choice include, for example, long-standing interpersonal difficulties, Axis II personality disorders, dysthymic disorder, and generalized anxiety disorder. The topography of the behavior (e.g., what the behavior looks like) is ultimately not as important as how the behavior might function for the individual in an interpersonal context. If the clinician assesses that the client's presenting problems may cause interpersonal difficulties due to discrimination deficits or a deficient, excessive, or aversive behavioral repertoire, the basic philosophical tenets of FAP suggest that it may be a valid and useful treatment.

TIME-LIMITED PSYCHOTHERAPY AND FAP

To date, the notion of time-limited psychotherapy has not been an area of great concern for behaviorally oriented scientists and practitioners. This is the case for a number of reasons. First, behavioral therapies typically have been tied to discrete outcomes and happen to be relatively short term. Second, time limits were never an issue because therapy persisted until the targeted changes were accomplished, a task which was generally easy to demonstrate because of the types of interventions and the problems (dependent measures) selected. Third, the issue of generalizability of the results of psychotherapy has always been an important value—encouraging behavior therapists to be sensitive to the bridge between therapy and change seen outside of therapy. This might have served to enhance the value that therapy is a bridge, and a short bridge, to getting clients to function better in their actual lives. Fourth, perhaps in part to distinguish itself from psychoanalytic psychotherapy, the social community of behavior therapists has focused on seeing clients for shorter rather than longer periods of time, a fact of which we are proud.

Until recently, behavioral treatments have tended to be relatively brief. Foa, Riggs, Massie, and Yarczower (1995) describe a treatment for posttraumatic stress disorder consisting of 9 twice-weekly sessions lasting 90 min each. Similarly, Chambless and Williams (1995) propose a treatment for agoraphobia based upon between sixteen to twenty 90-min sessions for those clients with severe agoraphobia, ten 90-min sessions for those clients with moderate agoraphobia, and ten 60-min sessions for those clients with mild agoraphobia. In the much-cited Treatment of Depression Collaborative Research Program, the number of sessions allocated to test the cognitive–behavioral therapy condition was between 19 and 20 sessions (Elkin, Gibbons, Shea, & Shaw, 1996).

However, as behavioral therapists grapple with more complex clinical issues, the length of treatment has tended to increase. Linehan's (1993b) treatment for the client with borderline symptoms generally requires 1 year for skills training to be mastered, and many clients graduate to other forms of treatment following that year, for an unspecified amount of time.

Kohlenberg and Tsai's FAP, as a stand-alone treatment, has most often involved clients who had problems in the area of intimacy. Further, these clients' intimacy problems did not fully emerge (as CRBs) within the therapeutic relationship until late in therapy. Thus, FAP cases typically exceeded what would be considered short-term psychotherapy guidelines.

From an FAP viewpoint, we break the short-term issue into two domains, one the actual therapy issues that arise when a time limit is placed on psychotherapy, and the other being raising general warnings regarding time-limited psychotherapy, based on data generated in experimental laboratories about the costs and benefits of learning through instructional control versus learning by way of exposure to the natural contingencies.

FAP does not take an a priori position on time limits and psychotherapy. Instead, an FAP perspective considers time limits in a more functional manner. That is, there are times when a time limit would be useful in therapy, and others when it would be harmful, and in all cases time limits are viewed as one of the many potentially evocative aspects of psychotherapy. If CRB1s are generated because of a time restriction, therapy could be actually improved by a time restriction. Conversely, if a CRB2 is punished because of a time restriction, therapy would have been damaged because of the time restriction. Clinical examples of each situation follow.

Consider a client who struggles with entering emotionally intimate relationships until the conditions are "perfect." The client has awareness of always seeking and finding flaws in potential partners, which result in their rejection and, ultimately, in the client's feeling distant and alone. After a screening interview with a new therapist, in which the client was quite excited and enthusiastic about beginning therapy, the client is informed that treatment is restricted to 16 sessions. The client's response is to state disinterest in continuing the therapy, and to markedly shut down emotionally.

This could be a therapeutic opportunity in which the therapist could, while respecting the client's right to decline treatment, encourage the client to take a risk and try to engage in treatment, fully knowing that the structure is not preferred by the client. The client's avoidance of therapy and emotional intimacy (CRB1), if noticed by the therapist, could provide a rich therapeutic opportunity. If the client continues in treatment, and in fact does take risks and tries to become fully involved in the treatment, even under these less-than-optimal conditions, a valuable opportunity has been given. If the client ends therapy having an awareness of the imperfection of all relationships, the inherent time restrictions present in all relationships, and that relationships can be satisfying even if imperfect, progress can be said to have been made. If the client engages in relationships more readily outside of therapy, a good therapy outcome can be said to have occurred.

Conversely, consider a client who has great difficulty knowing and expressing wants and needs and who demonstrates a high degree of compliance in therapy. The client, of course, agrees readily to a 16-session bout of treatment. At the end of therapy, the client timidly asks if there is any way therapy can continue—stating that therapy has been of great benefit and asking if the therapist would consider extending treatment. This is an example of a CRB2—the client stating a desire for therapy despite an awareness that it could be a problem for the therapist. In this case, extending treatment would be indicated. Ending treatment as agreed could be viewed as punishing a true, in-session demonstration of improvement (CRB2). Extending treatment could serve to reinforce the client's initial stab at stating wants or needs even when others might be inconvenienced by them.

In any case, time limits or lack thereof are viewed as one of the many potential evocative events that can occur in treatment. No time limits at all are potentially as evocative as time limits. A therapist being late to a session, forgetting a session, forgetting something important to the client, being pregnant, being ill, being tired and distracted, being seen in public by the client, all of these instances are grist for the mill and are potential sources of CRB1. Without CRB1, there cannot be CRB2, and thus therapy stands still.

Although FAP would not take a position on time-limited psychotherapy, other than by viewing the time limit as potentially evocative of clinically relevant behavior, FAP therapists do tend to see clients for a long time. This is likely because the kinds of clients most often seen by FAP therapists tend to have difficulty in the broad area of interpersonal relations, an area that is hard to isolate and work on when therapy is brief. We do have appreciation for the fact that some clients will do best in short-term types of treatment, and some will do worse. Being able to distinguish between these two groups may be more of an inductive endeavor, based on response to treatment restrictions than on a priori groupings.

In any event, we do believe that nearly any treatment—short or long term—will be enhanced by the focus on CRB called for by FAP. In effect, a focus on CRB takes advantage of the well-established fact that learning takes place better in vivo. For example, Kohlenberg and Tsai (1994b) used FAP to enhance Beck's cognitive therapy for depression and found that

> The client–therapist relationship provided in vivo opportunities for learning new behaviors called for in the behaviorally reconceptualized cognitive therapy. The enhanced treatment improved clinical efficacy and increased the client's focus on his [her] deficits in interpersonal repertoires. (p. 305)

BASIC RESEARCH AND TIME-LIMITED PSYCHOTHERAPY

Given that behaviorally oriented clinicians have historically practiced short-term therapies, it is surprising that out of the behavioral research tradition comes some very strong support for longer, rather than shorter, psychotherapy. In the human operant laboratory, researchers have been investigating the differences in learning that occur when skills are taught by way of instructional control or contingency shaping. It has been discovered that behavior can be acquired more rapidly when the participant is told what to do in order to succeed in the experiment. However, this behavior is not sensitive to changes in experimental demands (i.e., does not generalize to other stimulus situations). Conversely, behavior that has been shaped through contact with the contingencies takes longer to meet criterion standards, but once the behavior is in place, it is sensitive to changes in experimental demands (e.g., Catania, Shimoff, & Matthews, 1989; for a more thorough discussion of this topic, see S. C. Hayes, 1989).

Similarly, behavioral researchers also have been studying the effects of contingency-based learning versus learning by way of rules in areas such as social skills training (Azrin & Hayes, 1984) and clinical supervision (Follette & Callaghan, 1995). These studies support the notion that more flexible behavior, behavior that is more responsive to the contingencies of the moment, rather than to instructions, is best brought about through lengthier procedures involving contingent shaping, rather than instructional control. We feel that the evidence collected in basic and applied behavioral laboratories is compelling and warrants caution in equating change brought about quickly, largely by way of instruction, versus change shaped slowly, by way of contact with natural contingencies.

Conclusion

Our impetus in the study of the process of psychotherapy is ultimately to help better alleviate human suffering. We feel that it is exciting to be involved in this pursuit, along with researchers and practitioners of many theoretical orientations. We contend that FAP is a parsimonious, pragmatic approach to the study and understanding of basic processes involved in the therapeutic relationship. We are hopeful that our approach is a promising one and that it will continue to be refined and improved on the basis of empirical research. We are encouraged by the convergence of scientists and practitioners of many theoretical orientations around the study of the therapeutic relationship and how it relates to the empirical investigation of therapy outcome. The notion of time-limited psychotherapy, we argue, is one example of many variables that influence the way psychotherapy is practiced—and its effect on therapy outcome must be investigated carefully. The business of psychotherapy should ultimately be concerned with alleviating human suffering.

References

Adler, G. (1980). Transference, real relationship, and alliance. *International Journal of Psychoanalysis, 61,* 547–558.

Alexander, F. (1963). The dynamics of psychotherapy in light of learning theory. *American Journal of Psychiatry,* 440–449.

Alexander, L. B., & Luborsky, L. (1987). The Penn Helping Alliance Scales. In L. S. Greenberg & W. M. Pinsof (Eds.), *The psychotherapeutic process: A research handbook* (pp. 325–366). New York: Guilford Press.

Azrin, R. D., & Hayes, S. C. (1984). The discrimination of interest within a heterosexual interaction: Training, generalization, and effects on social skills. *Behavior Therapy, 15,* 173–184.

Blatt, S. J., Stanislow, C. A., III, Zuroff, D. C., & Pilkonis, P. A. (1996). Characteristics of effective therapists: Further analysis of data from the National Institute of Mental Health Treatment of Depression Collaborative Research Program. *Journal of Consulting and Clinical Psychology, 64,* 1276–1284.

Bordin, E. S. (1979). The generalizability of the psychoanalytic concept of the working alliance. *Psychotherapy: Theory, Research and Practice, 16,* 252–260.

Brenner, C. (1980). Working alliance, therapeutic alliance, and transference. In H. Blum (Ed.), *Psychoanalytic explorations of technique* (pp. 137–158). New York: International Universities Press.

Callaghan, G. M., Naugle, A. E., & Follette, W. C. (1996). Useful constructions of the client–therapist relationship. *Psychotherapy, 33,* 381–390.

Catania, A. C., Shimoff, E., & Matthews, B. A. (1989). An experimental analysis of rule-governed behavior. In S. Hayes (Ed.), *Rule-governed behavior: Cognition, contingencies, and instructional control* (pp. 117–150). New York: Plenum Press.

Chambless, D. L., & Williams, K. E. (1995). A preliminary study of African Americans with agoraphobia: Symptom severity and outcome of treatment with in vivo exposure. *Behavior Therapy, 26,* 501–515.

Day, W. (1969). Radical behaviorism in reconciliation with phenomenology. *Journal of the Experimental Analysis of Behavior, 12,* 315–328.

Day, W. (1983). On the difference between radical and methodological behaviorism. *Behaviorism, 11,* 89–102.

Dougher, M. (1993). Interpretive and hermeneutic research methods in the contextualistic analysis of verbal behavior. In S. Hayes, L. Hayes, H. Reese, & T. Sarbin (Eds.), *Varieties of scientific contextualism* (pp. 211–221). Reno, NV: Context Press.

DeVoge, J. T., & Beck, S. (1978). The therapist–client relationship in behavior therapy. *Progress in Behavior Modification, 6,* 204–248.

Elkin, I., Gibbons, R. D., Shea, M. T., & Shaw, B. F. (1996). Science is not a trial (but it can sometimes be a tribulation). *Journal of Consulting and Clinical Psychology, 64,* 92–103.

Ferster, C. B. (1972). An experimental analysis of clinical phenomena. *The Psychological Record, 22,* 1–16.

Foa, E. B., Riggs, D. S., Massie, E. D., & Yarczower, M. (1995). The impact of fear activation and anger on the efficacy of exposure treatment for postraumatic stress disorder. *Behavor Therapy, 26,* 487–499.

Follette, W. C., & Callaghan, G. M. (1995). Do as I do, not as I say: A behavior–analytic approach to supervision. *Professional Psychology: Research and Practice, 26,* 413–421.

Follette, W. C., Naugle, A. E., & Callaghan, G. M. (1996). A radical behavioral understanding of the therapeutic relationship. *Behavior Therapy 27,* 623–641.

Gelso, C. J., & Carter, J. A. (1994). Components of the psychotherapy relationship: Their interactions and unfolding during treatment. *Journal of Counseling Psychology, 41,* 296–306.

Greenberg, L. S. (1994). What is "real" in the relationship? Comment on Gelso and Carter (1994). *Journal of Counseling Psychology, 41,* 307–309.

Greenberg, L. S., & Safran, J. D. (1987). Emotion in psychotherapy. *American Psychologist, 44*, 19–27.

Greenson, R. (1965). The working alliance and the transference neurosis. *Psychoanalytic Quarterly, 34*, 155–181.

Greenspoon, J., & Brownstein, A. J. (1967). Psychotherapy from the standpoint of a behaviorist. *The Psychological Record, 17*, 401–416.

Hanly, C. (1992). *The problem of truth in applied psychoanalysis.* New York: Guilford Press.

Hartley, D. E., & Strupp, H. H. (1983). The therapeutic alliance: Its relationship to outcome in brief psychotherapy. In J. Masling (Ed.), *Empirical studies in analytic theories* (pp. 1–37). Hillside, NJ: Erlbaum.

Hayes, L. (1992). The psychological present. *The Behavior Analyst, 15*, 139–145.

Hayes, L. (1993). Reality and truth. In S. Hayes, L. Hayes, H. Reese, & T. Sarbin (Eds.), *Varieties of scientific contextualism* (pp. 35–44). Reno, NV: Context Press.

Hayes, S. C. (1987). A contextual approach to therapeutic change. In N. Jacobson (Ed.), *Psychotherapists in clinical practice: Cognitive and behavioral perspectives* (pp. 327–387). New York: Guilford Press.

Hayes, S. C. (1989). *Rule-governed behavior: Cognition, contingencies and instructional control.* New York: Plenum Press.

Hayes, S. C., Hayes, L., & Reese, H. (1988). Finding the philosophical core: A review of Stephen C. Pepper's *World Hypotheses. Journal of the Experimental Analysis of Behavior, 50*, 97–111.

Hayes, S. C., Streusal, D., & Wilson, K. G. (in press). *Acceptance and commitment therapy: Treating human suffering.* New York: Guilford Press.

Hobbs, N. (1962). Sources of gain in psychotherapy. *American Psychologist, 17*, 741–747.

Horvath, A. O. (1995). The therapeutic relationship: From transference to alliance. *In Session: Psychotherapy in Practice, 1*, 7–17.

Horvath, A. O., & Luborsky, L. (1993). The role of the therapeutic alliance in psychotherapy. *Journal of Consulting and Clinical Psychology, 61*, 561–573.

Horvath, A. O., & Symonds, B. D. (1991). Relation between working alliance and outcome in psychotherapy: A meta-analysis. *Journal of Counseling Psychology, 38*, 139–149.

Howard, K. I., & Orlinsky, D. I. (1972). Psychotherapeutic processes. *Annual Review of Psychology, 23*, 615–658.

Jacobson, N. S., Dobson, K. S., Truax, P. A., Addis, M. E., Koerner, K., Gollan, J. K., Gortner, E., & Prince, S. E. (1996). A component analysis of cognitive behavioral treatment for depression. *Journal of Consulting and Clinical Psychology, 64*, 295–304.

Klee, M. R., Abeles, N., & Muller, R. T. (1990). Therapeutic alliance: Early indicators, course, and outcome. *Psychotherapy, 27*, 166–172.

Kohlenberg, R. J., & Tsai, M. (1991). *Functional analytic psychotherapy: Creating intense and curative therapeutic relationships.* New York: Plenum Press.

Kohlenberg, R. J., & Tsai, M. (1994a). Functional analytic psychotherapy: A behavioral approach to treatment and integration. *Journal of Psychotherapy Integration, 4,* 175–201.

Kohlenberg, R. J., & Tsai, M. (1994b). Improving cognitive therapy for depression with functional analytic psychotherapy: Theory and case study. *The Behavior Analyst, 17,* 305–320.

Kohlenberg, R. J., Tsai, M., & Dougher, M. J. (1993). The dimensions of clinical behavior analysis. *The Behavior Analyst, 16,* 271–282.

Kohlenberg, R. J., Tsai, M., & Kohlenberg, B. (1996). Functional analysis in behavior therapy. In M. Hersen, M. Eisler, & P. Miller (Eds.), *Progress in behavior modification* (pp. 1–24). New York: Plenum.

Linehan, M. M. (1993a). *Cognitive behavioral treatment of borderline personality disorder: The dialectics of effective treatment.* New York: Guilford Press.

Linehan, M. M. (1993b). *Skills training manual for treating borderline personality disorder.* New York: Guilford Press.

Meissner, W. W. (1996). *The therapeutic alliance.* New Haven, CT: Yale University Press.

Moore, J. (1981). On mentalism, methodological behaviorism, and radical behaviorism. *Behaviorism, 9,* 55–77.

Mowrer, O. H. (1939). A stimulus–response analysis of anxiety and its role as a reinforcing agent. *Psychological Review, 46,* 553–565.

Newirth, J. (1995). Impasses in the psychoanalytic relationship. *In Session: Psychotherapy in Practice, 1,* 73–80.

O'Donohue, W. (1995). The scientist–practitioner: Time allocation in psychotherapy. *The Behavior Therapist, 18,* 117–119.

Omer, H. (1995). Troubles in the therapeutic relationship: A pluralistic perspective. *In Session: Psychotherapy in Practice, 1,* 47–57.

Orlinsky, D., & Howard, K. (1986). Process and outcome of psychotherapy. In S. Garfield & A. Bergin (Eds.), *Handbook of psychotherapy and behavior change: An empirical analysis.* New York: Wiley.

Pepper, S. C. (1957). *World hypotheses.* Berkeley: University of California Press.

Rimm, D. C., & Masters, J. C. (1979). *Behavior therapy: Techniques and empirical findings.* (2nd ed.). San Francisco: Academic Press.

Rosenfarb, I. S. (1992). A behavior analytic interpretation of the therapeutic relationship. *The Psychological Record, 42,* 341–354.

Safran, J. D., Crocker, P., McMain, S., & Murray, P. (1990). The therapeutic alliance rupture as a therapy event for empirical investigation. *Psychotherapy, 27,* 154–165.

Safran, J. D., & Muran, J. C. (1995). Resolving therapeutic alliance ruptures: Diversity and integration. *In Session: Psychotherapy in Practice, 1,* 1–12.

Safran, J. D., & Muran, J. C. (1996). The resolution of ruptures in the therapeutic alliance. *Journal of Consulting and Clinical Psychology, 64,* 447–458.

Salter, A. (1963). *The case against psychoanalysis.* New York: Citadel Press.

Sandler, J., & Sandler, A. M. (1984). The past unconscious, the present unconscious, and the interpretation of the transference. *Psychoanalytic Inquiry, 4,* 367–399.

Schafer, R. (1982). The relevance of the "here and now" transference interpretation to the reconstruction of early development. *International Journal of Psychoanalysis, 63,* 77–82.

Shaffer, L. F. (1947). The problem of psychotherapy. *American Psychologist, 2,* 459–467.

Shaw, F. (1946). A stimulus–response analysis of repression and insight in psychotherapy. *Psychological Review, 53,* 36–42.

Shea, T., Elkin, I., Imber, S. C., Sotsky, S. M., Watkins, J. T., Collins, J. F., Pilkonis, P. A., Beckman, E., Dolan, R. T., & Parloff, M. B. (1992). Course of depressive symptoms over follow-up: Findings from the NIMH Treatment of Depression Collaborative Research Program. *Archives of General Psychiatry, 49,* 782–787.

Shoben, E. J. (1949). Psychotherapy as a problem in learning theory. *Psychological Bulletin, 46,* 366–392.

Skinner, B. F. (1945). The operational analysis of psychological terms. *Psychological Review, 52,* 279–294.

Skinner, B. F. (1953). *Science and human behavior.* New York: Macmillan.

Skinner, B. F. (1957). *Verbal behavior.* New York: Appleton-Century-Crofts.

Strupp, H. H. (1996). Some salient lessons from research and practice. *Psychotherapy, 33,* 135–138.

Turkat, I. D., & Brantley, P. J. (1981). On the therapeutic relationship in behavior therapy. *The Behavior Therapist, 4,* 16–17.

Watson, J. C. (1996). The relationship between vivid description, emotional arousal, and in session resolution of problematic reactions. *Journal of Consulting and Clinical Psychology, 64,* 459–464.

Watson, J. C., & Greenberg, L. S. (1995). Alliance ruptures and repairs in experiential therapy. *In Session: Psychotherapy in Practice, 1,* 19–31.

Wilson, T. G., & Evans, I. M. (1977). The therapist–client relationship in behavior therapy. In A. Gurman & A. Razin (Eds.), *Effective psychotherapy: A handbook of research* (pp. 544–565). New York: Pergamon Press.

Wilson, T. G., & O'Leary, K. D. (1980). *Principles of behavior therapy.* Englewood Cliffs, NJ: Prentice Hall.

Wolpe, J. (1958). *Psychotherapy by reciprocal inhibition.* Stanford, CA: Stanford University Press.

Wolpe, J. (1981). Behavior therapy verses psychoanalysis: Therapeutic and social implications. *American Psychologist, 36,* 159–164.

Zetzel, E. R. (1956). Current concepts of transference. *International Journal of Psychoanalysis, 37,* 369–376.

Cory F. Newman

The Therapeutic Relationship and Alliance in Short-Term Cognitive Therapy

5

Since the early, classic volumes on cognitive therapy in the 1970s (A. T. Beck, 1976; A. T. Beck, Rush, Shaw, & Emery, 1979), the role of the therapeutic relationship in cognitive therapy (CT) has undergone evolutionary changes. Originally conceived and tested by Aaron T. Beck as a short-term, outpatient, psychosocial treatment for uncomplicated, unipolar depression, CT has grown to be applied and researched across a plethora of diagnostic areas (e.g., anxiety disorders, Hawton, Salkovskis, Kirk, & Clark, 1989; substance abuse, A. T. Beck, Wright, Newman, & Liese, 1993; bipolar disorder, Scott, 1996; schizophrenia, Kingdon & Turkington, 1994; personality disorders, A. T. Beck, Freeman, & Associates, 1990) and modalities (e.g., couples therapy, Datillio & Padesky, 1990; family therapy, Epstein, Schlesinger, & Dryden, 1988; group therapy, White, 1995; inpatient treatment, Wright, Thase, Beck, & Ludgate, 1993). In order to meet the needs of these heterogeneous populations, and of diverse applications, the CT model has developed to incorporate new techniques and more sophisticated methods of case formulation (Layden, Newman, Freeman, & Morse, 1993; Persons, 1989). Further, the therapeutic relationship has been reconceptualized (to some degree) as well.

The early writings and research trials on CT present the therapeutic relationship as almost a given in the process of therapy, as something that is routinely, easily established, and that serves as the positive background for the so-called actual work of therapy. The assumption was that the cognitive therapist would communicate warmth, respect, genuineness, and confidence in the therapeutic process and that the patient would be readily responsive to this interpersonal stance, such that a healthy, collaborative, therapeutic relationship would ensue. Further, early researchers of CT assumed that this positive, uncomplicated relationship would remain a fait accompli, and that the work of therapy would not entail examining the vicissitudes of the therapeutic relationship, or necessitate the repairing of setbacks or ruptures in the therapeutic relationship.[1]

However, as CT came to be applied to populations who were more likely to have experienced chronic, interpersonal problems (e.g., borderline personality disorder, cf. Layden et al., 1993; substance abuse, cf. A. T. Beck, Wright, et al., 1993), the therapeutic relationship was no longer viewed as routine or as in the background. Entire sections of the above-mentioned texts were devoted to establishing, conceptualizing, maintaining, and troubleshooting the therapeutic relationship. The therapeutic relationship no longer was seen as a prelude to the treatment, but as part and parcel of the process. Misunderstandings, misperceptions, and magnified reactions (positive, negative, and mixed, both in the patient and in the therapist) in the interactions between the therapist and patient became targets for case formulation and intervention in themselves.

With these changes in the therapeutic relationship's place within the realm of CT came the acceptance of the notion that treatment could be long term. Although the standard model of CT—indeed, most of the controlled, outcome research on CT—on average calls for between 12 and 20 hour-long weekly sessions, the actual practice of CT is witness to a far wider range of sessions. In fact, some of our patients at the University of Pennsylvania Center for Cognitive Therapy continue their work for 2 years or more.

However, true to the CT goals of empowering the patient and of continually evaluating the efficacy of the treatment, great emphasis is placed on boosting the levels of the patient's self-confidence, *especially* in long-term cases where overdependency on the therapist is a risk. This entails strategies such as tapering off the frequency of sessions,

---

[1]Interestingly, an early demonstration videotape on CT from the 1970s shows Beck skillfully repairing what could have been a damaging episode of mistrust in the therapeutic relationship. In the *"Janice" Tape, Session #2* (A. T. Beck, 1977), the patient believed that Beck's interventions were "manipulating" her feelings, such that she felt out of control. Beck tuned into this problem immediately, validated the patient's concerns, and then Socratically helped the patient to reconstrue his techniques as being *empowering and instructive* of the self-help skills to be learned in CT. Apparently, the actual practice of CT was richer in its handling of the therapeutic relationship than the textbooks would have had us believe, even then.

having the patient take greater control over the therapeutic agenda (both in session and across sessions), and having the patient devise his or her own homework assignments.

Now, unfortunately, financial considerations (e.g., limited insurance reimbursements for patients, markedly lesser revenues for therapists, institutional pressures to end therapy quickly, and so forth) have made the use of short-term therapy more necessary, even when longer term therapy otherwise may be indicated. This situation forces mental health professionals to rethink their therapeutic agendas, such that there is a greater emphasis on building the patient's psychological skills for the future, and relatively less emphasis on focusing on the therapeutic relationship and its relation to the patient's developmental history. As noted earlier, this model was presented as the norm in the early writings and studies on CT of unipolar depression, and the model worked extremely well. However, now that cognitive therapists regularly treat individuals who otherwise would be candidates for long-term treatment, it is necessary to find a way to incorporate the best that the therapeutic relationship has to offer, in the most time-effective way. The present chapter addresses this issue.

Conceptualization of the Therapeutic Relationship

Cognitive therapists endeavor to engage their patients in a process of "collaborative empiricism" (A. T. Beck et al., 1979, p. 6). This means that the therapists facilitate a sense of teamwork with their patients, so that together they may investigate the patients' lives, formulate hypotheses about how and why problems have arisen (and are maintained) and test possible solutions. The therapists emphasize to their patients that an active partnership will facilitate the best progress toward their patients' goals. This is so, in part, because although the therapist is the expert in CT, the patient is the expert about his or her own life story. Each participant benefits from the other's font of knowledge. Together, they achieve a better, more constructive understanding of the patient's unique difficulties, as well as of how to effect change.

I have often said to my supervisees in CT training that in order to be good cognitive therapists, they have to be "part Sherlock Holmes and part Marcus Welby" (the latter being a compassionate, caring, family doctor in a 1970s American television series). To be explicit, this means that they need to be the wise, benevolent doctor who inspires trust, confidence, and a sense of safety, while also exhibiting a probing, systematic, critical thinking process toward the "solving of the case." Having said that, one should add that the patients need to be "part Dr. Watson and part Steven Kiley" (Dr. Welby's junior partner)— that is to say, to be *colleagues* in this process. Patients exemplify this when they engage in between-sessions homework assignments; when they come prepared with an agenda for each session; when they self-monitor their moods, thoughts, and actions; and when they willingly formulate hypotheses, rather than being content to say, "I don't know." Patients also facilitate this process when they reciprocate their therapists' healthy, positive regard. However, as we shall see, this is not a given, and therapists must have methods by which to deal with problematic, strained, conflictual therapeutic relationships.

THE ROLES OF THE THERAPIST AND PATIENT

At the start of a course of CT, the therapist serves as a teacher, coach, mentor, and role model. Likewise, the patient takes the role of a student, team player, protégé, and role observer. This is congruent with the psychoeducational approach that is inherent in CT.

Therapists teach their patients about the cognitive theory of emotional disorders (A. T. Beck, 1976), and the patients come to learn the nomenclature, spotting their automatic thoughts, generating rational responses, enacting behavioral experiments, recognizing when they are falling prey to dichotomous thinking, and the like. Patients' application of this knowledge provides them with a sense of empowerment, which further solidifies the sense of partnership in the therapeutic relationship.

Therapists coach their patients by giving them feedback about attempts to understand and help themselves. They give their patients instruction, nonjudgmental positive regard, and corrective feedback when they struggle in session (or in their between-sessions homework assignments), and they give their patients enthusiastic (but decidedly nonpatronizing) kudos when they make progress.

Therapists mentor their patients by working toward the ideal goal of the patients learning to become their own cognitive therapists. The metamessage from the therapist may be stated as follows: "I am the person to whom you have come for assistance, and I will gladly offer it; however, I am going to pass the baton to you, as you will become more and more responsible for, and capable of effecting, the long-term self-application of CT."

Therapists serve as role models by demonstrating personal qualities and skills such as (a) consistency, (b) humble self-confidence, (c) direct, clear communication, (d) the capacity for unexaggerated, but unfailing optimism, (e) a mind toward problem solving, (f) flexibility in incorporating new data and in revising hypotheses, (g) patience and perseverance, (h) proactivity, (i) genuine warmth, and (j) trustworthiness, to name a few. These are high standards of behavior, to be sure. Nevertheless, these therapist characteristics increase the probability that patients will extend themselves to do their best to contribute to the process of treatment (the message to "do as I do" is significantly more effective than giving the message merely to "do as I say"). Further, they give patients—some of whom may come from developmental backgrounds where healthy, adult functioning was anything but the norm—the sense of safety that they need before they can fully, deeply communicate their concerns, fears, and pain. If patients come to imitate their therapists' most adaptive behavioral and cognitive styles, this is an additional bonus, provided that the patients accept the notion that their own unique styles need to be respected.

HYPOTHESIZING THE PATIENT'S BELIEFS ABOUT RELATIONSHIPS

As CT has advanced to treat more challenging populations such as those for whom interpersonal relations pose chronic difficulties, the conceptualization of the therapeutic relationship in CT has broadened and deepened. For example, the therapeutic relationship is seen as a source of information about the patient's "unwritten rules for relationships," including their basic beliefs and schemas pertinent to relating to others. In addition, to the extent that the therapist can maintain the necessary self-awareness to avoid becoming entangled in the patient's dysfunctional interpersonal cycles (cf. Safran & Segal, 1990), the therapeutic relationship can serve as the basis for modifying the patient's beliefs about relationships.

For example, one of the author's patients was remanded to CT as a condition of his parole. From the outset, "Vic" was guarded and mistrustful of the therapist, making it very clear that coming to therapy was not his favorite activity. One day after Vic failed to show up for a session for the third time, the therapist wrote him a letter in which he empathized with Vic's reluctance to put himself under the psychological spotlight, and nicely entreated him to return so that he could maintain his freedom (i.e., not violate parole).

Vic returned to therapy upon receiving the letter, but admitted that the letter disturbed him greatly, precisely because the tone was so respectful and compassionate. This seemingly paradoxical reaction led to a productive discussion about Vic's beliefs about relationships, specifically, that people (especially those in positions of authority) were malevolent and that it was self-protective for Vic to expect the worst in people. When Vic received the therapist's polite letter, it stirred up a sense of vulnerability because he felt "off guard" and "out of control." In other words, Vic's idiosyncratic belief was that he was safer if people were indeed hostile toward him, provided that he was expecting such behavior. By contrast, if someone were to act nicely toward him, as the therapist had done, it would feel more dangerous, because it confounded Vic's expectations. The discovery of this belief system, born of an evaluation of the interactions between Vic and the therapist, led to lengthy discussions about alternative ways to view and manage relationships.

Another illustration of using the therapeutic relationship as a way to understand the patient's beliefs about relationships is the case of a woman with highly conflicted, contradictory views of herself. "Shayna," who suffered from bipolar disorder, sometimes viewed herself as one of *les misérables* in life: a poor, lonely, deprived, unfortunate soul who needed a great deal of attention, sustenance, and care. Conversely, she sometimes perceived herself to be of the highest intellect, resourcefulness, and respectability, a person who was capable of great independence. When the therapist would respond to Shayna's emotional pain and neediness, she would take offense at "not being treated as an equal." On the flip side, when the therapist would demonstrate confidence in the patient's coping skills, she would rail at him for having "blindly optimistic" expectations for her.

As a result of the processing of these scenarios in the therapeutic relationship, a great deal was learned about Shayna's relationships with the people closest to her. Specifically, Shayna believed that others should be able to ascertain by intuition her cycling moods and concomitant states of mind and that this was the so-called true sign of caring. If someone empathized with one polar aspect of Shayna's experience, she would not see this as a supportive gesture, but rather as a deliberate invalidation of the opposite pole of her experience. In this manner, Shayna's internal double bind came to double bind the significant others of her life as well, including the therapist. This revelation set the stage for Shayna to begin the process of revising some of her most time-honored beliefs about herself and about her interactions with others.

CT patients sometimes have stereotyped, preconceived notions about what the therapeutic relationship will entail, often based on articles or books that they have read prior to seeking CT (e.g., Burn's, 1980, *Feeling Good*). Patients who have explored the literature on CT often expect that therapy will focus almost exclusively on "rational thinking." As a result, many of these patients express surprise when their course of CT also focuses on emotions and interpersonal issues (including the therapeutic relationship), even in short-term treatment. Clearly, the reputation of CT is of heavy emphasis on the "rationality" aspect, and misleadingly light emphasis on the emotional and inter-personal variables (Gluhoski, 1994; Newman, 1991).

Implications of a Short-Term Approach in Conceptualizing the Therapeutic Relationship

CT does not fall prey to the uniformity myth, as it pertains to patients and therapies (cf. Kiesler, 1966; Safran & Segal, 1990). It is clear that "one size does not fit all"—the therapist's approach needs to be tai-lored to fit the specific needs of a given patient. Some patients are more well suited for short-term treatment than others (Muran, Segal, Samstag, & Crawford, 1994). One hypothesis is that patients who respond best to short-term treatment are more likely to have come from developmental backgrounds where their needs for nurturance and safety were more readily met by significant caregivers (Stern, 1993). For these patients, issues about basic trust (e.g., in relating to the therapist) are not primary. Therefore, if therapists give them the proper support, guidelines, and structure, they can "dive right into" therapy and make significant changes in a relatively short span of time.

By contrast, there are patients who necessitate a much longer period of warm-up time in treatment before they will open up suffi-ciently to deal with the most pressing issues. Such patients are look-ing for signs that the therapist will neither ridicule, judge, nor other-wise harm them. This process requires that therapists act with consistency over a period of time.

Another intriguing hypothesis put forth by Edbril (1994) suggests the short-term model of psychotherapy is geared toward the develop-mental needs of men, and alternately, is detrimental to the develop-mental needs of women. She argues that separation from a nurturer (e.g., mother, therapy) is part of the male's process of individuation, although the female needs continuity of connection over time in order to mature and grow. Interestingly, this theory dovetails with the demographic data above, whereby men may tend to self-select for CT, assuming that it is quick, efficient, rational, and not much else.

Naturally, if therapy is limited to "*x*" number of sessions, this imposes an artificial barrier for the patient who seeks a more long-term attachment, or who requires a longer time to establish trust. Recognizing this, cognitive therapists generally do not view CT as a short-term therapy per se, but more appropriately as a time-effective treatment. In this vein, cognitive therapists do pay close attention to time, as time is a precious commodity in life, but they do not rush their patients unduly. The goal is not to *waste* time, but instead to spur on a process of achieving therapeutic goals as promptly as is reasonably possible, whether it takes a single session, a month, a year, or more.

Of course, this is a theoretical goal, because there is no perfect way to measure whether time is being used well or wasted. However, there are general principles and procedures to which most Beck-trained cognitive therapists adhere so as to be time effective. For example, cognitive therapists formulate an agenda for each therapy session, so as to minimize the possibility that the session will drift into peripheral tangents, minutiae, or idle chat—which patients (and sometimes therapists) often find to be more comfortable. As I have heard more than one CT trainee exclaim, "This treatment requires a lot of work!" Indeed, it does, and this is part of its efficacy.

Further, cognitive therapists ask their patients many open-ended questions (in order to stimulate their ability to think through a problem), give them direct feedback (in order to make full use of the therapist's knowledge, rather than allow it to lie dormant until such time as the therapist believes that the patient is "ready" to hear something), often do not accept "I don't know" for an answer (which otherwise would maintain the patient's status quo of perceived helplessness; cf. Newman, 1994, 1996), and assign between-sessions homework, which is associated with better and more sustained treatment outcome (Burns & Auerbach, 1992; Persons, Burns, & Perloff, 1988; Fennell & Teasdale, 1987; Primakoff, Epstein, & Covi, 1989).

The above strategies are congruent with the psychoeducational model of CT, whereby the therapeutic relationship is very much akin to that of a professor–graduate student, or senior partner–junior partner dyad. While it is true (given the acknowledged heterogeneity of patients) that some patients respond more readily to this model than others, it is apparent that most CT patients move toward empowerment and autonomy. The length of time it takes to achieve this goal may be variable, but the goal itself is not.

Having said the above, what do cognitive therapists do when the length of therapy is fixed and short? For example, some patients can afford only their limited allotment of insured outpatient sessions, and that is that. Similarly, patients who take part in research protocols often have to adhere to a fixed limit of sessions (unless ethical issues dictate otherwise). In such instances, cognitive therapists endeavor to prepare their patients for termination from the outset. At first, this may seem less than nurturing; however, it is honest, and it facilitates goal-directedness. Further, it prevents the problem of too much time in therapy spent on negotiating an ambiguous termination time (A. T. Beck et al., 1979; Safran & Segal, 1990). Therapists necessarily handle such planned terminations with great sensitivity. They must give their patients a clear rationale for this approach, so that the chance that the patient will feel personally rejected or abandoned will be minimized.

As a graduate student, I was a protocol therapist in a CT study (later published in Beach, Sandeen, & O'Leary, 1990), where each patient received 16 sessions. One patient cried during the third session, explaining that "I'm already thinking that I'm going to lose you in thirteen more sessions." Witnessing and managing this patient's emotional reactions to a planned termination—even one that was more than three quarters of the length of treatment away—was an important learning experience. Anticipated separation and loss are big issues for some patients, whether they are in CT or not. Cognitive therapists must be able to attend to these feelings, even as they pursue their usual, problem-focused agendas. One approach does not preclude the other, but it does require more creativity, sensitivity, and a willingness to adopt a more integrative approach in therapy (cf. Norcross & Goldfried, 1992).

In the previous example, the patient overtly called attention to the therapeutic relationship and its impending dissolution. Therefore, it behooved the therapist to include this issue on the therapeutic agenda and to explore the meaning of the attachment, as well as the anticipated loss. It also led to the discussion of a more common topic in CT, namely, enhancing the patient's social-support system, so that the patient would not feel isolated, helpless, and unloved. However, if the patient herself had not brought up the issue of her anticipatory grief regarding the ending of the therapeutic relationship, I (as most cognitive therapists) would not have called attention to the therapeutic relationship as a matter of course. I certainly would have continued to behave in such a way as to provide a positive (perhaps corrective) interpersonal experience, but it would have remained a covert factor in the treatment, not an overt point of discussion in session.

This, perhaps, represents the general rule-of-thumb in short-term CT: If the patient wishes to discuss the therapeutic relationship (or otherwise shows subtle, important reactions to it), the cognitive therapist should not sidestep the issue, but rather link it to interpersonal issues that will be pertinent to the patient in the long run (with relatively greater emphasis on the future, rather than on the past). On the other hand, cognitive therapists, by and large, do not bring up the topic of the therapeutic relationship without first being prompted in some demonstrable way.

Establishing an Alliance in Short-Term CT

The demands of short-term CT[2] necessitate the therapist's immediately working hard to show that he or she is making every effort to understand and help the patient. The therapist is expected to demonstrate *simple empathy*, by listening, reflecting, and offering words of kindness, concern, and encouragement. However, it is even more facilitative if the therapist can provide *accurate* empathy from the very outset of treatment. *Accurate empathy* requires a potent admixture of data and therapist intuition. It is one thing to say to a patient, "That must have been very difficult for you." It is even more powerful to be able to hypothesize *why* a given situation "must have been very difficult" for the patient. The latter method is more readily achievable if the therapist has obtained clinical information about the patient prior to the first session.

At the Center for Cognitive Therapy, patients who call for an initial evaluation are informed that they will receive an extensive battery of inventories and open-ended questionnaires in the mail. They are asked to complete all of these forms and to bring them to their intake session. These data provide the therapist who performs the intake with information that typically goes beyond the scope of structured, diagnostic interviewing (e.g., historical or developmental issues, incidents of prior trauma, self-identified patterns in romantic relationships, beliefs about the self, others, and the future, and so forth). The intake therapist integrates this information with the diagnostic findings to produce a report that provides a fairly sophisticated, preliminary case conceptualization. The report, in turn, allows the therapist to "hit the ground running" with the patient in the first therapy session. In our experience here at the Center for Cognitive Therapy, for every patient who complains about the arduous intake procedures, there are four or five who exclaim that they have never before been attended to so thoroughly and carefully, or ever understood so quickly.

As an illustration, take the example of a patient who, in the first therapy session, was prone to making a high rate of self-deprecatory remarks. Any observant, empathic cognitive therapist could have said,

---

[2]The terms *therapeutic relationship* and *therapeutic alliance* are nearly synonymous in CT. If there is a subtle distinction, it is that the *alliance* emphasizes that part of the therapeutic relationship that entails the participants' active collaboration toward goals. For the purposes of this chapter, the terms will be used interchangeably.

"Gee, you're very down on yourself." However, because this patient had indicated on his intake questionnaires that his father had made these same, derogatory remarks to him, the therapist was able to say, "The things you're saying to yourself sound like the sorts of verbally abusive comments your father used to make to you. Did you realize that? I wonder if that adds an even deeper degree of emotional pain to your self-recriminations." This latter approach is an example of *rapid, accurate empathy*. It not only shows that the therapist has a heart, but also that the therapist has really done his or her homework. The patient is more likely to realize that the therapist is making a serious investment in the therapeutic process, and the alliance can be established quite quickly. Although it may be true that an astute therapist can achieve rapid, accurate empathy based solely on a first-time, face-to-face meeting with a patient, it is more likely to happen if the therapist is armed with preliminary data.

One of the inventories that has proved useful in ascertaining how to establish an immediate alliance with a new patient is the Sociotropy–Autonomy Scale (SAS; A. T. Beck, Epstein, & Harrison, 1983). When patients score significantly higher than the norm on the factor of Sociotropy, and lower than the norm on the factor of Autonomy, it indicates that the patient places much more emphasis on affiliation than on achievement or autonomy. The reverse is also true: The high Autonomy scorers place more value on achievement and independence, and relatively less emphasis on relationships.

Therapists who have patients' SAS scores can tailor their approach to be compatible with each patient's personal values, so as to facilitate an early, positive alliance. For example, if a therapist knows that a patient is highly autonomous, they may spend the early sessions of CT focusing heavily on problem solving, reviewing the techniques of rational responding, and emphasizing the ultimate goal of the patient's learning to become his or her own therapist. This allows the patient to "play to strength," which instills confidence and enthusiasm. After a solid alliance has been formed, the therapist then may choose to focus on the other side of the spectrum (i.e., interpersonal issues), so that the patient's psychological lacunae are not ignored.

Similarly, when therapists ascertain from the SAS that a patient is markedly sociotropic, it may be wise to focus initially on the patient's emotional and interpersonal life and to go easy on the rational, individual, problem-solving techniques. The therapist can teach the model of CT to such patients by examining their automatic thoughts and core beliefs in the context of their important relationships. Later, after a solid therapeutic relationship has been formed, the therapist can help the patients to improve their areas of weakness by focusing on the standard CT skills of self-help, self-instruction, and problem solving.

In sum, by using measures such as the SAS, therapists can behave in such a way as to maximize the patients' sense that their therapists are compatible with them, a perception that may be very important to the establishment of optimism and a commitment to work toward change (Horn-George & Anchor, 1982). This strategy, of course, requires that the therapist have a flexibility of style.

Maintaining an Alliance in Short-Term CT

Given that the number of sessions in which the patient and therapist have the chance to interact regularly, face-to-face, is limited, the maintenance of the therapeutic relationship is a concept that transcends the active life of therapy. It is important, and quite a challenge, for the therapist to make a significant, positive impact on the patient's life, the likes of which will carry on long after weekly sessions have concluded. The therapeutic relationship is maintained in the sense that the patients remember things they have learned in their work with their therapists, constructively utilize these lessons, and feel a warm, nostalgic connection with their therapists when they do this. Such a process is very similar to the positive experience that people have when they reminisce about a strategy that a former coach had taught them, or wise advice that they got from a great aunt at a family reunion, or a pep talk they received from a camp counselor. These are all short-term encounters, but very powerful in their own ways. So too is the short-term relationship in CT.

How are patients and therapists supposed to accomplish this everlasting bond, based on such a brief period of time? After all, how many therapists have had the experience whereby a new patient reviews his or her history of outpatient therapies and claims that he or she cannot remember the names of previous therapists? I have heard this statement more than a few times, and yet I have always been struck by the implication (assuming that the patient is being open and honest in pleading forgetfulness) that there really wasn't an important connection between this patient and his or her ex-therapists. It also provokes the thought, "How can I make this therapy experience *different* for this patient, so that it will be worthy of being remembered in all its most important detail? How can we make this experience *endure*, even if our time together is limited?"

CONVEY POSITIVE REGARD AND HOPE

One answer to the above question is quite basic, although not necessarily easy. Simply put, therapists have to exude warmth, genuineness, and positive regard—the humanistic qualities (Rogers, 1957; Truax & Carkhuff, 1967) that often are associated with the establishment of a long-term therapeutic relationship. However, in short-term CT, therapists also have to be active, directive, quick to share their knowledge, and above all, hopeful. To be truly hopeful means that therapists have to resist the temptation to imply (e.g., with a given patient who may have serious problems) that short-term therapy will not be enough, "but, alas, that's all we have." To the contrary, it is vital for short-term cognitive therapists to express at least a moderate level of optimism, focusing on what can be accomplished during the course of treatment, rather than on what will get short shrift. Given that we know that hopelessness is a significant predictor of suicidality in depressed patients (A. T. Beck, Steer, Beck, & Newman, 1993), it behooves us to be purveyors of hope.

For example, a therapist can say

> We have been allotted 10 sessions, so we really have to put our heads together to make the best use of our time. I have looked over all of the questionnaires and inventories you filled out— and by the way, thank you for enduring the thousand-and-one questions, but it really helps me get a picture of who you are, and what your life is like—and I have some ideas about what we can focus on in order to make the best progress possible. However, before I get into that in more depth, I'd like to hear what *your* goals for therapy are, and what your thoughts are about our having 10 sessions in which to help you move in the directions you want to go.

This statement doesn't promise the patient the moon, but it conveys confidence, sincerity, respect, and positive expectations for treatment. This is the stuff that builds hope and that creates a long-term influence out of a short-term therapy.

THERAPISTS DO THEIR HOMEWORK

Therapists can maximize the probability of maintaining a positive therapeutic alliance by demonstrating that they are investing their energy and their attention to each and every session (as well as between sessions). This involves the therapist's showing a strong work ethic, at least a moderate degree of urgency, and an aptitude for remembering important details about the patient from session to session. When time is of the essence, it is a strong gesture of goodwill when therapists are on time for sessions and are active (and alert) in the sessions. This is basic, but not to be underestimated.

Similarly, therapists earn their patients' trust when they show their concern for the limited time allotment by working hard between sessions—in effect, by doing their own share of the therapy homework. This may be as simple as the therapists taking accurate, detailed notes on each session, reviewing these notes religiously, and therefore being "sharp" and on target with their feedback or questions in each session. It may also entail therapists giving themselves parallel homework assignments between sessions and saying, for example:

> In sum, as we agreed, your assignment is to prepare a thoughtful series of questions for your supervisor, so you can begin to solve your dilemma at work in the most peaceable manner possible, and my assignment is to track down that magazine article, to which I alluded, on the subject of dealing with impossible bosses.

Another way in which therapists communicate their involvement is by sharing the thoughts they have had about the patients while preparing for a session. For example, it is a powerful experience for patients to hear their therapists say

> I have been thinking about some of the things that you said last session, and I was struck by the degree to which you repeatedly negate the importance of your accomplishments. Were you aware of that? I think we should add this topic to today's agenda, if you agree.

Aside from showing patients that the therapists are "working on their case" even when they are not together in the same room, such a comment also serves a modeling function in that it encourages patients to process the work of therapy on a regular basis as well. This increases the sense of collegiality between therapists and patients, and serves to make the best use of their limited time together. To make good use of time is not only a boon to therapy, but also a life skill in general. When we use our time effectively, we increase the chances of achieving more of our goals, both in and out of therapy. The achievement of goals, in and of itself, strengthens and maintains the therapeutic relationship. As the saying goes, "Nothing succeeds like success."

KEEP WRITTEN RECORDS AND TAPES

How else is the therapeutic relationship maintained? An important answer is that therapists and patient must not rely solely on the "oral history." If the therapist and patient merely talk to each other, much of what was said will fade away, along with the most potentially powerful aspects of their shared collaboration. Instead, the therapist and patient need to make use of the "written history," as well as audiotapes and videotapes. It is standard practice for therapists to document the process and the progress of therapy. Given that CT views patients as active collaborators, it becomes the norm for patients to keep a variety of records of their sessions (and of their between-sessions homework) as well.

Patients in short-term CT often do some or all of the following:

1. Take notes during session;
2. Write flashcards of new rational responses (and other good ideas) in session;
3. Keep a folder of all of their homework, which they bring to session for selective review;
4. Keep a running journal of their experiences in therapy and between sessions;
5. Audiotape their own sessions, so as to listen to the contents of the session a second or third time, perhaps taking notes along the way, so as to facilitate transfer of therapeutic material to long-term memory and to bring clarity to complicated, fleeting interactions that occurred in session;
6. Collect the audiotapes of their own sessions, so as to create an archive of their therapy sessions, with each tape being labeled by topic, assignment, or other meaningful markers to which the patient later can refer quickly; and
7. Purchase selected book(s) from the self-help genre, with the CT therapist's guidance, the contents of which they can review together, and which the patient always can have as a useful reminder of the work that was done with the therapist.

I have often recommended that my patients save the best examples of their writings and recordings and to think of them as being akin to *The Best of Carson* or *The Best of Saturday Night Live*—in other words, a special series of their favorite moments in therapy. This, too, builds an enduring relationship that extends beyond the temporal bounds of short-term, face-to-face CT.

BOOSTER SESSIONS AND TAPERING SCHEDULES

Even when the number of sessions is limited, it is sometimes possible to extend the span of time over which the therapist and patient interact through the use of "booster" sessions. Depending on the constraints of third-party payers' regulations or the therapist's research protocol, this may take the form of tapering off the frequency of sessions, or it may involve discrete follow-up periods, or both. For example, a 12-session therapy can be divided into 4 weekly sessions, followed by 4 biweekly sessions, followed in turn by 4 monthly sessions, over the course of 6–7 months. Alternately, the same allotment of appointments can be configured to allow for 8 weekly sessions, followed by 2 monthly sessions, and concluding with follow-up meetings held at 3 months and 6 months "posttherapy," respectively. The particulars of such arrangements are quite variable.

The rationales for planning a tapering schedule or booster sessions are many. First, it provides for a lengthier, face-to-face therapeutic relationship. For some patients, this arrangement provides a degree of "continuity of connectedness" that compensates them somewhat for the limited number of hours of actual therapy time (cf. Edbril, 1994). Second, it gives patients a chance to adapt gradually to the completion of treatment, rather than being cut off abruptly. Third, it provides for the assessment of the patient's maintenance of therapeutic gains, the likes of which could not be ascertained if there were no arranged follow-up period. Fourth, both the therapists and patients can observe the latter's consistency in using self-help skills over time, the likes of which may help extend the benefits of therapy (Burns & Auerbach, 1992; Fennell & Teasdale, 1987; Persons et al., 1988; Primakoff et al., 1989). In fact, some patients anecdotally indicate that they are more inclined to practice their self-help skills— and therefore have such skills become more a part of their everyday routines—if they know that they will be seeing their therapists again down the road.

Ideally, patients have some control over the manner in which the frequency of therapy sessions is decreased. For example, therapists ask their patients, "How would *you* like for our latter three sessions to be arranged?" or "What sorts of goals would you like to pursue on your own, after which you could come back for a follow-up session to review with me?" This is a clear indication to patients that the responsibility for utilizing the knowledge gained in therapy is shifting primarily to their hands. At the same time, it gives the message that the therapist is still involved and wants to know how the patient is faring over a longer period of time. Similarly, the therapist tries to make a distinction between the patient's being "independent" and being "alone." As therapy goes through a planned, fade-out period, the patients learn that they must become the prime-movers in creating and maintaining positive changes in their lives. However, the prospect of booster sessions adds the element of "togetherness," such that patients are reminded that their therapists are still "in their corner."

Alliance Ruptures in
Short-Term CT

OVERWHELMING THE PATIENT WITH ACTIVITY AND OPTIMISM

Given that cognitive therapists try to help their patients accomplish so much in a relatively short period of time and given that cognitive therapists often are quite active and directive, patients sometimes can feel unduly "bombarded" with information, expectations, and perceived demands. Patients who already feel encumbered with problems and injured by life's "slings and arrows" sometimes view therapy solely as a place to relax, vent, and get unconditional support. Therefore, when they ascertain that CT also involves a rather rigorous learning process, they may feel mistreated or at least misunderstood (e.g., "If you really understood how worn-out and depressed I am, you wouldn't ask me for summary statements, you wouldn't request that I fill out questionnaires, and you certainly wouldn't expect me to do homework").

Practitioners of CT do, indeed, ask a great deal of their patients. Cognitive therapists attempt to find the patient's "ceiling" of functioning and to pursue it with hopefulness and vigor. Cognitive therapists attempt to do this with the utmost respect and without negative judgment.

Nevertheless, cognitive therapists are very sensitive to the possibility that patients may have adverse reactions to what they perceive as the therapist's unbridled, unwarranted hopefulness or excessive expectations for high-level functioning. Therefore, one of the central tasks of the cognitive therapist is to check for feedback (in fact, this is one of the items on the Cognitive Therapy Rating Scale, which monitors the cognitive therapists' activities in session; Young & Beck, 1980). Therapists ask, "What is your reaction to what I am saying so far?" or "What went through your mind as I was talking about the homework?" or "Do you have any qualms, concerns, or misgivings about my suggested approach to therapy?" Then, when the patient answers, the therapist pays attention, not only to what the patient actually says, but also to the nonverbal cues. A patient may say, "It sounds okay to me" with a hesitant tone, or may simply shrug his or her shoulders, to name a couple of reactions. This is the therapist's cue that the patient may be experiencing some unspoken discomfort.

Therefore, the therapist explores this area, taking great care to be supportive and understanding. The therapist emphasizes that he or she will not criticize the patient for not doing therapy homework, nor will he or she chastise the patient for being "too negative." The goal is to find the upper limits of the rate of change, but not at the expense of the patient's well-being. The therapist and patient go through the process of treatment in tandem. Whatever struggles they encounter and whatever successes they achieve, the patient and therapist are a team.

Along the lines of the above, some patients of cognitive therapy take issue with the therapist's enthusiasm and optimism. Rather than viewing the therapist's stance as supportive, progressive, and energizing, they view it as Pollyannaish, patronizing, or invalidating. The patient's thoughts on the matter can be summed up as follows: "You just don't get it—my life *really* is terrible," "I don't want to be told to 'Look on the bright side of life,'" and "If you're not sharing my misery with me, then you're not on my side."

In such instances, it behooves the therapist to explain that CT does not encourage the patient to engage in idle, positive thinking (Newman & Haaga, 1995). To do so would be to engage in denial, which is the opposite or polar extreme of the problem of catastrophizing. CT, in fact, eschews such all-or-none extremes, looking instead for the healthy, middle ground. This latter view holds, "Problems need to be acknowledged, but kept in perspective, so that people can bring all of their best personal resources to the forefront in order to address problems constructively."

Further, therapists need to emphasize that they are not minimizing the patient's sense of distress and hopelessness, but rather are trying to teach the patients how not to succumb to such experiences. I have at times told my patients a facsimile of the following:

> I do empathize with you. If I were in your life situation and I thought the way you are thinking right now, I am quite certain I would be very unhappy. However, I know that people who are depressed tend to get locked into thinking that their problems are unmanageable and that there is no solution. One of my most important responsibilities, in addition to giving you my undivided attention and support, is to show you the way out of this hopeless, defeated state of mind. To do that, I have to help you explore alternative ways to look at yourself and your life. I also have to assist you in doing whatever you can do to help yourself. This is a tried-and-true way to overcome depression. However, I am very open to hearing your points of view, and I will try to be as flexible as possible in taking things at a pace that you believe is realistic for you. I am on your side, but I will not collude with the part of you who is against yourself.

PERCEIVED COMPETITION FOR CONTROL

Another potential rupture in the therapeutic alliance is in the area of autonomy and control. Although patients may be very dissatisfied and unfulfilled in their lives and therefore acknowledge that they need the help of a therapist, they may nonetheless be very protective of their world view. As such, they may not take kindly to the therapist's implication that they need to change the way they think. The sentiment can be expressed as, "Hey, I may not be a happy person, but I know what I know and don't try to tell me otherwise."

Here, therapists must do all they can to steer clear of a power struggle over "who is right and who is wrong." Instead, therapists must acknowledge that patients have a wealth of experience about themselves to which the therapist may never be privy; therefore, the patient's perceptions must be taken seriously. Nevertheless, therapists explain that, as professionals, they bring a high level of objectivity to the exploration of the patient's life. The patients, by definition, are going to be much more subjective about themselves, and, while this is not a personal failing, they will be prone to bias, especially under duress. I frequently add that "This is why mental health professionals sometimes seek the help of other mental health professionals—not because the former lack intelligence, experience, autonomy, or knowledge of the human psyche—but rather, because they may be lacking objectivity, and they understand that they may be able to get it from another clinician."

For good measure, cognitive therapists go further by adding that they do not always assume that their opinions are optimally objective or "correct." They admit that all humans (including therapists) are prone to their own, idiosyncratic perspectives, some more adaptive than others. Therefore, cognitive therapists present their views as hypotheses to be tested, rather than as indisputable facts. In order to strengthen a sense of collaboration, therapists then can request that patients agree to view their own perceptions as hypotheses as well. Following this, therapists and patients can work together to test many of their collective hypotheses, as an investigative team. This reduces the struggle over autonomy and control.

PATIENTS FEEL RUSHED INTO TASKS BEFORE THEY ARE READY

Cognitive therapists teach their patients a variety of psychological skills, including communication, assertiveness, self-monitoring, self-instruction, systematic problem solving, and others. Accomplishing this in a short-term framework is eminently possible, but it may be a tall order for many patients. Therefore, another way in which the therapeutic alliance may be ruptured occurs when patients feel rushed into doing tasks that they feel they are not ready to do.

The therapists' response to this problem is similar to their response to other sources of misalliance: Validate the concern, but provide a rationale for viewing it a different way. In this case, the therapist notes that therapy may, in fact, be hurried along more than would be ideal. At the same time, it is important that the patient receive as much of the "full package" as possible, even if it means that the patient has to do much of the work of therapy after regular sessions have concluded. If this is the case, follow-up sessions are a major boon in overcoming the patient's concerns that he or she isn't correctly applying the skills learned in therapy.

When patients plead that they are not ready to engage in the nuts-and-bolts techniques of CT, therapists must tune into the patients' fears and lack of confidence, which themselves become focal points of therapeutic discussion. In this way, pursuing the tasks and learning the skills of CT pose a win–win situation, even if the patients feel intimidated or otherwise put off. It is a "win" if the patients surprise themselves with their efficacy, thus providing themselves with evidence that their self-doubts may be poor reflections of their actual capacity for growth. It is also a "win" if the patients choose not to engage in the tasks and skills of CT, in that their self-inhibitory beliefs may come to the fore, thus providing "hot cognitions" (Safran & Greenberg, 1982) that otherwise may have been inaccessible for therapeutic exploration. The implications of the above are clear: Opportunities for change are lost mainly when therapists choose to be inactive themselves, perhaps out of an untested fear that the patients are too fragile to have their positive limits tested and an untested belief that the therapist will be unable to manage a patient's adverse reaction.

One also should add that the notion of "readiness" is an elusive concept. Oftentimes, patients will maintain that they are not "ready" to engage in the most active parts of treatment, without any criteria for what "ready" means, other than their subjective impressions. Therefore, I openly discuss the issue of "what constitutes readiness" with some of my patients who demonstrate low self-efficacy. Typically, patients come to realize that a sense of readiness often is a *result* of trying something new (perhaps in a graded fashion), and that it is a much less adaptive use of the short-term therapy (and our short-term lives as human beings) to wait for a sense of readiness as a prerequisite to doing something new.

ANTICIPATION OF ABANDONMENT

In any short-term therapy—and CT is no exception—abandonment issues may be relevant (hearken back to the aforementioned example of the patient who cried, "I'm already thinking that I'm going to lose you in thirteen more sessions"). In some instances, patients will be hesitant to commit themselves to the work of therapy, believing that this will create a sense of dependency, followed shortly by a devastating loss. Therefore, they go through therapy in half-hearted fashion and reap fewer of the benefits. On the flip side are patients who immerse themselves in therapy and in the therapeutic relationship. As short-term therapy winds to a close, they experience great unrest, feeling anticipatory grief, and believing strongly that they will not be able to care for themselves in the absence of the therapist.

Cognitive therapists strive to help their patients find the middle ground between these extremes, where the patients make an optimal investment of themselves in treatment, form a mutually respectful alliance with the therapist, and gain a greater sense of confidence in being able to "carry the baton" after regular sessions have ended.

However, this goal is not always achieved. Those who keep their therapists at arm's length emotionally sometimes leave treatment early. Others remain in therapy, but seem to go through the motions. When therapists make note of patients' flat affect, they may be disinclined to discuss the matter, or slough it off as just being indicative of who they are (in a future treatment, many of these patients will be the ones who can't remember their previous therapist's name).

Those patients who come to feel very dependent upon their therapists, and who fear the imminent end of therapy, may have a number of reactions. Some try to convince the therapist to extend the length of therapy (whether the therapist has any control over this issue is another matter altogether), others react with sadness or anger; while still others try overtly to minimize the importance of the loss and may try to "go out on their own terms."

An example of the last reaction was a patient who was in a 16-week therapy research protocol. At the end of each of the first 14 sessions, "Catherine" would politely say "thank you" to the therapist and would exit the office, leaving the door open. At the end of the 15th session, Catherine recorded the time and date of the final appointment in her datebook, said "goodbye" to the therapist, and exited the office, *closing* the door behind her. Catherine never showed up for the 16th session, and she never responded to follow-up phone calls. An obvious hypothesis is that Catherine took control of the termination in a way that gave her a modicum of empowerment. Other interesting hypotheses may be ventured, but I sincerely regret that I never got the opportunity to explore them with Catherine. However, it taught me a lesson about how sad it can be when you lose a therapeutic relationship and you have no say in the matter.

In another instance, "Matthew" angrily exclaimed to me, "How can you do this for a living? How can you be people's friend, hearing about their most private thoughts and feelings, and then just say goodbye over and over? I don't understand it. Do you have real feelings?"

I addressed this plea in two ways. First, I honestly admitted that while my feelings were "real," I didn't actually know how I had come to adapt to multiple losses, adding something like:

> I know it must seem cold-hearted of me to just be able to say goodbye and accept it, but I really do like my patients and miss them when they're gone. Being a therapist is one of the most unusual jobs a person can have, and I guess I wouldn't be able to do it if I couldn't deal with saying goodbye to people. I do practice what I preach, in that I use CT on myself, so that I take solace in focusing on all of the good things that go on between myself and my patients, and I carry those experiences with me in my memory. So I look at my relationships with my patients as a blessing and a privilege, even though there is a cost. Does that make sense?

Having heard me be open in this manner, Matthew was willing to engage in the second area of discussion, which entailed his own struggling with trust, closeness, and loss, along with his sense of anger when he perceived that he was more invested in a relationship than the other person in the dyad.

Additional Interventions for Alliance Ruptures

Some of the traditional, standard techniques of CT are well-suited to examine and repair problematic interactions between therapists and patients. For example, when the therapist detects a negative, affective shift in the patient (e.g., rolling of the eyes, using sarcasm, orienting of posture away from the direction of the therapist), the therapist can ask the quintessential CT question: "What was going through your mind just then?" Sometimes this will be sufficient to open the discussion. However, if the patient says, "I don't know," the therapist can add that he or she noticed that the patient's reaction indicated some displeasure and that the therapist is open to hearing about this. The therapist may need to spell out that he or she is sorry if anything was said that hurt the patient's feelings and that the therapist would welcome the opportunity to get some corrective feedback from the patient.

One of the standard, structured methods by which CT patients monitor and evaluate their thinking processes is the Dysfunctional

Thought Record (DTR; cf. J. S. Beck, 1995). As a gesture of goodwill, as well as a means by which to do some self-exploration, therapists can offer to do their own DTR, in parallel with the patient, in an attempt to resolve a rift in the therapeutic relationship. If the therapist stays close to the task at hand, which is to understand the problem in the therapeutic relationship, this can be an appropriate, collaborative, reparative technique.

For example, "Amelia" became uncharacteristically tearful in session. I was taken aback, as I had not anticipated that Amelia, who always seemed so naturally composed, would have this reaction. When I asked her what she was thinking and feeling, Amelia offered that she was deeply disappointed that I was "ignoring" her. Dumbfounded, I asked what she meant. Amelia replied, "Haven't you been paying attention to my answers on the Beck Depression Inventory?" (BDI; A. T. Beck, Ward, Mendelson, Mock, & Erbaugh, 1961). I had no choice but sheepishly to admit that I had been lax in this area lately. When I looked at Amelia's written responses on the inventory, I was shocked to find that her depressive symptoms had gone up significantly. Given that it was time to end the session, and therefore there was no time to process the situation, I suggested that each of us do a DTR about the situation, and to share our responses at a session that should be scheduled as soon as would be convenient for Amelia.

At the next session, I shared my DTR responses, in which I spelled out that my emotions were guilt, sorrow, apprehension, and embarrassment. I also added the following:

> *Automatic thoughts:* I have been taking Amelia's feelings for granted. I got so accustomed to her being so composed that I failed to look at other signs that might indicate that she was struggling. Now she thinks I am neglectful and that I don't care, and all of our good work that we have done together is in danger of going down the drain. Maybe I was so invested in seeing Amelia as a "success case" that I filtered out anything I didn't want to see. What I did was terrible.

> *Rational response:* Although I made a mistake by overlooking Amelia's BDI responses, I am willing to own up to the mistake and to do everything I can to help her deal with her depression. I am still very dedicated to helping her, just as I am still very respectful of the way that she comports herself, even when she is in great emotional pain. I know I am not neglectful, but I have learned a valuable lesson about paying closer attention and staying vigilant. I know that I have not trivialized Amelia by thinking of her in terms of being a "success case." First and foremost, Amelia is a person, someone I value. I have faith in Amelia and in our work together, and I refuse to catastrophize that this will spell doom

for our relationship. I know we can work this out. This is not a terrible thing. Rather, it's a wake-up call, which is something entirely different.

After therapy ended, Amelia wrote me a letter, stating that she was doing very well and that she was actively, successfully applying the principles that she had learned in CT. Notably, Amelia pointed to the session in which I shared my thoughts on a DTR as a "turning point" in therapy. She indicated that it showed that I was humble enough to admit a mistake, that by doing a CT technique on myself I showed I was not "hypocritical," and that I was willing to leave myself open to criticism in order to honestly appraise and solve a difficult situation.

Note that the vignette above also demonstrates that (as mentioned earlier) therapists can give homework assignments to themselves. This also serves a valuable function in reestablishing goodwill in response to a problem in the therapeutic relationship. Such a strategy not only reemphasizes the collaborative nature of the relationship, but also provides the therapist with a way to gain some time and distance to think through the problem more clearly, just as we ask patients to do.

Another standard method of CT is to conceptualize patients' problems in terms of their core beliefs and to examine how these beliefs, born of past experiences, interact with the patients' current life situation (J. S. Beck, 1995; Persons, 1989). This same method can be used to examine rifts in the therapeutic relationship, such as when there is a power struggle over homework (Newman, 1994).

For example, "Bart" seemed to taunt me by stating that, although he complied with the therapy assignment to read *Feeling Good* (Burns, 1980), he threw the book in the trash minutes after buying it. Rather than simply assuming that Bart was being spiteful, I tried to conceptualize the patient's behavior. After asking a few open-ended questions about Bart's thoughts about buying and then trashing the book, it became clear that Bart's mistrust was the salient issue. When he read the information about the author, he mistakenly believed that the proceeds from the book's sale would go straight to the Center for Cognitive Therapy. Bart concluded that the homework assignment was nothing more than a money-making scheme and that I was simply taking advantage of my patients. This conceptualization opened the door to a great deal of productive, corrective discussion, and the therapeutic relationship was temporarily repaired (until the next crisis of mistrust, when the reparative process of conceptualizing the problem was repeated).

Conclusion

Although short-term CT historically has had the reputation of being long on technique and short on relationship issues, the reality (in practice) is that the therapeutic relationship is a vital part of the process. Cognitive therapists understand that providing warmth, genuineness, and positive regard is only a starting point and that many other issues may emanate from the vicissitudes of the therapeutic relationship. Experienced cognitive therapists, similar to experienced therapists of other orientations, know that they have to pay close attention to their patients' reactions to the relationship, that they have to conceptualize such reactions in the context of the patient's history and current life situation, that they need to take stock of their own role when problems occur with their patients, that making repairs to a damaged therapeutic relationship is an extremely high priority if therapy is to proceed, and that there are appropriate means by which to "use themselves" in dealing with therapeutic alliance ruptures.

Short-term CT, by definition, does not allow for a lengthy process of identifying and working through issues in the therapeutic relationship. However, this does not mean that the therapeutic relationship is not a meaningful aspect of short-term CT. The cognitive therapist serves as a teacher, coach, mentor, and role model, thus paving the way for patients to learn many of the psychological skills that they will need in order to help themselves in the long run. Further, the cognitive therapist creates a secure environment in which it is safe to discuss difficult issues, including rifts in the therapeutic relationship.

Although the active time of the face-to-face therapeutic relationship is brief, it can produce a powerful, positive impact on the lives of patients. We are all familiar with stories about how "brief encounters," or "chance meetings with a stranger" have changed people's lives. Similarly, and perhaps even more so, the short-term therapeutic relationship in CT can change patients' lives in profound ways. By teaching patients skills that increase their self-efficacy and that help them to manage life's problems, a bond of trust, respect, and positive regard is established. By carefully and sensitively addressing the issues surrounding the tensions and conflicts in the therapeutic relationship, as well as the meaning of the end of therapy, this positive connection can endure.

References

Beach, S. R. H., Sandeen, E. E., & O'Leary, K. D. (1990). *Depression in marriage: A model for etiology and treatment.* New York: Guilford Press.

Beck, A. T. (1976). *Cognitive therapy and the emotional disorders*. New York: International Universities Press.

Beck, A. T. (1977). *Cognitive therapy with a depressed patient: The "Janice" tape, Session 2*. Center for Cognitive Therapy Videotape archives, University of Pennsylvania.

Beck, A. T., Epstein, N., & Harrison, R. (1983). Cognitions, attitudes, and personality dimensions in depression. *British Journal of Cognitive Psychotherapy, 1*, 1–16.

Beck, A. T., Freeman, A., & Associates. (1990). *Cognitive therapy of personality disorders*. New York: Guilford Press.

Beck, A. T., Rush, A. J., Shaw, B. F., & Emery, G. (1979). *Cognitive therapy of depression*. New York: Guilford Press.

Beck, A. T., Steer, R. A., Beck, J. S., & Newman, C. F. (1993). Hopelessness, depression, suicidal ideation, and clinical diagnosis of depression. *Suicide and Life-Threatening Behavior, 23*, 139–145.

Beck, A. T., Ward, C. H., Mendelson, M., Mock, J., & Erbaugh, J. (1961). An inventory for measuring depression. *Archives of General Psychiatry, 4*, 561–571.

Beck, A. T., Wright, F. D., Newman, C. F., & Liese, B. S. (1993). *Cognitive therapy of substance abuse*. New York: Guilford Press.

Beck, J. S. (1995). *Cognitive therapy: Basics and beyond*. New York: Guilford Press.

Burns, D. (1980). *Feeling good: The new mood therapy*. New York: William Morrow.

Burns, D. D., & Auerbach, A. H. (1992). Does homework compliance enhance recovery from depression? *Psychiatric Annals, 22*, 464–469.

Dattilio, F., & Padesky, C. (1990). *Cognitive therapy with couples*. Sarasota, FL: Professional Resource Exchange.

Edbril, S. D. (1994). Gender bias in short-term therapy: Toward a new model for working with women patients in managed care settings. *Psychotherapy, 31*(4), 601–609.

Epstein, N., Schlesinger, S. E., & Dryden, W. (Eds.). (1988). *Cognitive–behavioral therapy with families*. New York: Brunner/Mazel.

Fennell, M. J. V., & Teasdale, J. D. (1987). Cognitive therapy for depression: Individual differences and the process of change. *Cognitive Therapy and Research, 11*, 253–272.

Gluhoski, V. L. (1994). Misconceptions of cognitive therapy. *Psychotherapy, 31*(4), 594–600.

Hawton, K., Salkovskis, P. M., Kirk, J., & Clark, D. M. (Eds.). (1989). *Cognitive behaviour therapy for psychiatric problems*. Oxford, England: Oxford University Press.

Horn-George, J. B., & Anchor, K. N. (1982). Perceptions of the psychotherapy relationship in long- versus short-term therapy. *Professional Psychology, 13*(4), 483–491.

Kiesler, D. J. (1966). Some myths of psychotherapy research and the search for a paradigm. *Psychological Bulletin, 65,* 110–136.

Kingdon, D. G., & Turkington, D. (1994). *Cognitive–behavioral therapy of schizophrenia.* New York: Guilford Press.

Layden, M. A., Newman, C. F., Freeman, A., & Morse, S. B. (1993). *Cognitive therapy of borderline personality disorder.* Needham Heights, MA: Allyn & Bacon.

Muran, C., Segal, Z., Samstag, L. W., & Crawford, C. E. (1994). Patient pretreatment interpersonal problems and therapeutic alliance in short-term cognitive therapy. *Journal of Consulting and Clinical Psychology, 62*(1), 185–190.

Newman, C. F. (1991). Cognitive therapy and the facilitation of affect: Two case illustrations. *Journal of Cognitive Psychotherapy: An International Quarterly, 5*(4), 305–316.

Newman, C. F. (1994). Understanding client resistance: Methods for enhancing motivation to change. *Cognitive and Behavioral Practice, 1,* 47–69.

Newman, C. F. (1996). A cognitive perspective on resistance in psychotherapy. *In-Session: Psychotherapy in Practice, 2*(1), 33–43.

Newman, C. F., & Haaga, D. A. F. (1995). Cognitive skills training. In W. O'Donohue & L. Krasner (Eds.), *Handbook of psychological skills training* (pp. 119–143). Needham Heights, MA: Allyn & Bacon.

Norcross, J. C., & Goldfried, M. R. (Eds.). (1992). *The comprehensive handbook of psychotherapy integration.* New York: Plenum.

Persons, J. B. (1989). *Cognitive therapy in practice: A case formulation approach.* New York: Norton.

Persons, J. B., Burns, D. D., & Perloff, J. M. (1988). Predictors of dropout and outcome in cognitive therapy for depression in a private practice setting. *Cognitive Therapy and Research, 12,* 557–575.

Primakoff, L., Epstein, N., & Covi, L. (1989). Homework compliance: An uncontrolled variable in cognitive therapy outcome research. In W. Dryden & P. Trower (Eds.), *Cognitive therapy: Stasis and change* (pp. 175–187). New York: Springer.

Rogers, C. R. (1957). The necessary and sufficient conditions of therapeutic personality change. *Journal of Consulting Psychology, 21,* 95–103.

Safran, J. D., & Greenberg, L. S. (1982). Eliciting "hot cognitions" in cognitive behavior therapy: Rationale and procedural guidelines. *Canadian Psychology, 23,* 83–87.

Safran, J. D., & Segal, Z. V. (1990). *Interpersonal process in cognitive therapy.* New York: Basic Books.

Scott, J. (1996). Cognitive therapy for clients with bipolar disorder. *Cognitive and Behavioral Practice, 3*(1), 29–52.

Stern, S. (1993). Managed care, brief therapy, and therapeutic integrity. *Psychotherapy, 30*(1), 162–175.

Truax, C., & Carkhuff, R. R. (1967). *Toward effective counseling and psychotherapy*. Chicago: Aldine.

White, J. R. (1995). *Overcoming depression and loss: A personal workbook for cognitive group therapy*. Palo Alto, CA: In Cognito Press.

Wright, J. H., Thase, M. E., Beck, A. T., & Ludgate, J. W. (Eds.). (1993). *Cognitive therapy with in-patients: Developing a cognitive milieu*. New York: Guilford Press.

Young, J., & Beck, A. T. (1980). *Cognitive therapy scale: Unpublished rating manual*. Philadelphia: University of Pennsylvania, Center for Cognitive Therapy.

Jeanne C. Watson and Leslie S. Greenberg

The Therapeutic Alliance in Short-Term Humanistic and Experiential Therapies

6

t is widely accepted that the working alliance is an important vehicle of change in therapy (Brodley, 1990; Greenberg, Rice, & Elliott, 1993; Henry & Strupp, 1994; Luborsky, 1994; Pinsof, 1994; Raue & Goldfried, 1994; Rogers, 1951). However, there are differences in the ways in which the therapeutic alliance is established and in the views that therapists have of its function within a therapeutic context. Bordin (1979) distinguished the working alliance from the transference and suggested that the former was a common factor across all therapies. He conceptualized the working alliance as consisting of three different components comprising the goals, tasks, and bonds of therapy. This formulation of the working alliance emphasizes the notion of collaboration: the idea that clients and therapists form a partnership to work to resolve clients' difficulties (Horvath, 1994; Watson & Greenberg, 1994).

The two aspects of the alliance that are emphasized in humanistic and experiential therapies are the *relationship conditions* and the *working conditions*. The former refers to the therapists' attitudes and behaviors that facilitate the development of the therapeutic bond and clients' change processes in therapy, the latter to the collaborative nature of the participants' interactions that facilitate clients' engagement in the work of therapy. This definition emphasizes both the quality of the relationship between the participants and more specifically therapists' attitudes and behaviors that promote change, as well as the tasks and goals of therapy that require collaboration between therapists and clients.

The relationship and working conditions that contribute to the alliance are emphasized differently within specific humanistic approaches. The degree to which each is emphasized is a function of how each approach conceptualizes the active ingredients of change and the role of the therapist.

In this chapter, we explore the role that the therapeutic alliance plays in short-term humanistic and experiential therapies. We begin by examining the way in which the therapeutic alliance is conceptualized in this tradition in general, as well as in three different modalities within the tradition: person-centered therapy, Gestalt therapy, and processes–experiential therapy. We then focus on the implications of a short-term format for the therapeutic alliance. We discuss how to form and maintain a working alliance in brief therapy by creating a safe environment, establishing a focus early in treatment, and balancing responsiveness with directiveness. Problems that therapists working within each of the modalities might experience in brief treatment are considered, and ways of dealing with these are addressed.

Person-Centered Therapy

According to Rogers (1951), one of the primary objectives of therapy is for clients to adopt an internal locus of evaluation. By this, he meant that in therapy clients need to begin to examine and evaluate their own perceptions, feelings, and actions, and in this way, learn to develop and apply standards for their behavior in the world independent of the judgment and evaluations of other sources, particularly of significant others. In this approach, the therapist suspends judgment and allows clients the freedom to be themselves so as to promote autonomy and independence. Rogers, like Perls, saw dysfunction occurring as a result of clients' internalizing the views and standards of others that are at odds with their own organismic experience, with the result that they are not attuned to their own inner experience, needs, goals, and values.

A second important goal in person-centered therapy is to help clients articulate the inner dialogue between their symbolic, reflective selves and their experiencing selves (Barrett-Lennard, 1997; Bohart, 1993; Watson & Rennie, 1994). In this way, person-centered therapists foster two client capacities: the ability to listen empathically to themselves and become aware of previously disowned aspects of experience, and the ability to reflect on themselves so as to break out of dysfunctional ways of being in the world (Watson & Rennie, 1994).

An important goal of person-centered therapy is to have clients become more aware of their inner experience.

In order for clients to achieve these tasks, Rogers emphasized the therapeutic relationship, which he saw as the primary vehicle of change. In person-centered therapy, the primary function of the relationship is to provide a context in which clients can learn new ways of interacting and being in the world. Rogers believed that clients are active agents capable of understanding and evaluating their behavior and perceptions and of devising new ways of acting in the world to enhance their functioning independently of their therapists. He suggested that given certain optimal conditions, clients would be able to reflect on and integrate diverse sources of information including perceptions, feelings, values, desires, and needs. However, to do this, clients need to feel safe and unthreatened by their therapists. According to Rogers, the best contribution therapists could make to the therapeutic process was to provide a secure environment for clients to perform these tasks by embodying and communicating the attitudes of empathy (responding empathically), prizing (valuing the client), and congruence (being congruent in the relationship so that there is harmony between what the therapist is feeling, thinking, and doing in the session). These were the necessary and sufficient conditions of client change. In his definition of the relationship, Rogers focuses on its function as a means of promoting change and less on it as a collaboration or working partnership. According to this view, the primary therapeutic task is to listen attentively and empathically to clients' phenomenological experiences and to communicate to them that they are prized and respected.

In addition to empathy and prizing, Rogers also advocated that therapists need to be congruent in their relationships with their clients, even if this means at times communicating negative feelings that they are experiencing toward their clients. *Negative feelings* were defined as those feelings that therapists experience as chronic or intrusive in their work with clients (Rogers, 1951). Other person-centered theorists caution that person-centered therapists need to exercise responsibility when being transparent and open in the relationship (Lietaer, 1993). Disclosures and observations about the process should not be blaming or critical of clients' participation. Although positive client-centered disclosures can enhance understanding of each other's perceptions about what is occurring between them and in the therapy and may clarify how their behavior impacts on each other, negative disclosures can rupture the alliance irrevocably. Positive therapist disclosures are seen as beneficial to clients' interpersonal growth.

Person-centered therapists are nondirective of client process; instead, they try to shadow their clients in order to provide a safe, secure working environment in which clients can pose questions, explore their experiences, and reflect on them to resolve their difficulties. The therapists' role is to follow their clients' lead and deepen their explorations. Person-centered therapists trust their clients to know and determine the best way to resolve the dilemmas that brought them into therapy in the first place (Bozarth, 1990; Brodley, 1990). To facilitate their clients' process in therapy, therapists are encouraged to reflect clients' statements, focusing on their feelings and cognitions. In this way, person-centered therapists check their understanding of what their clients are saying and validate their clients' perspectives. This type of responding can help clients perceive how they interact with others and identify their particular styles of being in the world as they actively reflect on their behavior. Clients in this approach are thus free to modify, correct, and extend their views as therapists attempt to help them explore the nuances of their thoughts, feelings, and behaviors.

Thus the working alliance as conceived within person-centered therapy emphasizes the bond and relationship conditions of the alliance as opposed to the tasks and goals of therapy. The alliance is nondirective, egalitarian, and encouraging of clients setting the goals of therapy, while therapists provide safe environments to facilitate the realization of these goals. This view emphasizes the quality of the relationship—particularly the presence of empathy, congruence, and prizing as the primary ways to facilitate change—and deemphasizes techniques. Collaboration is assumed to flow naturally out of the implementation of the three therapeutic conditions. Numerous person-centered therapists continue to subscribe to Rogers's view of the relationship. These theorists actively oppose the use of specific techniques to deepen clients' experiences, arguing that their use subverts the nature of the relationship and interferes with clients' autonomy and potential for self-determination (Bozarth, 1990; Brodley, 1990). Other person-centered therapists in an attempt to stimulate clients' reflective processes have begun to use empathic questioning as a way of having clients think about and evaluate their assumptions, cognitions, values, and perceptions (Toukmanian, 1992; Watson & Rennie, 1994).

Gestalt Therapy

In contrast to person-centered therapists, Gestalt therapists emphasize working conditions, including the tasks and goals of therapy, as opposed to bond and relationship conditions. Initially, Gestalt therapists had a less clearly defined theory of the relationship than their person-centered colleagues. Gestalt therapists focused more on how to promote client processes of awareness, deeper experiencing, and the resolution of unfinished business than on the quality of the bond. More recently, an interpersonal form of Gestalt therapy has replaced the more classical approach in which the active experiment was the cornerstone of treatment.

The classical approach included experiments such as two-chair dialogues and dream work, as well as experiments created in the moment to help clients intensify and embody their experiences. This might involve having a client who complained of feeling walled off from others play as if he were the wall and trying to give it words and form, or having clients express desires (to make them more vivid), or helping clients to access and experience the interruptive processes that prevent them from expressing themselves, or acting upon their needs and desires. In this experiment-oriented approach the task and goal elements of the alliance were emphasized, while the bond component was assumed to be present. When problems emerged in the alliance, these were seen as projective, transferential processes that needed to be worked on in therapy.

More recently, Gestalt therapists have promoted the view of the therapeutic relationship as a real, existential encounter between two people. This perspective is guided by Buber's view of an I–thou relationship that emphasizes that encounters between individuals should be characterized by qualities of presence, inclusion, nonexploitativeness, and authenticity (Yontef, 1991). Practitioners of the more recent form of Gestalt therapy, rather than viewing relational problems as client projections, are far more field-oriented and see relational contact as occurring in an interpersonal field (Wheeler, 1991). Here, breaks in contact are seen as "micro" ruptures of the alliance, and therapy is focused on healing these ruptures through the therapist's identifying them and responding supportively.

The goal of this approach is to support clients' emerging experience and sense of personal validity. Thus, Gestalt therapists highlight the immediate interaction between the participants as the vehicle for change in therapy by focusing on present contacts between clients and therapists and attending to disruptions in these contacts. Therapists' and clients' experiences of the disruptions are then explored and become the focus of treatment. In this view, clients' awareness of patterns in their experiences and how they interrupt themselves, as well as the corrective experience of a helping dialogue, are seen as curative. As in person-centered therapy, the relationship is seen as the vehicle for change in Gestalt therapy, although it is thought to promote change differently in each approach.

Process–Experiential Therapy

Recently, an experiential approach to therapy, which represents a merger of Gestalt and person-centered approaches, has begun to be articulated. Although process–experiential therapists distinguish between the relational conditions and the working conditions, they believe that each contributes uniquely to client change. This approach emphasizes all three components of the alliance including tasks, goals, and bonds. Following from Rogers's and Perls's conceptualizations of dysfunction as resulting from aspects of experience that are disowned or denied to awareness, it emphasizes the need for clients to become aware of their inner experience in therapy in order to promote optimal client functioning. An important objective in process–experiential therapy is to have clients integrate information from their experiential or emotional processing systems and their rational or cognitive systems. Clients integrate emotional and cognitive processes by symbolizing their inner subjective experiences in words and then reflexively examining the symbolic representations of their experiences, their needs, goals, and values (Greenberg & Pascual-Leone, 1995; Greenberg et al., 1993; Watson & Greenberg, 1996).

This approach integrates the person-centered relational conditions with the active interventions from Gestalt therapy. A number of interventions have been intensively studied and developed to promote the integration of the cognitive and emotional aspects of information processing. These include focusing to resolve an unclear felt sense (Gendlin, 1981, 1996), systematic evocative unfolding to resolve problematic reactions (Rice & Saperia, 1984; Watson & Rennie, 1994); two-chair work to resolve conflict splits, empty-chair work to resolve unfinished business toward a significant other (Greenberg et al., 1993), the creation of meaning to resolve challenges to cherished beliefs (Clarke, 1989), and being responsively attuned to ruptures and misunderstandings in the relationship (Safran, Muran, & Samstag, 1994).

Process–experiential therapists recognize that the therapeutic relationship is a vital ingredient of the change process; however, they see other processes as equally important in helping clients to resolve the specific cognitive–affective problems that brought them to therapy (Gendlin, 1981; Greenberg et al., 1993; Lietaer, 1990; Mahrer, 1989). Experiential therapists emphasize the roles of emotional arousal and clients experiencing in the change process, and they have devised techniques to heighten clients' access to their inner experiences. They see the use of more active interventions as integral to therapy. As they balance more active interventions with the therapeutic relationship's conditions of empathy, prizing, and congruence, process–experiential therapists constantly need to assess whether they should focus on a specific task (e.g., a conflict split or problematic reaction) and implement more active interventions, or simply remain responsively attuned to exploring their clients' inner phenomenological worlds. Process–experiential therapists face a special challenge in that they walk a tightrope between actively directing their clients' process (while still mirroring their clients' experiences during the intervention) and offering the relationship's conditions of empathy, prizing, and congruence.

Thus, although process–experiential therapists see the relationship's conditions of empathy, prizing, and congruence as necessary and vital to the therapeutic process, they use other interventions at specific cognitive–affective problem markers or client statements indicating a specific problem, like unfinished business to assist, clients in accessing parts of their experiences that may not be in awareness, but that are readily available. Although it has been argued that the use of other more directive interventions violates clients' autonomy within the therapeutic relationship (Brodley, 1990), it should be stressed that process–experiential therapists grant primacy to the clients' subjective experiencing. Thus, while directing clients' attention to various aspects of their functioning, process–experiential therapists encourage clients to use their own experience as the final arbiter and touchstone both in the session and outside it. To the degree that process–experiential therapists use a variety of techniques to facilitate clients' experiencing in the session, they must be carefully attuned to clients' ways of responding and signs of opposition or reluctance and other breaks in the therapeutic process. By noticing and attending to breaks in the alliance, process–experiential therapists can facilitate its successful development.

It has been argued elsewhere that in fact the sensitive implementation of the more active interventions enacts the therapeutic relationship's conditions of empathy and prizing to the extent that therapists are able to perceive accurately the specific problems clients are grappling with and are able to implement tasks to facilitate their clients' goals in therapy (Watson & Greenberg, 1994). The view of process–experiential therapists being advanced here is that the more active interventions, in tandem with the relationship conditions, enable clients and therapists to establish productive working alliances. A successful working alliance is established as therapists and clients clearly articulate the goals of therapy and implement appropriate therapeutic tasks. However, there may be an optimal therapeutic balance between leading a session and following a client's responses that therapists need to maintain in order to be effective. If therapists are overly directive, they may interfere with the establishment of a good working alliance and hinder clients from working productively in therapy. This has been observed both in work with groups and with individuals (Lietaer, 1990; Watson, 1996). Moreover, agreement on the goals and tasks of therapy facilitates the development of the therapeutic bond to the degree that clients feel that their therapists are collaborating actively with them to help them resolve their difficulties. We now examine how person-centered and process–experiential therapists forge and maintain a working alliance in brief treatments.

CREATING A SAFE WORKING ENVIRONMENT

Just as they do in longer term therapies, clients in short-term therapy require a safe working environment and a sense that they can trust their therapists in order to access and symbolize potentially difficult and threatening inner experiences. However, one of the special demands of short-term therapy is that there is less time for these conditions to develop. Person-centered and process–experiential therapists establish trust and safety by responding empathically to the live, poignant aspects of clients' experiences. Empathic responding may consist of reflecting the feelings, perceptions, or behaviors of clients, as well as the use of metaphor to distill the essence of the clients' experiences of being in the world. By attending to the special significance that events have for their clients, person-centered and process–experiential therapists are able to convey their sensitive understanding and awareness of their clients' phenomenological experiences. In the early stages of therapy, process–experiential therapists are concerned with developing safety and identifying the goals of treatment. It is important that clients have a secure base before they begin to engage in some of the microtasks, such as two-chair work, that facilitate experiencing.

Experiential therapists have developed a number of ways of being alert to their clients' processes and resources over and above attention to the content of clients' narratives. The ways that humanistic therapists have developed to alert them to the salient, poignant aspects of clients' experiences and to assess their capacity for turning inward to do the work of therapy include attending to (a) clients' vocal quality, (b) clients' stance toward their experience during the session, (c) the words clients use, and (d) other aspects of nonverbal expression.

Rice and Wagstaff (1967) identified four different types of vocal quality indicative of different client processes during the session: focused, externalizing, limited, and emotional. Clients' use of focused voice can alert therapists that their clients are exploring and carefully examining potentially new aspects of their experience. There is a slow, hesitant quality, as clients try to render their experiences in words. These moments provide the gateways to potentially productive paths for further exploration. The other vocal style that is indicative that clients are engaged in the process of articulating their experience of emotionality. These are times in therapy when clients' vocal patterns are distorted by the expression of emotion. Clients may be unable to speak or can only do so in a distorted fashion because they are crying or expressing anger in the session (Rice, Koke, Greenberg, & Wagstaff, 1979; Watson & Greenberg, 1996).

In contrast to focused and emotional vocal quality, clients' use of an externalizing or limited vocal quality indicates that they are not in touch with their inner experience at that particular moment. When responding in an externalized vocal style, clients seem to have turned their attention outside of themselves and appear to be recounting their experiences in a rehearsed fashion. There is no sense of an active experiential search; rather the client appears to be delivering a rehearsed speech. At these times the therapists may need to employ interventions that can heighten clients' access to their inner experiences, for example, by focusing or by evocative descriptions of their experiences. Limited vocal quality is similar to an externalizing pattern, but here clients seem to have far less energy. Rather than trying to produce an effect on the outside world, these clients appear fragile, as if they are on the run from their experience in general (Rice et al., 1979). It is possible that clients who have this as a predominant vocal style may not be good candidates for short-term experiential therapy, because more time might be necessary to help them become comfortable with the task of representing their experience and giving it form within the limits of the therapy hour.

To further distinguish clients' statements that reflect their attendance to and expression of immediate inner experience as opposed to making more experience-distant, general observations about self and others, Rice, Watson, and Greenberg (1996) developed the *clients' expressive stance measure*. This measure differentiates clients' statements in terms of three different dimensions: first, whether clients' attention is focused on their inner or outer experience; second, whether they are engaged and actively involved in their experience or disengaged and observing their experience; and third, the type of processing activity in which clients are engaged, for example, whether they are evaluating, explaining, or observing their experience. By monitoring the focus of clients' attention and the words they use, therapists are able to get a clear sense of whether their clients are focused on their inner or outer experience. This provides a guide to therapists of where to direct clients' attention, so that if clients are focused outside of themselves, therapists can help to turn their attention inward. Thus, it provides an indication of how accessible clients' experiences are to them at different points in therapy.

Moments when clients are expressing an immediate inner awareness of feelings, reactions, and assertions of self are good indicators that not only are they productively engaged in working through problematic issues, but also that these statements alert therapists to those aspects of clients' experiences that are available for exploration and poignantly alive for them in the session. In contrast, if clients are speaking about their experiences in analytical and experience-distant ways, this can indicate to therapists that they need to increase their efforts toward having their clients turn inward, either by focusing on the subjectivity of perceptions, or by using more evocative and metaphoric language, or by using more active interventions that will direct clients' attention inward (Angus & Rennie, 1988; Gendlin, 1981; Greenberg et al., 1993; Leijssen, 1996; Rice, 1974; Watson, 1996). Being alert to the processing activities that clients are engaged in moment-to-moment in the therapy hour enables therapists to identify the experiential questions clients are asking and also to determine the kinds of activities that clients are seeking to perform. Some examples are whether they are trying to examine, evaluate, or explain and understand their behavior. Knowing this helps therapists determine which activities and tasks would be most productive for clients at different moments in therapy.

ESTABLISHING A FOCUS

To enhance the efficacy of short-term treatments, experiential therapists need to establish a focus early in treatment and actively work toward an agreement with their clients on the goals of therapy in the first few sessions, enabling them to implement those tasks that will help clients achieve their desired ends. In our 16–20-week treatment study of depression (Greenberg & Watson, in press; Watson & Greenberg, 1996) that compared a person-centered approach with a process–experiential approach, we found that those clients with the poorest outcome in both therapeutic modalities had not established agreement with their therapists on the goals of treatment early on in therapy according to clients' self-reports on the Working Alliance Inventory (Horvath & Greenberg, 1989), nor was this lack of agreement rectified over the course of treatment. This was manifest in the absence of a focus in the treatments on an underlying determinant or problematic issue involved in generating the clients' depression. This was in sharp contrast to those clients with the best outcomes, who felt that they had established agreement about the goals of therapy with their therapists by the fifth session and who worked consistently on a specific focus. Interestingly, failure to establish a focus and clear goals did not affect clients' ratings of the quality of their bonds with their therapists. Both groups reported that they experienced their therapists as supportive and caring (Weerasekera, Linder, Greenberg, & Watson, 1997). Person-centered therapists may have difficulty defining a focus of inquiry early on in therapy given their reluctance to structure their clients' experiences and their belief that clients should engage in therapy at their own pace. In contrast, process–experiential therapists may be able to establish a focus early on but need to be careful to balance responsive reflections with more directive responses.

An important component of establishing a focus and helping clients to track their experience is the therapist's ability to develop a sense of direction. This requires some criterion that enables the therapist to recognize the significance of events and experiences in their clients' lives that might be contributing to their symptoms and current distress. Good therapists seem to have an ability to attend to their clients' use of language, level of emotional arousal, as well as their own inner sense of what is meaningful and salient as indicators of what is significant to their clients. Process–experiential therapists use their own inner sense as an internal barometer of what to respond to in the session. This reflects their capacity for experiencing and their tacit knowledge of human functioning, which is an amalgamation of their practical experience with clients, their own life experiences, and their theoretical knowledge. These capacities guide therapists' understanding and interventions.

In addition to their own experience, experiential therapists use their clients' inner experiencing as a guide to what fits and what feels right in the session (Gendlin, 1996; Leijssen, 1990; Watson & Rennie, 1994). Person-centered, Gestalt, and process–experiential therapists use clients' affective responses as a compass to direct them where to focus attention. By tracing clients' affects, experiential therapists help them access and track seemingly disparate but highly significant aspects of their experience.

In addition to tracking clients' affects, experiential therapists need to be alert to those particular questions that clients are posing about their experience in order to identify treatment goals and a focus in therapy (Klein, Mathieu-Coughlan, & Kiesler, 1986). Although some clients may be less clear, others may be explicit about the questions that are troubling them; for example, they may be perplexed about why they became depressed in a particular situation. Although questions may not always be clearly formulated by clients, if therapists can nonetheless pay attention to the domains of inquiry that clients are mapping out for themselves, they will be able to forge a collaborative bond sooner than if they are not attentive to the specific focus of clients' inquiries.

Process–experiential therapists are alert to "markers," which are statements in the session that indicate clients are experiencing particular cognitive–affective problems. For example, client statements that they cannot carry out a decision or a self-critical comment may indicate that clients are experiencing conflict splits and that they may benefit from exploring these with the aid of the two-chair technique (Greenberg et al., 1993). Alternatively, clients' statements that they harbor unresolved negative feelings toward a significant other may indicate that empty-chair work might be productive. The use of marker-guided interventions in process–experiential therapy can help to identify a focus of inquiry early in therapy.

However, therapists need to be finely attuned to their clients and be quick to alter course if they detect that their clients are not responding to their interventions. If therapists are unable to correct or modify the frames they have developed of clients' issues and develop alternative ways of responding to their clients, they then risk rupturing the alliance.

For example, one client, who was depressed as a result of losing his job and experiencing severely strained financial circumstances complained that he felt he had failed his family and at times felt that they would be better off without him (Watson, 1996). His circumstances were exacerbated by the fact that he had expected to benefit from a sizeable inheritance on his father's death; however, this had been inherited by a step-sibling. He was very aware that his lifestyle was in sharp contrast to that of other members of his family. Moreover, he felt that he might still inherit money from his mother, but he had a difficult and tenuous relationship with her, which left the client feeling powerless and uncertain of how to act to maintain the relationship and ensure his mother's goodwill.

The therapist chose to emphasize the client's unfinished business with his parents instead of his client's monetary concerns. The disparity between the therapist's and client's focus occurred in the first session, when the client describes the source and nature of his depression:

> CLIENT. My-self worth is pretty low at times, and it comes from not being able to provide for the family in a manner in which I would like to have done.

The therapist responds empathically, but then attempts to formulate the goals of treatment in terms of the client's difficulties with his parents.

> THERAPIST. So you're feeling somehow that you've not measured up as a provider, is that it? Okay, I guess from where I'm sitting, uh, you know, the struggle that you are having around employment and so on is a hard cold fact.

CLIENT. Yeah.

THERAPIST. But I'm struck with, you know, your drawing my attention to these two major traumas with your parents—ah, which you're leading me to feel that you didn't really resolve—you didn't finish them and life is tough enough . . . in the here and now without carrying around this baggage. Perhaps your depression would be lighter without it, I think we should focus on these issues in here. (Watson, 1996, p. 8)

The primary focus of the therapy was the client's disappointment at being disinherited by his father and his difficulties with his mother. This focus was achieved by using unfinished business events. Although these were important aspects of the client's situation and the focus on them probably contributed to a reduction in the number of interpersonal problems that the client reported at the end of therapy, his depression scores did not change at termination. It seems that the more intense and poignant aspects of his experience of depression concerned his own loss of power and identity as the breadwinner in his family. He appeared to feel "ground down" by his inability to provide for himself and his wife and to remedy the situation by securing a well-remunerated position. Moreover, his current situation was impacting negatively on his relationship with his wife and children. The therapist, by focusing on the client's unfinished business with his parents, did not focus on the client's critical introject by means of which he castigated himself for failing. It is likely that these internal processes may have precipitated and intensified his current depression, rather than his unfinished business with his parents (Watson, 1996).

The therapist accurately perceived that the client was distressed about his employment situation. However, by calling it a "hard cold fact," he is dismissing it as something to be worked on in therapy. In doing so, he ignores the psychological sequelae of the client's situation, for example, the client's loss of identity and lowered self-esteem because of his inability to provide adequately for his family. The therapist's continued focus on the client's family of origin resulted in a rupture in the alliance at midtreatment. In the 10th session, the client tries to make his economic plight more focal, and the therapist conceptualizes it as symbolic:

CLIENT. I really don't know where we are going at this point . . . um . . . I think this is the tenth session. Is it? I don't know whether we are on track as far as you are concerned.

THERAPIST. Over the course of the last nine sessions, we seem to pick certain objectives and begin to move toward them and then break off. So I am not sure at this point what you want to accomplish, what it is you want to deal with.

CLIENT. Well, I think we identified last week that quite significantly that there is a single thread running through all of them and that is the lack of money; however you manipulate it, it generally means my inability to provide it.

THERAPIST. Well, it seemed to me money was a thread but it was more symbolic.

CLIENT. Well, I can assure you it is far from symbolic; it's very real.

The therapist tried to refocus the treatment after this, and the alliance appeared to improve so that the client was able to engage in some new interpersonal behaviors; however, the two never seemed able to come to grips with the client's depression.

ESTABLISHING AGREEMENT ON TASKS

Clients and therapists need to establish agreement on the tasks of therapy early in treatment. The metatask is to help clients turn inward to symbolize experience in new and fresh ways and to attend to alternative sources of information that initially may be unfamiliar to them. The task of attending to clients' emotions is essential to experiential therapies. In longer term therapies, there is more time to initiate clients into the metatask of self-disclosure, adopting an internal focus and engaging in self-exploration. However, this has to be done more quickly in short-term therapy if the treatment is to be successful. An important component of helping clients to turn inward is the establishment of safety and trust between the participants so that clients feel free to self-disclose and focus on themselves (Rennie, 1993; Watson & Rennie, 1994).

Therapists may also need to inform clients explicitly of the nature of these relationships and specifically talk about the tasks and goals of therapy. The importance of therapists and clients sharing congruent expectations for the therapeutic alliance was demonstrated in a study by Al-Darmaki and Kivlighan (1993). These authors found that congruence in expectations between therapists and their clients predicted the quality of the alliance on the dimensions of Tasks and Bonds, although not for agreement on Goals. Several authors have noted in reviews of research on the therapeutic relationship that in order to establish a working relationship, counselors might need to manifest behaviors complementary to those shown by their clients. Thus they may need to be more assertive of boundaries when their clients appear overly friendly, or conversely, they may need to be able to respond with empathy and gentleness when their clients are more hostile (Henry, Schacht, & Strupp, 1990; Sexton & Whiston, 1994). Some clients may take time to understand the requirements of different types of therapies and may even have difficulty with the metatask of being the person who engages in self-disclosure as the therapist intervenes in more structured ways. These clients may need to learn about the process before they can engage productively.

Clients' positions relative to the change process have important implications for the type of work that can be accomplished in short-term therapy (Prochaska, DiClemente, & Norcross, 1992). For example, one client who presented with depression and seemed motivated to participate in treatment would willingly engage in various therapeutic tasks suggested by her therapist, but would become unfocused and very emotional during the tasks. It was only once the client was able to acknowledge her fears about being in therapy and to negotiate a greater sense of safety both with herself and her therapist that she was able to concentrate on the issues that were contributing to her depression. Initially, she and her therapist were working at cross-purposes to the extent that the therapist understood that her focus was her depression, but the client had not yet even fully committed to the process of being in therapy.

Engaging in an experiential search is particularly difficult for clients who have never learned to use their inner experience as a guide or who have actively dissociated from their inner experience as a way of coping with traumatic and difficult early life situations. Clients suffering from specific disorders such as psychosomatic disorders (Sachse, in press), anxiety disorders (Wolfe & Sigl, in press), and obsessive–compulsive personality disorders may have particular difficulty referring to their inner experience as an important source of information with respect to their problems in living. Yet other clients who suffer from posttraumatic stress may flit from topic to topic, finding it difficult to explore a theme or idea through to its completion, as they actively try to avoid the feelings and memories associated with the traumatic incident (Elliott et al., 1996). These clients may benefit from the use of more directive interventions to help them focus on their inner experiences or on issues of concern.

When working with clients who have obsessive tendencies or difficulty focusing on their inner experience, it is sometimes more helpful to frame interventions that are intended to turn them inward in the form of questions, as opposed to reflections. This may be even more important at the beginning of therapy, as these clients may be frustrated by the use of reflections because these reflections require them to engage in tasks that are unfamiliar and uncomfortable. Other ways therapists can assist these clients are by using more structured interventions, such as focusing (Gendlin, 1981) or two-chair work to highlight the effects of the obsessive process on their self-experience.

Therapists can also make observations about their clients' processes. For example, they might say that it seems difficult for them to dwell on or think about their problems and inner experience. However, therapists need to be careful that these observations do not sound critical or blaming (Henry et al., 1990; Lietaer, 1993; Watson, 1996).

A difficulty that person-centered therapists might encounter in short-term therapy is that their clients may feel frustrated by their nondirectiveness. This frustration may be exacerbated by the time pressure to resolve problematic issues that is imposed by brief therapy. Clients' frustration at their therapists adopting a more nondirective stance can be especially difficult if clients have been exposed to more structured, didactic forms of therapy. One client, who had previous experience with cognitive–behavioral therapy, was particularly disappointed by her therapist's approach, stating that she wished he would be more didactic and point out her irrational beliefs and suggest ways that she might remedy her thinking patterns. However, at follow-up, she commented that in retrospect she valued her therapist's approach because she had learned to validate her own experience and had gained in self-confidence. Thus it may not always be useful to alter course if clients are disgruntled by what they perceive to be a less didactic and more egalitarian stance.

BALANCING DIRECTIVENESS AND RESPONSIVENESS

As stated earlier, process–experiential and Gestalt therapists need to balance directive responding with following their clients' leads (empathic responses). These therapists can risk rupturing the relationship sometimes irreparably if they are too directive. It seems that there may be an optimal ratio of directive to empathic responses, as well as an optimal therapeutic range of these behaviors. Bischoff and Tracey (1995) have observed that clients' resistance increases as therapists become more directive. The potentially negative effects of being overly directive were highlighted in another study conducted by Watson (1996). The structural analysis of social behavior (Benjamin, 1974) was used to identify differences in therapists' and clients' interpersonal process between a good-outcome and a poor-outcome case in process–experiential therapy. In those sessions in which therapists were actively involved in helping clients to engage in specific tasks such as two-chair work, systematic evocative unfolding, or empty-chair work, there were significant differences in the type of therapist responses in the good- versus the poor-outcome case.

In the former, 64% of the therapists' responses were classified as *affirming* and *understanding*, and 36% as *teaching* and *controlling*, whereas in the bad-outcome case, 42% of the therapist responses were classified as *affirming* and *understanding,* and 58% were seen as *teaching* and *controlling.* A similar disparity in type of responses was observed in those sessions in which therapists and clients were not engaged in one of the tasks. In these sessions, therapists were required to implement the relationship conditions as advanced by person-centered therapy. In the good-outcome case, 82% of therapist responses were classified as *affirming* and *understanding,* and 18% as *teaching* and *controlling,* whereas in the bad-outcome case, 60% of responses were identified as *affirming* and *understanding,* and 40% as *teaching* and *controlling.* Therapists may need to err in favor of more affirming and understanding responses, taking care not to be too controlling or critical of their clients in session.

Another difficulty process–experiential and Gestalt therapists may experience as they try to implement the active interventions is that clients may feel self-conscious talking to an empty chair. Initially, it may be difficult for clients to see the benefits of separating out different aspects of their experience so concretely. At these times therapists should not try to coerce their clients to engage in the specific tasks, but rather try to work with their clients to get around their feelings of shyness and self-consciousness. This enables both therapists and clients to become aware of the self-statements that clients make to themselves to inhibit certain responses and ways of acting. Clients' reluctance to engage in certain tasks are seen as indications that more time and work has to be done to build the alliance. Reluctance may be a sign that clients and therapists are not in synchrony about the goals of therapy and how these are to be achieved within the specific modality being used.

Together with responsive reflections, metacommunication has been suggested as a way that therapists can talk to their clients about what is transpiring between them and as a way to inform them of the purpose and function of certain interventions that might at first seem odd or artificial (Rennie, 1993; Safran et al., 1994; Watson & Greenberg, 1994). Horvath, Marx, and Kamann (1990) found that clients' understanding of therapists' intentions was significantly related to their ratings of counselor helpfulness. Although metacommunication is useful in establishing agreement between the participants, Rennie has observed that it may not always be effective. This failure is probably more likely if metacommunication is used with the intent of persuading another to engage in certain exercises. However, metacommunication may have other functions that can be very useful in building the alliance. First, it can increase understanding between the participants so that they can appreciate each other's perspectives on the client's problems and can begin to negotiate a shared understanding of the methods that can be used to realize the client's goals. Second, metacommunication can function to clarify misunderstandings between the participants and thereby facilitate the development of the alliance and validate the client's experiences (Safran et al., 1994). Third, metacommunication can illuminate clients' processes and help them become aware of certain behaviors or styles of responding that may be contributing to their difficulties.

LIMITING THE GOALS OF SHORT-TERM THERAPY

The brevity of short-term therapy and the imminence of termination may cause difficulties for certain clients. For example, clients suffering from borderline personality disorder may feel abandoned and rejected once they are terminated from a brief treatment. Thus experiential therapists have to assess carefully the depth and severity of clients' interpersonal problems and weigh the benefits and potential costs of engaging in short-term treatment. Process–experiential and Gestalt therapists need to be attuned more sensitively to their clients in short-term therapy.

The nature and quality of clients' experiences with early caretakers may have a bearing on the degree to which they are able to undertake and achieve changes in their inter- and intrapersonal functioning in brief therapy. Therapists find it is useful to examine the quality of clients' introjects at the beginning to help evaluate the appropriateness of short-term therapy to achieve the clients' goals. Clients who are hostile and rejecting of themselves and who do not seem to have any complementary affirming, understanding, or nurturing attitudes toward themselves may not be good candidates for short-term therapy. These clients may need a longer term of treatment in order to develop more nurturing and caring ways of behaving toward themselves.

Given the time limitations of short-term treatment, therapists may need to examine carefully the clients' internal representations of self and others and then discuss the limitations of short-term therapy to establish agreement on realistic goals for the therapy.

Conclusion

In this chapter, we examined the objectives and goals of humanistic and process–experiential approaches to therapy and have demonstrated their implications for the working alliance. We have specified two functions of the alliance that are emphasized differently in person-centered, Gestalt, and process–experiential therapies: the relational conditions and the working conditions. Although both contribute to the development of the bonds between therapists and clients, working conditions focus more on establishing agreement about the goals and tasks of therapy than do relational conditions.

Person-centered therapists emphasize relationship factors as providing the "soil" for client change and growth. They do not emphasize the collaborative nature of the alliance, and they downplay the importance of techniques and specific interventions. In contrast, Gestalt therapists emphasize the task and goal component of the alliance and have only recently begun to attend to the relationship dimensions of the alliance. Process–experiential therapists, on the other hand, see the relationship and specific task interventions as equally important and as leading to client change. To the extent that process–experiential and Gestalt therapists highlight the role of different techniques in facilitating clients' processes in therapy, they are more aware of the need for a collaborative working alliance with their clients to facilitate positive outcomes in therapy.

We have discussed ways of facilitating the development of good working alliances in short-term therapy and dealing with some of the difficulties that can emerge. More intensive study of therapist and client in-session behavior begun by a number of research groups (Henry & Strupp, 1994; Rennie, 1993; Safran et al., 1994; Watson, 1996) will be important in determining at a more specific level those behaviors that contribute to and those that interfere with the formation of positive working alliances across different therapeutic modalities.

References

Al-Darmaki, F., & Kivlighan, D. (1993). Congruence in client–counselor expectations for relationship and the working alliance. *Journal of Counseling Psychology, 40,* 379–384.

Angus, L., & Rennie, D. (1988). Therapist participation in metaphor generation: Collaborative and non-collaborative styles, *Psychotherapy, 25,* 552–560.

Barrett-Lennard, G. T. (1997). The recovery of empathy—Towards others and self. In A. Bohart & L. Greenberg (Eds.), *Empathy reconsidered: New directions in psychotherapy* (pp. 103–121). Washington DC: American Psychological Association.

Benjamin, L. S. (1974). Structural analysis of social behavior. *Psychological Review, 81,* 392–425.

Bischoff, M. M., & Tracey, J. J. (1995). Client resistance as predicted by therapist behavior: A study of sequential dependence. *Counseling Psychology, 42*, 487–495.

Bohart, A. (1993). Experiencing: The basis of psychotherapy. *Journal of Psychotherapy Integration, 3*, 51–67.

Bordin, E. S. (1979). The generalizability of the psychoanalytic concept of the working alliance. *Psychotherapy, 16*, 252–260.

Bozarth, J. (1990). The essence of person-centered therapy. In G. Lietaer, J. Rombauts, & R. Van Balen (Eds.), *Person- centered and experiential psychotherapy in the nineties* (pp. 54–64). Leuwen, Belgium: Leuwen University Press.

Brodley, B. (1990). Person-centered and experiential: Two different therapies. In G. Lietaer, J. Rombauts, & R. Van Balen (Eds.), *Person-centered and experiential psychotherapy in the nineties* (pp. 87–107). Leuwen, Belgium: Leuwen University Press.

Clarke, K. (1989). Creation of meaning: An emotional processing task in psychotherapy. *Psychotherapy, 26*, 139–148.

Elliot, R., Sutter, R., Manford, J., Radpour-Markert, L., Siegel-Hinson, R., Layman, C., & Davis, K. (1996). A process–experiential approach to post-traumatic stress disorder. In R. Hutterer, G. Pawlowsky, P. Schmid, & R. Stipsits (Eds.), *Client-centered and experiential psychotherapy: A paradigm in motion* (pp. 235–254). Frankfurt: Peter Lang.

Gendlin, E. (1981). *Focusing.* New York: Bantam Books.

Gendlin, E. (1996). *Focusing-oriented psychotherapy: A manual of the experiential method.* New York: Guilford Press.

Greenberg, L. S., & Pascual-Leone, J. (1995). A dialectical constructivist approach to experiential change. In R. A. Neimeyer & M. J. Mahoney (Eds.), *Constructivism in psychotherapy* (pp. 169–194). Washington, DC: American Psychological Association.

Greenberg, L. S., Rice, L. N., & Elliott, R. (1993). *Facilitating emotional change: The moment by moment process.* New York: Guilford Press.

Greenberg, L. S., & Watson, J. C. (in press). Experiential therapy of depression: Differential effects of person-centered conditions and active experiential interventions. *Psychotherapy Research.*

Henry, W., Schacht, T. E., & Strupp, H. (1990). Patient and therapist introject, interpersonal process, and differential psychotherapy outcome. *Journal of Consulting and Clinical Psychology, 58*, 768–774.

Henry, W., & Strupp, H. (1994). Therapeutic alliance as interpersonal process. In A. Horvath & L. Greenberg (Eds.), *The working alliance: Theory, research and practice.* New York: Wiley.

Horvath, A. (1994). Research on the alliance. In A. Horvath & L. Greenberg (Eds.), *The working alliance: Theory, research and practice.* New York: Wiley.

Horvath, A., & Greenberg, L. (1989). Development and validation of the working alliance inventory. *Journal of Counseling Psychology, 36,* 223–233.

Horvath, A., Marx, R., & Kamann, A. (1990). Thinking about thinking in therapy: An examination of clients' understanding of their therapists' intentions. *Journal of Consulting and Clinical Psychology, 58,* 614–621.

Klein, M., Mathieu-Coughlan, P., & Kiesler, D. (1986). The Experiencing Scales. In L. Greenberg & W. Pinsof (Eds.), *The psychotherapeutic process: A research handbook.* New York: Guilford Press.

Leijssen, M. (1990). On focusing and the necessary conditions of therapeutic personality change. In G. Lietaer, J. Rombauts, & R. Van Balen (Eds.), *Person-centered and experiential psychotherapy in the nineties* (pp. 225–250). Leuwen, Belgium: Leuwen University Press.

Leijssen, M. (1996). Characteristics of an inner healing relationship. In R. Hutterer, G. Pawlowsky, P. Schmid, & R. Stipsits (Eds.), *Client-centered and experiential psychotherapy: A paradigm in motion.* Vienna: Peter Lang.

Lietaer, G. (1990). The client-centered approach after the Wisconsin Project: A personal view on its evolution. In G. Lietaer, J. Rombauts, & R. Van Balen (Eds.), *Person-centered and experiential psychotherapy in the nineties* (pp. 10–46). Leuwen, Belgium: Leuwen University Press.

Lietaer, G. (1993). Authenticity, congruence, and transparency. In D. Brazier (Ed.), *Beyond Carl Rogers: Towards a psychotherapy for the twenty-first century* (pp. 17–47). London: Constable.

Luborsky, L. (1994). Therapeutic alliances as predictors of psychotherapy outcomes: Factors explaining the predictive success. In A. Horvath & L. Greenberg (Eds.), *The working alliance: Theory, research and practice.* New York: Wiley.

Mahrer, A. (1989). *How to do experiential psychotherapy: A manual for practitioners.* Ottawa: University of Ottawa Press.

Pinsof W. M. (1994). An integrative systems perspective on the therapeutic alliance: Theoretical, clinical, and research implications. In A. Horvath & L. Greenberg (Eds.), *The working alliance: Theory, research and practice* (pp. 173–198). New York: Wiley.

Prochaska, J. O., DiClemente, C., & Norcross, J. (1992). In search of how people change: Applications to addictive behaviors. *American Psychologist, 47,* 1102–1114.

Raue, P., & Goldfried, M. (1994). The therapeutic alliance in cognitive–behavior therapy. In A. Horvath & L. Greenberg (Eds.), *The working alliance: Theory, research and practice.* New York: Wiley.

Rennie, D. (1993). Clients' deference in psychotherapy. *Journal of Counseling Psychology, 41,* 427–437.

Rice, L. N. (1974). The evocative function of the therapist. In D. Wexler & L. Rice (Eds.), *Innovations in client-centered therapy* (pp. 289–312). New York: Wiley.

Rice, L. N., Koke, C., Greenberg, L. S., & Wagstaff, A. K. (1979). *Manual for client vocal quality classification system*. Toronto: York University, Counseling & Development Center.

Rice, L. N., & Saperia, E. (1984). Task analysis and the resolution of problematic reactions. In L. N. Rice & L. S. Greenberg (Eds.), *Patterns of change* (pp. 29–66). New York: Guilford Press.

Rice, L. N., & Wagstaff, A. (1967). Client vocal quality and expressive style as indexes of productive psychotherapy. *Journal of Consulting Psychology, 31,* 557–563.

Rice, L. N., Watson, J. C., & Greenberg, L. S. (1996). *A measure of clients' expressive stance.* Unpublished manuscript, York University, North York, Ontario, Canada.

Rogers, C. (1951). *Client-centered therapy.* Boston: Houghton-Mifflin.

Sachse, R. (in press). Goal oriented client-centered psychotherapy of psychosomatic disorders. In L. S. Greenberg, G. Lietaer, & J. C. Watson (Eds.), *Experiential psychotherapy.* New York: Guilford Press.

Safran, J., Muran, J., & Samstag, L. (1994). Resolving therapeutic alliance ruptures: A task analytic investigation. In A. Horvath & L. Greenberg (Eds.), *The working alliance: Theory, research and practice* (pp. 225–255). New York: Wiley.

Sexton, T. L., & Whiston, C. S. (1994). The status of the counseling relationship: An empirical review, theoretical implications, and research directions. *The Counseling Psychologist, 22,* 6–78.

Toukmanian, S. (1992). Studying the client's perceptual process and their outcomes in psychotherapy. In S. Toukmanian & D. Rennie (Eds.), *Psychotherapy process research: Paradigmatic and narrative approaches* (pp. 77–107). Newbury Park, CA: Sage.

Watson, J. C. (1996, June). *An analysis of therapist interventions using the SASB model of interpersonal behavior in a good and poor outcome case in the experiential therapy of depression.* Paper presented to the International Meeting of the Society for Psychotherapy Research, Amelia Island, FL.

Watson, J. C., & Greenberg, L. S. (1994). The alliance in experiential therapy: Enacting the relationship conditions. In A. Horvath & L. Greenberg (Eds.), *The working alliance: Theory, research and practice,* (pp. 153–172). New York: Wiley.

Watson, J. C., & Greenberg, L. S. (1996). Pathways to change in the psychotherapy of depression: Relating process to session change and outcome. *Psychotherapy Research, 33,* 262–274.

Watson, J. C., & Rennie, D. (1994). A qualitative analysis of clients' reports of their subjective experience while exploring problematic reactions in therapy. *Journal of Counseling Psychology, 41,* 500–509.

Weerasekera, P., Linder, B., Greenberg, L., & Watson, J. (1997). *The development of the working alliance in the experiential therapy of depression.* Manuscript in preparation.

Wheeler, G. (1991). *Gestalt reconsidered.* New York: Gardner Press.

Wolfe, B., & Sigl, P. (in press). Experiential psychotherapy of anxiety disorders. In L. S. Greenberg, G. Lietaer, & J. C. Watson (Eds.), *Experiential psychotherapy.* New York: Guilford Press.

Yontef, G. M. (1991). *Awareness, dialogue and process: Essays on Gestalt therapy.* New York: The Gestalt Journal Press.

James C. Coyne and Carolyn M. Pepper

The Therapeutic Alliance in Brief Strategic Therapy

7

We . . . see our work as very strategic. This is not in the military sense, since we view treatment as a cooperative endeavor, not an adversarial one. But the broader dictionary definition refers to strategy as "a careful plan or method," which certainly proposes forethought, judgment, and deliberate choices of one's actions.

WEAKLAND, 1992, p. 142

s a discussion of the therapeutic alliance in strategic therapy written by authors including a former member of the Mental Research Institute (MRI) Brief Therapy Center staff, this chapter represents a first of sorts. In their writings, strategic therapists have emphasized *techniques* to the exclusion of *relationship*. To readers familiar with the approach, a discussion of the therapeutic alliance in strategic therapy might seem as odd as discussions of the therapeutic alliance in behavior therapy would have been in the early 1970s, prior to Goldfried and Davison's (1976) seminal chapter on the topic. We will start by arguing that the reluctance of strategic therapists to discuss their approach in terms of a therapeutic alliance has been principled, but that it has had some unfortunate consequences. We next provide an overview of the basic assumptions and conduct of strategic therapy. We then proceed to a strategic perspective on the therapeutic alliance more generally, and specifically, on what occurs in strategic therapy itself.

The Therapeutic Alliance in
Strategic Therapy: An Oxymoron?

Writings concerning the strategic therapy developed by the MRI (Coyne, 1989; Coyne & Segal, 1982; Fisch, Weakland, & Segal, 1982; Watzlawick & Coyne, 1980; Watzlawick, Weakland, & Fisch, 1974; Weakland, Fisch, Watzlawick, & Bodin, 1974) have been curiously silent about the nature of the therapeutic alliance in this form of brief therapy (Duncan, 1992). The term *strategic* was chosen for this approach because of its emphasis on therapists accepting responsibility for their role in the change process by making deliberate choices about which strategies and tactics to adopt in assisting clients (Haley, 1973; Weakland, 1992). Considerable attention has been paid to specific therapist behaviors and broader strategies such as therapists preserving their maneuverability by adopting a *one-down position*, that is, taking steps to diminish the implied distance from clients and conveying a sense that strategic therapists themselves are modest people with insecurities and shortcomings of their own. Strategic therapy also involves the prescription of distinctive therapeutic assignments to clients, assignments often of a paradoxical nature. It would seem that an understanding of how to select and implement such interventions would require a focus on the therapeutic relationship within which they occur. Yet there is a consistent lack of discussion of the therapeutic alliance as an interpersonal relationship throughout the writings of the MRI group (for one brief exception, see Coyne, 1986).

This omission is particularly striking, given the strong Sullivanian roots of strategic therapy (Coyne & Segal, 1982). The interpersonal theory of Harry Stack Sullivan involved a key shift from viewing the individual in isolation as the focus of study and treatment to the patterning of interpersonal relationships. The founder of MRI, Don Jackson, was directly supervised by Harry Stack Sullivan. Richard Fisch, who joined the group later and who was instrumental in forming the MRI Brief Therapy Center, was also a Sullivanian by training. In the early 1960s, the MRI group began exploring how they could intervene directly in clients' lives to modify the interpersonal contexts, complex feedback processes, and characteristic responses of others that were maintaining clients in their predicaments. This was something Sullivan himself was reluctant to do (Wachtel, 1977). The MRI group's experimentation grew into strategic therapy as we now know it. Yet the Sullivanian emphasis on the interpersonal relationship as the irreducible unit of study was not extended to therapy itself.

The MRI group's eschewal of any discussion of therapy as an inter-personal relationship was a part of a deliberate effort to refocus attention on the interface between therapy and the everyday lives of clients rather than on therapy as an autonomous system of communication separate from this life. The MRI approach construes therapy as a brief series of consultations with the purpose of providing clients with a staging area to plan and begin to implement changes in their every-day lives. Strategic therapists assist clients in reframing their coping tasks so that their existing values and orientation can lead to new behaviors. Yet, therapists are skeptical of apparent change that is discussed in the therapy session, unless there is evidence that these changes have been implemented in the everyday contexts where clients' problems have been occurring. This is one of the reasons for their emphasis on therapeutic homework assignments to be completed between sessions.

The MRI group was also eager to distance themselves from the ways in which the therapeutic relationship had been construed in more conventional approaches to therapy. Both psychodynamic and humanistic therapy have tended to view the quality of the therapeutic alliance as more important than what the therapist specifically does or what is occurring in clients' lives between sessions (Bordin, 1982). One derivative of strategic therapy, solution-focused therapy, has reverted to such an exclusive focus. It analyzes what goes on between the therapist and the client. Thus, de Shazer (1993) stated:

> There are no wet beds, no voices without people, no depression. There is only talk about wet beds, talk about voices without people, talk about depression. . . . There is nothing outside of the therapy session that can help us understand what is going on in the session. (p. 89)

Yet, it is precisely this position that the MRI group rejects because of concerns that such a conceptualization reduces therapy to mere conversation, rather than a basis for clients' developing plans and making a commitment to action. Furthermore, this view of therapy excludes the actual changes relative to wet beds, voices without people, and depression that strategic therapists and their clients view as the goals of therapy.

It may well be that the same qualities of the therapeutic relationship determine a major portion of the variation in outcome across diverse therapeutic orientations (Horvath & Symonds, 1991). Surely, some basic level of trust and therapist credibility is required by all forms of therapy. There is some evidence that in strategic therapy, as in other therapies, client ratings of therapist warmth predict subsequent improvement (Green & Herget, 1991). Yet from a strategic perspective, too exclusive a focus on such ratings would leave some key questions unanswered. First, what are strategic therapists actually doing that is reflected in client ratings of the therapeutic relationship, and how might this differ from what is done by therapists of other orientations? Second, how are these qualities of the therapeutic relationship related to what clients are able to achieve in their everyday lives, and how, in turn, do events in clients' lives determine the kind of therapeutic relationship that can be achieved?

Another reason strategic therapists have avoided much discussion of the therapeutic relationship is that traditional writings on the topic have often been associated with the assumption that therapy is, of necessity, a long-term process. The gradual development of the therapeutic relationship is assumed to be a precondition for the therapist's breaching of sensitive topics and the client's responding in a nondefensive manner. In contrast, strategic therapists immediately take steps with clients to decrease some of the social distance. With humor, irony, and calculated irreverence, they encourage clients to join with them in acknowledging what might otherwise remain obvious, but unspoken. As early as the first session, homework assignments may be negotiated as a way of gathering information, defining the nature of the therapeutic contract, or simply beginning the process of change.

Strategic therapists' reluctance to discuss the therapeutic alliance in traditional terms has been principled and defensible. Yet, such a position has distinct disadvantages when it becomes a barrier to teaching and refining strategic therapy. It is difficult to evaluate and generalize from strategic therapists' provocative case vignettes when no sense is provided of the therapeutic context in which interventions were developed, implemented, and followed up. Open-minded, but skeptical readers are left wondering how a strategic therapist could possibly have come up with an intervention in a particular situation and why the client accepted it. Obviously, the nature and effectiveness of such interventions are inextricably intertwined with the kind of relationship within which they are formulated and delivered. It is known from studies of therapists of other orientations that poorly timed and otherwise inappropriate interventions may damage the therapeutic alliance (Piper, Azrin, Joyce, & McCallum, 1991), and the influence of the quality of the alliance on the appropriateness of intervention is undoubtedly reciprocal. Moreover, when its proponents remain silent on the quality of the therapeutic relationship in which strategic interventions are delivered, the approach becomes vulnerable to caricature and distortion by critics who claim that it is manipulative and noncollaborative (see, for instance, Goolishian & Anderson, 1992). More than therapists of most orientations, strategic therapists have exposed their actual sessions with clients to scrutiny in transcripts (Fisch et al., 1982), videotapes, and observation through one-way mirrors. Nonetheless, misperception and misinterpretation have been fostered by written presentations of their interventions in brief vignettes that grant little acknowledgment of how the therapists and clients collaborated in reaching the point of intervention and in its follow-up.

Another disadvantage of strategic therapists' reluctance to discuss the nature of the therapeutic relationship is that it has prevented others from appreciating the potential contribution of this approach to more eclectic and integrative models of therapy. As we argue in this chapter, strategic therapists sometimes simply use different terms to describe what they do in therapy; yet in other ways, they do indeed operate with some assumptions that differ from those guiding traditional forms of therapy. In some instances, strategic therapists are best seen as utilizing alternative means to achieve goals that are shared with other approaches. In other instances, strategic therapists are operating in ways that truly challenge traditional assumptions. Regardless, one cannot adequately explore such similarities and differences unless there is first greater acknowledgment of the nature of the therapeutic relationship in strategic therapy.

Some Basic Assumptions of Strategic Therapy

Strategic therapy is a pragmatic, goal-oriented, short-term approach that focuses on how clients' miscarried coping efforts are perpetuating their problems and how these efforts can be redirected. The aim of therapy is to resolve clients' presenting complaints as briefly and efficiently as possible so that the clients can get on with their lives. Yet, the focus of case formulations and therapy more generally is typically not on the presenting complaint, but rather on what clients are doing about it. Thus, the focus with a depressed client is not likely to be depression per se, but rather what the client has been attempting to do to feel better. This could be, for instance, efforts to renegotiate an unsatisfactory intimate relationship by alternately futilely arguing with the partner and then avoiding any direct expression of discontent because it only leads to futile arguing.

The assumption is that if these ineffective means of coping—these *attempted solutions* or *problem-maintaining solutions*—are redirected, then the clinical problem will resolve itself. A further assumption is made that clients persist in these ways of coping because they have become involved in the situation in a way that validates for them that this is the only or the best way they can cope. It is not assumed that they lack the requisite skills for more effective problem solving, but rather that they fail to see the relevance of their existing skills or fail to appreciate that they are entitled to respond differently in the situation. Thus, upon careful inquiry, it might be established that a depressed woman is quite nurturant of her friends, deeply empathizes with them, and would take offense if they were to tolerate mistreatment in a close relationship. Confronted with a friend remaining in a verbally abusive relationship, the woman would undoubtedly protest that the friend should look after herself and not accept such mistreatment. Yet, the depressed woman might be in such a predicament herself because she does not similarly feel entitled to look after herself and instead accepts abusive and exploitative behavior from a partner.

Working goals are typically specific small changes in behavior, but these strategic changes are intended to instigate change of a more general nature (i.e., a fundamental shift in clients' attempted solutions). Exploring the role of the past, working through emotional issues, and teaching problem-solving or communication skills are not emphasized (Shoham, Rohrbaugh, & Patterson, 1995). Insight, increased self-awareness and emotional release may accompany change in strategic therapy, but they are not considered necessary. They often prove insufficient, and pursuit of them as ends in themselves may distract the therapists from their fundamental task: to redirect clients' miscarried efforts to cope with their problems. Clients may ultimately feel they have gained insight from therapy, but the insight is more likely the result of having effectively dealt with their situation, rather than the trigger for a behavior change.

A wide variety of interventions are used, and, most distinctively, some of them are paradoxical in nature (see Fisch et al., 1982, for actual transcripts of sessions). A key element of many of these interventions is *reframing* (Coyne, 1985; Watzlawick et al., 1974). This involves the therapist's grasping the client's interpretation of the problematic situation, actively acknowledging an acceptance of this view, and then introducing some new element into this view that leads to very different behavior. Thus, in the example of the depressed woman just presented, reframing might begin with the therapist eliciting reports of how she looks after friends, praising this virtue, and then lamenting that the woman does not have a friend immediately available to look after her in the same way. The crucial element that would be added is the suggestion that when dealing with her partner, the woman should step back, adopt the role of a friend, and follow the friend's advice. In subsequent sessions, the therapist might revert to a query such as "What would a friend say?" when the client voiced discontent about her treatment by her partner. The therapist would also assist the client in identifying instances in which she had adopted such a perspective herself. Taken literally, such reframes may seem to request little or no change in behavior; yet, when such reframes are successful, clients are likely to give a markedly different answer to the question "What is going on here?" and their experience of the predicament and their tendencies to behave in particular ways are likely to change significantly (Coyne, 1985).

This approach assumes that clients persist in ineffectual attempted solutions because they have become committed to a particular perspective on their predicament. This perspective or framing of their situation is both the basis for the persistence of their problem and the basis of engaging them in the process of therapeutic change:

> [Clients'] existing framing of their situations reflects some mixture of what their situation affords; socioculturally provided, commonsense understanding; and the validation available in their interaction with others. Their existing frames maintain their problems, but are also the means for communicating with them and finding new solutions. Thus, in order to provide viable frames, the therapist must acknowledge some key aspects of [clients'] existing frames and link reframes to it. For reframes to endure, they must be proposed in such a manner that they validate [clients'] interactions with their everyday environments. (Coyne, 1985, p. 343)

For our present purpose of understanding the therapeutic alliance in strategic therapy, some points deserve emphasizing. Therapeutic change involves what is at least a covert challenge or unsettling of clients' existing perspective. Whatever else strategic therapists do, they try to persuade clients to take action or to adopt views that will advance the clients' interests. Therapy is inherently rhetorical, and to draw on a classic rhetoric text,

> You persuade a man only so far as you can talk his language by speech, gesture, tonality, order, image, attitude, idea, *identifying your ways with his.* . . . True, the rhetorician may have to change an audience's opinion in one respect, but he can succeed only insofar as he yields to that audience's opinions in other respects. Some of their opinions are needed to support the fulcrum by which he would move other opinions. (Burke, 1950, pp. 55–56)

Although strategic therapists strive to modify or transpose key elements in clients' understanding of their situation ("I will be a friend to myself and do what that friend suggests, rather than what I would otherwise be inclined to do"), they can succeed only if they accept key aspects of clients' own interpretations and actively communicate this acceptance. Unfortunately, writings on strategic therapy have sometimes exaggerated therapists' cleverness in formulating reframes and have downplayed the role of careful information gathering, clarification, negotiation, shaping of clients' willingness to accept intervention, and timing. Furthermore, the outcome of a case is rarely set with the client's acceptance of a single reframe or assignment. Much depends on how the therapist subsequently nurtures incipient change, negotiates the client's interpretation of resultant new experiences, and manages termination (Shoham et al., 1995).

The Conduct of Strategic Therapy

Strategic therapy sessions are relatively low-key, with the therapist taking an active role in obtaining the particulars of the client's every-day life, highlighting the specific exchanges that are seen as problematic, and identifying the client's problem-maintaining solutions. An effort is made to move from abstract definitions of the problem such as the client feeling depressed or not being able to communicate with an intimate partner to specific incidents that illustrate these problems, exactly how they are distressing, and what the client has tried to remedy the situation. What is first sought is a concrete, action level of description, essentially an elaborated answer to the question, "*Who* is doing *what* that presents a problem, to *whom*, and *how* does such behavior constitute a problem?" (Fisch et al., 1982, p. 70). Additionally, the client needs to be committed to a workable goal, and an explanation is sought for why the client is seeking change now rather than previously or putting the matter off until some future time.

The therapist guides this process by requesting examples, indicating confusion when complaints are left abstract, or suggesting that therapy would proceed better if the therapist could visualize the occurrence of a problematic situation. The emphasis is on what is occurring currently in the client's life, rather than in the distant past. The most relevant situations and problem-maintaining solutions are current ones, but the therapist is also likely to at least touch upon solutions that have been tried and discarded, as well as touch upon how analogous situations have been successfully handled in the past. The intent is to reveal resources and past achievements that are relevant, but are unnoticed by the client.

Clients define their problems, even though therapists may take a key role in clarifying just what behavior is involved and in identifying what is most important to the client but initially expressed in a vague or confused manner. Ultimately, "the client is the expert on and basic determiner of the *ends* of treatment" (Weakland, 1992, p. 144). However, strategic therapists are sensitive to the possibility that in exploring precisely how a particular problem is troubling to a client, it may be revealed that the client is personally not particularly troubled at all, but coming for therapy only because of pressure from others. The ability to define behavior as problematic and people as troubled and in need of therapy is not necessarily evenly or fairly distributed in social systems (Lakoff & Coyne, 1992). If in a particular case the therapist and client jointly conclude that a problem is mainly a problem for others, therapy may become refocused on solving the problem of the client feeling harassed, coerced, or simply misunderstood by others. Strategic therapy is decidedly nonnormative and nonjudgmental in the definition of clinical problems. The radical acceptance of the client's perspective is often subtle, but pervasive. Occasionally, this attitude on the part of strategic therapists becomes explicit. When a client opens with "I think I am kinda weird," the therapist might counter with "I have come to think we all probably are. Are you 'weird' in a way that is interesting or in a way that is troubling to you?"

As the problem becomes defined, an attempt is also made to formulate some concrete, minimal goal for treatment with answers to the question, "What would it take to indicate to you that you were on the right path, even if you were not out of the woods?" Alternatively, it might be suggested that "There is a lot of difficulty and uncertainty in your life, and we cannot expect to take care of it all. Is there one problem such that if we were able to make some small progress in dealing with it, you would feel a bit more able to cope with everything else?" When clients are facing situations that appear largely intractable to their efforts, the question of goals may be a matter of "What would it take to allow you to feel that you were handling this situation as well as you could?" In the initial interview, a therapist may realize that a pessimistic stance better matches client expectations than to propose goals that hint of an optimistic prospect. Being flexible, a strategic therapist might shift to

> It doesn't look like things will ever be the way you want them to be again. What's your bottom line? What could you live with if you really have to? (Efron & Veenendaal, 1993, p. 16)

From the start, the therapist calls attention to the time-limited nature of therapy. This brief nature of therapy can be structured in a number of different ways. At the MRI Brief Therapy Center, clients are offered 10 sessions with an understanding that they can complete therapy in fewer sessions and leave the rest "in the bank." Clients seem to find security in leaving some sessions in the bank. Even when not actually drawing on these sessions, clients' merely knowing that they are available seems to give a sense that they are not alone and that they can proceed with the assurance that they have this resource. This may give them a greater confidence in their own efficacy. Furthermore, they may sense that whatever they do is in a context of a continued relationship with the therapist, and this relationship serves as a reference point, where the therapist becomes a significant other. Clients' coping efforts may be positively affected by how they would potentially explain themselves to the therapist, and this possibility is heightened by their having the option of returning to claim their sessions in the bank. Often, when clients do eventually use their remaining sessions, they report having resolved problems in the interim in which they engaged in imagined dialogues with the therapist.

An alternative to a limited number of sessions is an agreement that therapy will proceed in short blocks, perhaps of three or five sessions, and that continuation will be based on making progress. The therapist may then make repeated reference to the time-limited nature of therapy and use this to prompt clients to think in terms of small, observable changes and to share in the responsibility for demonstrating that therapy is not a waste of time:

> I would like to think that what we are going to do here will make a difference, but we can not be sure. I don't want it to be a waste of your time, and so maybe we should plan to assess our efforts in five sessions and decide whether we have got enough evidence that we are getting somewhere to justify continuing. What would be a sign to you that we were getting somewhere? (Coyne, 1988)

The sign that is negotiated may be a goal of therapy or simply an identifiable step toward it. What is important is that continuation of therapy be justified by progress, not the lack of it. With a positive assessment of progress, a new target can be identified for the next block of sessions.

Strategic therapists proceed with an acute sense that they are not simply eliciting an account of the clients' beliefs in an interview, but also are actively shaping clients' formulation of those beliefs. In an important sense, therapists and clients are together *creating* what clients experience as a *reporting* of their beliefs. The particular questions therapists ask focus clients' attention on specific details, while distracting them from others, and a line of questioning implicitly challenges some assumptions that have been taken for granted, while leaving others unexamined. Likewise, therapists' selective responses and choices of whether to accept clients' language or introduce new language of their own shape not only the course of the discussion that follows, but also clients' understanding of themselves. Thus, in gathering information, therapists are simultaneously structuring clients' *framing* or definition of the problems, preparing them for reframes, and defining the nature of the therapeutic relationship. The interventions that can be designed by therapists and the extent to which they can be made palatable to clients depend upon how these intermediate steps are accomplished.

In the course of the interview, strategic therapists are sensitive to the nuances of clients' choice of words. They are alert for language that reveals clients' key values and commitments in a situation—their position (Watzlawick et al., 1974)—and other language that can be adapted to their purposes. Thus, a client's presenting complaint of chronic fatigue was not ostensibly related to her divorce from a domineering ex-husband 2 years earlier. However, in a digression, she spontaneously mentioned the difficulty she had faced in convincing her ex-husband that the relationship was over, even after the divorce was final. Asked how she finally succeeded, she described a telephone conversation: "I just refused, again and again, I just refused to see him." At the end of the session, the therapist commented that she was not sure how the client would unleash the relevant resources to reclaim some of her life from the dominance of her fatigue, but that in dealing with her husband, she had shown that she had what it took. Undoubtedly, her resistance to being dominated by the fatigue would start with a defiant "I refuse." The client was then encouraged to practice saying that phrase until it no longer stuck in her throat and to notice what initiatives occurred over the next week.

Strategic therapists do not take for granted that they have achieved a sufficient understanding of clients' existing framing of their predicaments or that they have adequately communicated an acceptance of it. Instead, in the course of questioning and making interpretations, they are constantly checking and refining this understanding, adjusting to the nuances of clients' responses. In the course of the interview, strategic therapists also deliberately introduce particular language and test and shape its acceptability so that it can become the basis for subsequent intervention. For example, a depressed client had frustrated all efforts by the therapist to activate him, despite that being his stated goal. Straightforward homework assignments to increase pleasurable activities had been readily accepted, but then routinely forgotten or thwarted in the course of the time between sessions. Finally the therapist observed, "You seem to be a man who doesn't like to be pushed around by others." His stubbornness was reframed as determination, a refuge for his self-respect in the face of health problems he could not control. The therapist then asked, "In fact, if someone told you to breathe, would you be inclined to hold your breath just to spite him?" The client quickly agreed with this depiction of himself, thereby setting the stage for paradoxical intervention. At the end of the session, the client was instructed in a mock authoritarian manner to go home and, "Do nothing, rest yourself, don't give into the urge to do something until it becomes absolutely irresistible." The following week this client reported numerous activities that had been attempted in spite of the therapist's admonition to do nothing and that he had some success. The therapist immediately backed down from his previous authoritarian stance, apologized for giving such bad advice, and pointed out that the client clearly already knew what he needed to do.

Reports of strategic interventions are easily misunderstood, particularly if they are taken as literal requests. It may seem as if clients are being instructed to do homework assignments that are bizarre and even counterproductive. Thus, a single mother complained that her 8-year-old son was demanding and disrespectful, particularly in the morning when she tried to get him ready for school. She was instructed that when the child's morning temper tantrums upset her, she should quietly make a peanut butter and tuna fish sandwich for his lunch. When the child came home and complained about his lunch, she was to apologize and state that she was so upset by the child's behavior that she must have gotten distracted and put peanut butter and tuna fish together, rather than peanut butter and jelly or tuna fish and mayonnaise. The therapist added that the woman would be doing her future daughter-in-law a favor in teaching her son now that if he mistreats women, they become less responsive to his needs. The goal was to empower the mother to take control of the situation. Although it would not have been a problem if the woman had actually made such a sandwich, doing this was considered unlikely. The expected outcome in such situation is that she would realize she has both the responsibility and the ability to regain control of a child's behavior. She would be more likely to exercise the existing option of intervening early and directly if he began misbehaving, even if she had previously denied that this was possible. Such assignments make explicit the mother's tendency to avoid conflict, even at her own expense. By giving her permission to confront the situation, even in an outlandish manner, the therapist is also implicitly communicating that she is responsible for her own behavior.

Strategic therapists are careful to follow up such therapeutic tasks in the next session with direct inquiries as to how clients interpreted them and what happened if they attempted to implement them. Yet, it is not assumed that literal interpretation and completion of such tasks as they have been prescribed are necessary or that a client's failure to complete these tasks represents sabotage or resistance. Strategic therapists are likely to react to such outcomes praising clients' assertion of their autonomy or creative reinterpretation of what has been asked of them. The therapist might even take a one-down position by apologizing for having been overcome with "therapeutic enthusiasm" in assuming that what had worked for others fit a particular client's needs. What is important with many assignments is that they commit clients to particular perspectives and plans of action, even if this is not manifested in completion of the assignment. Thus, an ex-Catholic man was asked to tackle his excessive scrupulosity and mildly compulsive behavior with a newspaper-buying ritual. On Mondays, he was to pay for two newspapers, but only take one from a machine; however, on Tuesdays, he should pay for one and take two. Wednesdays were labeled as the most difficult day of the week: He was to take two papers, pay for one, and hope that he did not die and go to hell before he could make up the difference on Thursday. What is important in his acceptance of this assignment is that he distance himself from his guilt and accept a certain amount of discomfort as part of the process of change, not that he pay for and retrieve newspapers in a particular order.

A Strategic Perspective on the Therapeutic Alliance

As we emphasized at the outset of this chapter, one would be hard pressed to find much in the way of explicit reference to the therapeutic alliance in existing writings on strategic therapy—unless we look for discussions of technique as therapeutic relationship. Yet, that is not to say that there is not much of relevance in these writings and in clinical materials such as videotapes. In the remainder of the chapter, we will discuss the therapeutic alliance from a strategic perspective. Some points apply more generally, across orientations, whereas others are particular to the strategic approach. However, in discussing the strategic perspective, we often had to go from descriptions of specific strategies and tactics by therapists to inferences about the kind of alliance in which these arise and which they foster. In doing so, we try to make explicit what is usually only implied in writings about strategic therapy. Strategic therapists sometimes seemingly make odd requests of clients, yet this is generally done without clients defecting from therapy. Clients often do not complete therapeutic tasks as they have literally been assigned; and not only is this not typically a source of a rupture in the therapeutic alliance, it may be met with praise and enthusiasm from strategic therapists. Strategic therapy is not typically characterized by any struggle between therapist and client, and traditional conceptions of client "resistance" are absent from key writings, except as a notion to be rejected. All of this assumes a well-developed, even if quickly developed, and sometimes unusual therapeutic alliance.

Perhaps the first step in understanding the nature of the therapeutic alliance in strategic therapy is to recognize that unless there is compelling evidence to the contrary, it is not assumed that the clients are fragile. Despite any distress, impairment, or self-derogation clients may present, there are nonetheless strengths, accomplishments, and competencies in who they are and what they have made of their experiences. Strategic therapists are careful to identify and cultivate these resources, paying more attention to the positive than the negative, and they attempt to engage clients as strong, accomplished, and resourceful. Strategic therapists are explicitly committed to persuading clients to undertake changes in behavior, but they are careful to recognize the limits of their influence and acknowledge their dependence on the cooperation of clients. They are careful not to replicate what has not worked in others' efforts to influence clients. Strategic therapists also strive to avoid seeming more powerful than they are or as if they are more committed to clients achieving particular goals than to the clients themselves. They are respectful of clients' ambivalence about proceeding and acutely sensitive to the possibility that clients have appeared to fail in previous efforts to attain their goals because the clients have mouthed conventional values without actually embracing them. Strategic therapists may introduce irreverence and paradox into clients' problem-solving efforts, but if so, these inteventions are often grounded in a shared sense that conventional values and ways of dealing with the client's predicament have paradoxically not worked.

AVOIDING OTHERS' PROBLEM-MAINTAINING SOLUTIONS

Strategic therapists' assumption that clients' attempted solutions are perpetuating their problems has an important corollary. Namely, if clients have persisted in their problem-maintaining solutions, it is because they have been unsuccessful in engaging others in ways that have freed them from their ineffective approach. Clients' self-defeating strategies may even be maintained and aggravated by others' responses. It becomes important, therefore, for strategic therapists to recognize what others have tried and to avoid replicating their unsuccessful efforts. Significant others may be hostile or adversarial, but it is also possible that their efforts have been normative, kind, and reasonable, at least at the outset, but ineffective in resolving clients' predicaments.

A specific patterning of client behavior and response from others has been spelled out for depression (Coyne, 1976), but it may have broader generality for situations in which one person attempts to relieve the distress of another. The obvious distress of depressed persons is compelling and invites efforts to soothe them and cheer them up. Similarly, their harsh denigration of themselves invites rebuttal: "You are not that bad of a person . . ." Their disclosure of ineptness invites constructive feedback and advice: "Why don't you . . ." Finally, their reports of victimization invite judgment about persons who are significant in their lives: "Your husband is an awful person. Why don't you . . ." Under some circumstances, these responses from others might do much to resolve transient distress. Yet, if these responses had proven sufficient, the client would not be presenting with depression. Such responses are likely to make them feel even more badly about themselves. As Watzlawick, Weakland, and Fisch (1974) have noted:

> What [others'] help amounts to is a demand that the client have certain feelings (joy, optimism, etc.) and not others (sadness, pessimism, etc.). As a result, what for the [patient] might originally only have been a temporary sadness now becomes infused with feelings of failure, badness, and ingratitude toward those who love him so much and are trying so hard to help him. (p. 34)

Like others in clients' lives, therapists are vulnerable to falling into these patterns of response. Therapists may find themselves slipping into countering depressed clients' negativity with phony reassurance and then getting into a dispute in which the depressed person gets more committed to justifying their negative view of themselves. Therapists may take the side of depressed persons in their disputes with others, only to have these depressed persons defend the people allegedly victimizing them. Finally, active, directive therapists may get more committed to plans of action than the depressed persons are, even while depending on the depressed persons to implement them. There can be a decay of helping so that therapists become frustrated, personalize depressed clients' difficulties, and ultimately become critical and rejecting (Coyne, Wortman, & Lehman, 1988).

The psychoanalysts Nacht and Racamier (1960) have unwittingly revealed taking this position with depressed clients:

> We wish to insist . . . that the depressed person . . . is always truly aggressive toward others through the very medium of the manifestations of his depression. His suffering is an accusation. His sense of incurableness is a reproach. His demands are perhaps humble, but devastating. His depression is tyrannical. He wallows in suffering, whilst trying to enmesh his object in it as well. (p 486)

Regardless of orientation, however, all therapists are potentially vulnerable to replicating these patterns. One important function for a theoretical framework for doing therapy is that it gives therapists a structure and focus to their relationships with clients so that they are buffered from falling into the compelling, but unhelpful response that may have characterized others. At the same time, however, they also need to avoid being perceived as aloof, indifferent, cold, or rejecting.

In strategic therapy, direct inquiry about others' past efforts to assist clients, including any recent psychotherapy, is an important part of the therapists' efforts to recognize and avoid becoming involved in unhelpful or miscarried helping. Other distinctive features of the therapists' contribution to the therapeutic alliance in strategic therapy serving this purpose include therapists taking a one-down position and maintaining a sense of irony and paradox.

TAKING A ONE-DOWN POSITION

Strategic therapists have some clear advantages over their clients. If they are justified in receiving a fee for their services, they presumably have some expertise. Clients seek help from them because they have decided that their own views have proved inadequate or inappropriate to resolve their problems. Perhaps most important, strategic therapists have the advantage of only empathically hearing about clients' problems, rather than having to live them out and be worn down by them. There is an inherent power imbalance in the client–therapist relationship, but anything that therapists do to aggravate this imbalance may reduce the client resources within which therapists must work. Strategic therapists, therefore, strive to create a relationship that clients experience as low-key and free of coercion. They assume that clients are cooperative and motivated to be relieved from their distress and that their task is to avoid interfering with this. Some clients prefer an authoritative, overtly directive approach, and strategic therapists are prepared to adapt to this. However, the working assumption is that clients will be more resourceful if they do not feel they are being pressured or simply following orders. Moreover, even if the goal is to shift clients' existing framing of their predicament, care is taken to avoid embarrassing or intimidating them or otherwise making them defensive.

From the perspective of other theoretical orientations, strategic therapists may seem to be overly respectful of clients' defensiveness and seem to encourage externalization of problems. To paraphrase Robert Frost, strategic therapists believe that good defenses make good clients. Thus, if a client tends to blame a spouse for all of the problems in the relationship, a strategic therapist is unlikely to challenge this directly. Instead, the therapist may acknowledge that the spouse sounds difficult or even impossible and then inquire how the client intends to deal with this. Without being required to take responsibility for the problem, the client is shifted into considering how to take responsibility for his or her own behavior in response to it.

Strategic therapists also operate on the assumption that clients will be more resourceful and accepting of what is asked of them in therapeutic tasks if the tasks are presented in a way that emphasizes both clients' choice in whether to accept them and the sacrifice involved in doing so. Thus, having gotten an agreement from the wife of a stroke victim that she would shift from her previous efforts to activate him with criticism and coercion, the therapist then immediately asked:

> I'm wondering . . . are we being carried away by therapeutic enthusiasm? Are we . . . demanding something that is so contrary to your outlook on how to help your poor husband that you will listen to us here but by the time you walk out of the building . . . your mind would have changed. . . . Think for a moment, how difficult this is going to be for you. (Fisch et al., 1982, p. 272)

If there are any doubts about the acceptability of a task, strategic therapists are inclined to express doubts about the suitability of it in a way that invites clients to offer reassurance that it is acceptable and that they are prepared to carry it out. Thus, in the above example, the woman's reply, "No, listen, I would be delighted to try anything you suggest . . ." (Fisch et al., 1982, p. 272), indicating that her commitment had been secured. The answer to the question "How do strategic therapists get clients to accept outlandish intepretations and assignments?" varies. First, they very often explicitly inquire whether clients are willing to accept a particular assignment and are prepared to clarify or retract the assignment if clients have any misgiving. Second, the offering of the assignment is likely to have been prepared in the exploration and rejection of more straightforward ways of tackling the problem.

In an important sense, the notion that clients are cooperative and that what appears to be resistance is a reflection of therapists' failure to engage them properly is not a readily falsifiable proposition, but a presumption in strategic therapy. It is the responsibility of the therapist to elicit and nurture this cooperativeness. What is paramount, however, is that the therapist avoid getting into struggles with clients and appear to pressure or criticize them. It may be seen as a first-order accomplishment that they avoid such traps, but a second-order accomplishment that they succeed in getting clients to demand a chance to attempt a task or to argue that they are responsible for their behavior in the face of therapists' polite suggestions to the contrary.

Protecting the clients' dignity and sense of cooperativeness is a working goal of strategic therapists, and task assignments reflect this.

When clients have ostensibly failed to undertake a task assignment, strategic therapists are likely in some way to avow responsibility for this; cite evidence that clients were actually being reasonable, creative, and cooperative in not completing the task; or simply retract the assignment as having been inappropriate. Assignments often have provisions built into them for making any response from the client a form of cooperation. Thus, a woman had returned to graduate school after having negotiated her husband's assumption of child rearing and household tasks that had previously been exclusively her responsibility. She felt she was not performing well enough in her studies to justify this and that she was also responsible for her husband's ineptness in looking after the family. Further, she felt that she was now neglecting both her studies and her family, basically retreating to bed. The therapist at first suggested that she make a choice and take a few days concentrating on either the family or the studies, but not both. However, when it could not be established that the client experienced this as permission to do what she wanted, rather than an additional burden, the therapist added what was meant to be face-saving for the client:

> And maybe you need a third choice. If you find that the next
> session is impending and you have not exercised either of your
> other options, you should come back and tell me that "No, I did
> not focus on my family or my schoolwork. I did a bit of both, or I
> just looked after myself." Maybe the issue is that you are inhibi-
> ted from getting anything done because you are not listening to
> yourself and feeling free to make choices for yourself. Maybe
> the first step is to decide not to be pushed around by anyone
> including me, and you will figure this out by the end of the week.

IRONY AND PARADOX: THERAPY AS DEAD-SERIOUS PLAY

A strategic conception of clinical problems and their treatment involves a number ironies or formal paradoxes (Coyne, 1987; Watzlawick, 1978; Watzlawick et al., 1974). Clients' problems and the associated distress are persisting because of what they (Wegner, 1997) and others (Shoham & Rohrbaugh, 1997) are doing to try to solve these problems. Clients present complaints that they cannot on their own change their behavior, and yet attempt to enlist the aid of therapists who can only work through clients' own behavior. It is assumed that clients have the resources to solve their problems, but they are either misapplying or failing to recognize these resources or not feeling entitled to use them. Yet, therapists' direct comments to clients about how their attempted solutions are perpetuating their problems can prove counterproductive. Such comments risk alienating or further demoralizing the client, aggravating their predicament and making it less likely they will be resourceful. Strategic therapists are more likely to focus on how the particulars of a given client's circumstances reveal resources and ironies that are useful in tackling the client's problems. A woman whose husband has abruptly left her for another woman may be distressed about having suddenly become a lonely single parent. However, it could be the case that her husband's lack of involvement had functionally made her an effective single parent long before his departure, and she was now free to claim a right of an "official" single parent: She no longer has to have sex with a man she detests.

All of this gives rise to the ironies and counterparadoxes that characterize strategic therapy. Many reframes and task assignments allow clients to recognize features of their behavior and circumstances that cannot readily be commented on directly. There is often a collusive quality to therapists' delivery of task assignments that goes beyond the subtle testing and negotiation that lead up to them. Far from being tricked, clients frequently nod approvingly or smile when given assignments. They are well aware of the absurdity of their having been trapped in ineffective problem-solving strategies and perceive how they are being given a way out. However, it is usually unwise for therapists to comment on this.

Strategic therapists are not averse to taking a stand and providing direct feedback when the feedback appears likely to be accepted, but they are sensitive to the risk of increasing clients' defensiveness. Even in the first session, strategic therapists begin to expand the bounds of what can be discussed with irreverence and a calculated unconventional sentimentality (Lakoff & Coyne, 1992). Thus, a woman was upset that her manipulative and hypochondriacal mother had scheduled a minor elective surgical procedure on the same day the daughter was planning to leave the country on a long-anticipated vacation. The daughter felt tremendous guilt that she would not be able to help her mother following the surgery and had even considered changing her vacation plans. The strategic therapist responded, with feigned indignation, "How could you leave your poor, sick mother in her time of need? How terrible!" The woman at first appeared shocked, but then laughed heartily and launched into a discussion of how angry she felt with herself for being so easily manipulated.

Strategic therapists may take increasing liberties, verbalizing what is obvious, but previously taboo for discussion. Thus, in a first session, a strategic therapist pushed the limits with a woman who had seemed to be indicating that she would be upset if her boyfriend was unfaithful, but that she would nonetheless tolerate his unfaithfulness:

THERAPIST. I know it would not be right, but could he get away
with it?

CLIENT. Possibly, maybe once. You can forgive and forget one
time, but not a second.

THERAPIST. You mean like . . . What do you think if I told [the
live-in boyfriend] "you have this deal that you are not going to
believe. You have a free one coming, but only one and so it
better be good . . ."

The discussion then turned to how the woman might make it convenient for the man to have his fling discretely. Her complicity became
explicit enough for her to realize that she really was not prepared to
accept this behavior from him and that she should stop tacitly encouraging the man to believe otherwise.

Strategic therapists are aware that praise and other positive comments are as risky as criticism in terms of leaving clients feeling defensive or misunderstood. As with criticism, therapists will not refrain
from praise if they believe that what they say will be credible and well-
received by clients. However, they tend to be sparing in their compli-
menting of clients and careful not to disrupt clients' budding efforts
by premature or overly generous praise. Therapists will, however, look
for opportunities to elicit material from clients that is not controver-
sial in its praiseworthiness:

THERAPIST. What is of interest to me is how, given all that has
gone wrong . . . why you are not more laid low than you are?

CLIENT. Because I decided not to be . . . The same way I decided
having my father molest me wasn't going to ruin the rest of
my life. . . . I don't mean that I don't get pissed off as hell
sometimes, just like I get pissed off that my father molested
me. And there are times when it really does affect me, but . . .
what I strive for is to be able to be depressed without being
suicidal.

THERAPIST. . . . Sure . . . I wish I could bottle whatever you've
got. I am sure that there would be a real demand for it. . . .
How about your husband, how is he dealing with things?

Notice how the therapist avoided engaging the client in a discussion
of her childhood sexual abuse. His intent was to elicit material from
her in order to compliment her on being a survivor, not to explore the
history or details of the abuse. Notice also that this valued attribute
was never named, and so the compliment was less vulnerable to being
dismissed, but more easily generalized to other situations.

Conclusion

> We are bound to influence our clients, and they are bound to influence us. The only choice is between doing so without reflection, or even with attempted denial, and doing so deliberately and responsibly. Clients come seeking change which they could not achieve on their own; expertise in influencing them to change usefully seems to us the essence of the therapist's job. (Weakland, 1992, p. 142)

Strategic therapists assume that clients are in therapy because they seek to be influenced in a way that reduces their distress and resolves their complaints. Clients' accomplishing these goals is facilitated by therapists being persuasive. Furthermore, therapeutic tasks are an important aid in ensuring that discussions in the therapeutic session lead to viable change in clients' everyday environment where their problems have been occurring. Being able to design, convey, and follow up on such therapeutic task assignments are important skills for the strategic therapist, and it is the development of these skills that writings on strategic therapy have emphasized. Yet, even if typically left implicit, much is being assumed about the resourcefulness of clients and the necessity of therapists engaging and recognizing this resourcefulness. In this chapter, we have tried to bring to the forefront of the discussion how this is done and the kind of therapeutic alliance it requires. Undoubtedly, much of what we have presented can be understood procedurally, in terms of the therapeutic alliance as a set of techniques. Yet, we hope we have also conveyed a sense of the attitudes and commitments that strategic therapists must bring to the relationship if they are to maximize their effectiveness. We are skeptical about the possibility of reducing these attitudes and commitments to a set of procedures. Effectiveness may depend upon them being held as core beliefs about people and therapy.

References

Bordin, E. S. (1982). A working alliance based model of supervision. *The Counseling Psychologist, 11,* 35–42.

Burke, K. (1950). *A rhetoric of motives.* Englewood Cliffs, NJ: Prentice Hall.

Coyne, J. C. (1976). Toward an interactional description of depression. *Psychiatry, 39,* 28–40.

Coyne, J. C. (1985). Toward a theory of frames and reframing: The social nature of frames. *Journal of Marital and Family Therapy, 11,* 337–344.

Coyne, J. C. (1986). The significance of the interview in strategic therapy. *Journal of Strategic and Systemic Therapies, 5,* 63–70.

Coyne, J. C. (1987). The concept of empowerment in strategic therapy. *Psychotherapy, 24,* 539–545.

Coyne, J. C. (1988). Strategic therapy. In G. Haas, I. Glick, & J. Clarkin (Eds.), *Family intervention in affective illness* (pp. 89–113). New York: Guilford Press.

Coyne, J. C. (1989). Employing therapeutic paradoxes in the treatment of depression. In M. L. Ascher (Ed.), *Paradoxical procedures in psychotherapy* (pp. 163–183). New York: Guilford Press.

Coyne, J. C., & Segal, L. (1982). A brief, strategic interactional approach to psychotherapy. In J. Anchin & D. Kiesler (Eds.), *Handbook of interactional psychotherapy* (pp. 248–261). New York: Pergamon.

Coyne, J. C., Wortman, C., & Lehman, D. (1988). The other side of support: Emotional overinvolvement and miscarried helping. In B. Gottlieb (Ed.), *Social support: Formats, processes, and effects* (pp. 305–330). New York: Sage.

de Shazer, S. (1993). Creative misunderstanding: There is no escape from language. In S. Gilligan & R. Price (Eds.), *Therapeutic conversations* (pp. 81–90). New York: Norton.

Duncan, B. L. (1992). Strategic therapy, eclecticism, and the therapeutic relationship. *Journal of Marital and Family Therapy, 18,* 17–24.

Efron, D., & Veenendaal, K. (1993). Suppose a miracle doesn't happen: The non-miracle option. *Journal of Systemic Therapies, 12,* 11–18.

Fisch, R., Weakland, J. H., & Segal, L. (1982). *The tactics of change: Doing therapy briefly.* San Francisco: Jossey-Bass.

Goldfried, M. R., & Davison, G. C. (1976). *Clinical behavior therapy.* New York: Holt, Rinehart & Winston.

Goolishian, H. A., & Anderson, H. (1992). Strategy and intervention versus no intervention. *Journal of Marital and Family Therapy, 18,* 5–15.

Green, R. J., & Herget, M. (1991). Outcomes of systemic/strategic team consultation: The importance of therapist warmth and active structuring. *Family Process, 30,* 321–336.

Haley, J. (1973). *Strategies of psychotherapy.* New York: Grune & Stratton.

Horvath, A. O., & Symonds, B. D. (1991). Relation between working alliance and outcome in psychotherapy: A meta-analysis. *Journal of Counseling Psychology, 38,* 139–149.

Lakoff, R., & Coyne, J. C. (1992). *Father knows best: The use and abuse of power in Freud's case of Dora.* New York: Teachers College Press.

Nacht, S., & Racamier, P. C. (1960). Symposium on "depressive illness": II. Depressive states. *International Journal of Psycho-Analysis, 41,* 481–496.

Piper, W. E., Azrin, H. F. A., Joyce, A. S., & McCallum, M. (1991). Transference interpretations, therapeutic alliance, and outcome in short-term individual psychotherapy. *Archives of General Psychiatry, 48,* 946–953.

Shoham, V., & Rohrbaugh, M. (1997). Interrupting ironic processes. *Psychological Science, 8,* 151–153.

Shoham, V., Rohrbaugh, M., & Patterson, J. (1995). Problem- and solution-focused couple therapies: The MRI and Milwaukee models. In A. S. Gurman & N. S. Jacobson (Eds.), *Clinical handbook of couple therapy.* New York: Guilford Press.

Wachtel, P. (1977). *Psychoanalysis and behavior therapy.* New York: Basic Books.

Watzlawick, P. W. (1978). *The language of change.* New York: Norton.

Watzlawick, P. W., & Coyne, J. C. (1980). Depression following stroke: Brief problem-focused family treatment. *Family Process, 19,* 13–18.

Watzlawick, P., Weakland, J. H., & Fisch, R. (1974). *Change: Principles of problem formation and problem resolution.* New York: Norton.

Weakland, J. H. (1992). Conversation—but what kind? In S. Gilligan & R. Price (Eds.), *Therapeutic conversations* (pp. 136–145). New York: Norton.

Weakland, J. H., Fisch, R., Watzlawick, P. H., & Bodin, A. (1974). Brief therapy: Focused problem resolution. *Family Process, 13,* 141–166.

Wegner, D. M. (1997). When the antidote is the poison: Ironic mental control processes. *Psychological Science, 8,* 148–150.

Douglas S. Rait

Perspectives on the Therapeutic Alliance in Brief Couples and Family Therapy

8

Often a marital therapist may feel like a labor negotiator, or a diplomat involved in conflictual issues. If he joins one side against the other, he becomes part of the problem rather than part of the solution. Yet inevitably he is personally involved in whatever the issues may be; and so he may find himself taking sides whether he likes it or not. What is so appealing, and yet so stressful, about marital counseling is the way the action draws on the feelings of the therapist. His own biases about men and women, and his own attitude about marriage, are forced out into the open as he struggles with marital issues.

> HALEY, 1976, p. 61

[The family therapist] knows that by becoming a member of the therapeutic system, he will be subjected to its demands. He will be channeled into traveling certain roads in certain ways at certain times. Sometimes he will be aware of the channeling; other times he will not even recognize it. He must accept the fact that he will be buffeted by the implicit demands that organize the family members' behavior. He will tend to talk to the central member, and smile secretly at the "schlemiel." He will feel the impulse to save the symptom bearer, or help in scapegoating him. His job as a healer requires him to be able to join the family in this way. But he must also have the skills to disjoin, then rejoin in a different way— and there's the rub.

> MINUCHIN AND FISHMAN, 1981, pp. 29–30

Portions of this chapter have been adapted from "The Therapeutic Alliance in Couples and Family Therapy: Theory in Practice," by D. Rait, *In Session: Psychotherapy in Practice, 1,* Copyright © 1995 John Wiley & Sons, Inc. Reprinted by permission of John Wiley & Sons, Inc.

As in all forms of psychotherapy, the success of brief couples and family therapy depends on the participants' ability to establish and maintain an open, trusting, and cooperative therapeutic alliance (Gurman, 1981; Pinsof & Catherall, 1986; Rait, 1995). However, one of the most difficult challenges that couples and family therapists face is learning how to manage therapeutic relationships with multiple family members in an environment characterized by conflict, emotionality, vulnerability, and threat. To new and experienced therapists alike, there appear to be so many ways to fail: by overidentifying with one family member, overprotecting another, or sharing in the family's experience of helplessness. Not surprisingly, the dropout rate in couples and family therapy is higher than in indivdual treatment (Bischoff & Sprenkle, 1993). The therapist can easily take a wrong step, inadvertently take sides, or become a disappointment to a client whose relationship is foundering.

Precisely because brief couples and family therapy requires a quicker read of the situation, the rapid development of a common perspective and language, and a shared commitment to therapeutic goals and a plan of action, forming a therapeutic alliance with a couple or family requires both conceptual clarity and interpersonal skill. Unfortunately, there has been diminishing consideration of the central role played by the therapeutic relationship in couples and family treatment. For example, Nichols and Schwartz (1991) observed that family therapists have become more technically oriented and "deemphasize the therapeutic relationship in their writing" (p. 547). Similarly, Minuchin, Lee, and Simon (1996) noted the recent "disappearance of the person of the therapist" and, by extension, the disappearance of a discussion of the therapeutic alliance. In their view, contemporary clinical models have tended to discount the personal qualities of the therapist and therapeutic alliance, placing greater emphasis on more readily observable dimensions of clinical technique.

Couples and family therapists routinely acknowledge principles found in most models of brief psychotherapy, such as the notion that many problems are situational, the belief that people coming for treatment are capable of change, the assumption that individuals always have more alternatives available to them than they recognize, and the expectation that considerable change can occur within a relatively brief period of time (Gurman, 1981). Like individuals who seek psychotherapy, couples and families presenting for therapy generally feel stuck, hopeless, and unsuccessful in their efforts to solve their problems. As a result, the therapeutic alliance in brief treatment may be even more crucial to reversing the family's demoralization and experience of failure by creating a competing momentum to counteract their spiraling despair. The practitioner of brief therapy must actively understand the family's predicament, appreciate client expectations that he or she will be able to repair even the most problematic relationships, and also instill hope that their circumstances can change.

Minuchin and Fishman (1981) view the family and therapist as forming a time-limited partnership that will support this process of exploration and transformation. From the structural family therapy perspective, *joining* is considered to be the glue that holds together the therapeutic system (Minuchin & Fishman, 1981). Although virtually every model of family therapy highlights the importance of developing a strong initial bond with the couple or family and its members, the subsequent therapeutic work requires alliances sturdy and flexible enough to support the therapist's challenges to the couple or family's preferred patterns of interaction. However, with regard to managing changes in this evolving, multifaceted alliance over time, the contemporary literature has been noticeably silent. As any therapist walking the tightrope between battling family members or competing coalitions knows, the most formidable clinical challenge involves not simply building these alliances, but also sustaining them over the course of therapy.

In this chapter, we will examine four important conceptual and practical features of brief couples and family therapy that continually influence the therapist's choices in maintaining a positive therapeutic alliance. These characteristics include the fact that the couples and family therapist must establish and maintain *multiple alliances,* adopt a conceptual framework that accounts for the interactions within *triangles* or three-person systems, recognize the *influence of the system* operating on him or her, and recognize how different models of family therapy define the *position of the therapist* in relation to the couple or family. After examining these points in greater detail, we will look at problems that can emerge in the therapeutic alliance. Finally, two general strategies for managing difficulties within the alliance in brief treatment with couples and families will be illustrated through case vignettes.

Conceptual and Clinical Issues

MULTIPLE ALLIANCES

Brief couples and family therapy can be demanding. Because there are multiple participants, the task of simply conducting the session can be arduous, especially for the beginning therapist. Couples and families in crisis predictably exaggerate the differences in their styles, and sessions tend to be noisier and more openly conflictual than the modal individual psychotherapy meeting. In addition to contending with the difficulties in managing the multisourced therapeutic conversation, the therapist immediately recognizes that not every family member comes to treatment with equal motivation, similar goals, or shared beliefs about how to change. Couples and family therapy is often conducted with some individuals who are, to some degree, hesitant or even involuntary clients.

Given the fact that family members are likely to differ in their levels of commitment, goals, and developmental stage, questions of technique must address not only when and how to form an alliance, but also with whom. For example, it is commonly accepted that the therapist must develop an alliance with every family member, especially in the initial session (Haley, 1976). Some clients experience an alliance with the therapist as a result of no more dramatic an intervention than the offering of warmth and empathy (Gurman, 1981). Others require more leadership and structuring by the therapist, the identification of problematic patterns, or the introduction of a provocative challenge. *Therapeutic joining* is a process by which a therapist uses him- or herself to create a context of trust and safety, so that exploration and experimentation are made possible (Minuchin & Fishman, 1981).

Because the therapist's alliance with one or two family members inevitably affects the alliance with other family members in a circular, reciprocal fashion, the systemically oriented clinician cannot consider any single dyadic alliance in isolation (Pinsof & Catherall, 1986). Falloon (1991) notes that because the therapeutic alliance in a family context must be looked at as a part of the system, the alliance "depends not merely on the relationship between the therapist and the family members, but also on the interrelationships among the family members themselves" (p. 84). The couples and family therapist therefore needs to develop different levels of alliance, including an alliance with each individual family member, the various subsystems within the family (e.g., the parents or siblings), and the couple or family as a whole.

Experienced therapists form and maintain these dynamic relationships in different ways. For example, the family therapist may affiliate with one family member while simultaneously addressing other family members, sometimes by using relational language that links their complementary behaviors (e.g., "Your wife seems so very sad. Can you speak to her in a way that does not depress her?"). Later on, the same therapist may choose to challenge the couple or family's pattern of interaction, while simultaneously supporting each member as individuals (e.g., "For two such intelligent and articulate people, you've certainly constructed an unsatisfying relationship!"). Finally, there may be instances where a therapist will choose to join with one family member in process (e.g., by moving his chair closer to an adolescent son) while, at the same time, supporting another family member in content (e.g., "You have something important to say to your son. Can you tell him now?"). In each instance, the couples and family therapist will opportunistically develop and elaborate different types of alliances in order to establish a sufficient foundation for therapeutic expansion.

TRIANGLES

To better characterize the dynamic, interpersonal milieu of treatment, the couples and family therapist makes an important conceptual shift; that is, dyadic exchanges are viewed within the context of triangular relationships. For example, although a two-person system may remain stable as long as it is free of tension, the dyad will immediately include "the most vulnerable other person to become a triangle" when anxiety surpasses the dyad's threshold (Bowen, 1976, p. 76). Understanding the dynamics of emotional triangles provides the therapist with a broader framework for looking at how dyadic interactions are embedded in larger systemic processes.

In considering the therapeutic alliance in the context of couples therapy, the therapist is also reminded that every therapeutic encounter involves, at the very least, a triangular relationship with the therapist as well. Extending Sullivan's (1953) notion that the therapist is always part of the field being observed, Haley (1976) has asserted that the therapist needs to include him- or herself in the description of the family: "When doing therapy with a couple, it is best for the therapist to consider that whatever the partners do in relation to each other is also in relation to the therapist" (p. 160). Unlike the therapist in individual psychotherapy, the couples therapist must be able to join and skillfully manage an alliance with each member of the couple, as well as with the couple as a unit. The therapist needs to be able to move freely back and forth between partners, alertly monitoring invitations to join one against the other.

In terms of clinical technique, Bowen (1976) suggested that the concept of triangles provides the therapist with a way of controlling his or her own automatic participation, described as emotional reactivity, in the couple or family's emotional process. Although the therapist might never remain absolutely unaffected by the family's emotional system, a knowledge of triangles makes it possible to "get outside," while staying emotionally in contact with and present for the family. By detriangling him- or herself, the therapist can induce a change in the couple's relationship by eliminating a preferred, maladaptive routine for regulating their anxiety (Kerr, 1981).

INFLUENCE OF THE SYSTEM

Couples and family therapy is often described as challenging because of the powerful emotional and social currents that influence the therapist. As in individual psychotherapy, the family therapist is always subjected to the social demands or "pull" of his or her clients. Bowen (1976) observed that "as soon as the vulnerable outside person comes into viable emotional contact with the family, he becomes part of it, no matter how much he protests the opposite" (p. 52). He noted that "it is easy for the family to wrap itself around the therapist emotionally, install the therapist in an all-important position, hold the therapist responsible for success or failure, and passively wait for the therapist to change the family" (p. 77). The expectations operating on the therapist to participate with the couple or family in a prescribed fashion can neither be ignored nor be underestimated.

At the outset, the therapist needs to observe the drama of the ordinary in the family by bringing "the family kitchen into the office" (Minuchin et al., 1996, p. 70). In particular, the therapist attends to the customary, stereotyped ways that members tend to relate to each other and to their environment. Family-systems approaches have traditionally held that couples and families in treatment can be characterized by a homeostatic conservatism that is expressed by their maintaining familiar patterns for as long as possible. Just as new developmental circumstances require changes in the family, the introduction of a catalyst for change (e.g., a therapist) into the system can therefore be expected to provoke behavioral responses aimed at returning the system to its accustomed, narrow range of functioning.

The experienced therapist entering the family system anticipates anxiety concerning the direction of change, questions about who is to be in charge, and challenges to his or her leadership. At the same time, he or she recognizes a crucial paradox; that is, the therapist is expected to help the couple or family to change their situation, while simultaneously responding to and potentially even operating under the same rules of interaction that preserve the problematic situation. In this regard, Andolfi and Angelo (1988) have contended that the family's implicit request to help them "change without changing" represents a wish to induce the therapist into playing complementary roles "most conducive to the maintenance of the status quo" (p. 237). Despite their best intentions, family therapists routinely find themselves inducted into and participating in the preferred patterns of interaction of the families.

POSITION OF THE THERAPIST

The particular relationship that emerges between therapist and couple or family is also influenced by the therapist's model of normal family processes and theory of change. Although not every clinical approach to couples and family therapy has something specific to say about the therapeutic alliance, practically every model does identify the position or stance the therapist should take in relation to the family. Some recommend an "interventionist" approach, where the therapist is viewed as an expert and the primary instrument of change (Minuchin et al., 1996). Others advocate a more inconspicuous, "restrained" role for the therapist (H. Anderson, 1994). These differing therapeutic stances can also be located on a continuum, ranging from those favoring proximity to those advocating a more distant relationship between therapist and family.

Anchoring one end of this spectrum is the humanistic tradition represented by Satir (1967), who suggested that the therapist "must first create a setting in which people can, perhaps for the first time, take the risk of looking clearly and objectively at themselves and their actions" (p. 160). Satir modeled warmth and support, valued give-and-take between family members, and emphasized that therapist and clients were equals in learning. From her perspective, the therapist needs to continually validate the expression of both positive and painful feelings and demonstrate respect for each family member.

In contrast to Satir's position of close proximity, Bowen (1976) proposed that the therapist take a more objective, differentiated position that approximated the role of a researcher or coach for the couple or family. He saw the therapist's role as striving to "stay out of the transference" and to avoid becoming affected by the family's emotional process. By reducing his or her own emotional reactivity, the therapist could serve as a calm, nonreactive presence for the family. Proponents of the Milan systemic approach also emphasized the therapist's vulnerability to the family's powerful influence and devised a team approach to counteract the expected induction (Tomm, 1984). The Milan therapist, described as the "conductor" of the session, assumed a disciplined stance of therapeutic neutrality in relation to family members' ideas, beliefs, goals, and values both to counteract these forces and to aid the family in discovering its own solutions.

Attending to the irrationality present in all couples and families that induces strong feelings in the therapist, Whitaker enjoined the therapist to be like the coach of the family team, not a player. In his view, every couple and family presented therapists with the challenge of finding the right therapeutic distance: "If he avoids the Scylla of overinvolvement, he is immediately faced with the Charybdis of isolation" (Whitaker, Felder, & Warentkin, 1965, p. 343). For this reason, Whitaker preferred co-therapy as a model of treatment because it provided the opportunity for the therapists to support each other, offered one therapist the freedom to think, while the other was emotionally engaged with the couple or family, and stimulated creativity. Whitaker believed the therapeutic encounter would not produce authenticity and growth without both immediacy and involvement.

Ackerman (1966) was one of the first family therapists to advocate a more flexible therapeutic stance. He suggested that the therapist not only needed to establish an atmosphere of support, but also had to be nimble enough to "move directly into the stream of family conflict, to energize and influence the interactional processes," reassume an observing position to "survey and assess significant events, and then move back in again" (p. 268). This perspective was further elaborated by Minuchin and his colleagues (Minuchin & Fishman, 1981; Minuchin et al., 1996) who encouraged therapists to join the family and allow themselves to experience its demands as temporary participants in the family's transactions.

In using themselves to form the therapeutic system, structural family therapists examine how their personal style, level of comfort, and preferred theoretical commitments might interact with the particular couple or family they are treating. Taking a flexible, rather than an invariant, stance in relation to the family, the therapist uses him- or herself openly and undefensively to support, coax, confirm, or challenge family members. In doing so, the therapist may take the role of therapist as a producer, stage director, protagonist, and narrator (Colapinto, 1991). At the same time, the structural family therapist demonstrates a respectful curiosity about the family's experience and strengths and maintains a solid commitment to help families change.

In contrast to the "interventionist" models described above, recent family therapy approaches based on recent social constructivist ideas emphasize the importance of collaboration and mutual respect in the therapeutic alliance (T. Anderson, 1987; White & Epston, 1988). Treatment is primarily conceptualized as a linguistic activity in which conversation about problems develops new meanings and new behaviors and where clients are viewed as equal participants in the co-construction of meaning (Sexton & Whiston, 1994). Narrative therapy prioritizes elegant reframes and the search for exceptions as primary elements of change, rather than treating the therapeutic relationship itself as a vehicle for understanding and lever for change. Because problems are often externalized, or redescribed as being situated "outside" of family members, the therapist helps galvanize the couple or family's focus on dissolving the corrosive effects of the problem on their patterns of relating (White & Epston, 1988).

The central role of the narrative therapist is, therefore, to manage therapeutic conversations in which fixed meanings are "given room, broadened, and changed" and where the goal of therapy "is to participate in a conversation that continually loosens and opens up, rather than closes down" (H. Anderson & Goolishian, 1988, p. 381). The *therapeutic alliance* is redefined as a collaborative relationship that allows for the deconstruction of confining narratives and the consideration and performance of new ones. Viewing the "we–they scenario" as an unfortunate consequence of traditional, interventionist models of psychotherapy, these constructivist approaches reject the therapist's expert role in favor of a more restrained and egalitarian relationship between therapists and clients (H. Anderson, 1994).

DIFFICULTIES IN THE THERAPEUTIC ALLIANCE

Even when the therapist clearly understands the family's process as well as his or her own "blindspots," problems in the therapeutic alliance inevitably arise. Although these impasses can be both frustrating and demoralizing, they also represent a potential learning opportunity for clinician and family alike. According to Safran (1993b), a therapeutic alliance rupture in individual psychotherapy can be defined as a negative shift in the quality of the therapeutic alliance or an ongoing problem in establishing one. These misalliances may "vary in intensity and duration from subtle, momentary miscommunications between client and therapist, to major barriers to the establishment of the alliance, which if unresolved, result in treatment failures and dropouts" (Safran, 1993b, p. 34). Markers of alliance rupture (or breaches, miscommunications, misunderstanding, and impasses) can include overt expression of negative sentiments, indirect communication of hostility, disagreement about the goals or tasks of therapy, noncompliance, avoidance maneuvers, self-esteem enhancing operations, and nonresponsiveness to intervention (Safran, Crocker, McMain, & Murray, 1990).

In the context of family treatment, Whitaker (1982) described the therapeutic impasse as a deterioration in the therapeutic relationship in which the therapeutic experience has lost its emotional voltage: "There is something about the impasse that is like an unhappy bilateral symmetrical dance. It's as though they're locked in and neither one can switch to being creative" (p. 45). Reacting to the powerful influence of the couple or family system, therapists may act to protect themselves through overinvolvement, increasing isolation, or overreliance on formal technique (Neill & Kniskern, 1982). Indications that the therapist is participating in a therapeutic rupture include insufficient joining, lack of therapeutic intensity, lack of pacing, inability to challenge the system, diffusing conflict, being "ahead" of the family, overidentifying with one family member, neglecting a family member or subsystem, lack of leadership, or taking too central and directive a position (Hodas, 1985). In each case, the fit between the therapist's and family's goals, style, and preferences contributes to the quality of the therapeutic alliance.

Rather than locating the source of difficulty in the couple or family, C. Anderson and Stewart (1983) direct attention to therapist–client interactions that inhibit the therapeutic system from achieving the family's goals for therapy. In addition, resistant interactions are valued because they reveal clues for how to generate a stronger alliance. As deShazer (1985) has proposed, there are no resistant families, only "misunderstood ones." This perspective is consonant with Safran's (1993a) notion that although ruptures in the therapeutic alliance can present a serious barrier to therapeutic progress, they also provide the therapist and client with "indispensable information" and the opportunity for genuine, corrective learning. Once the impasse is identified, it is the therapist's responsibility to prevent or terminate it (Whitaker, 1982).

CASE ILLUSTRATIONS

We now look at two case examples that illustrate how attention to issues within the therapeutic alliance can facilitate the process and progress of treatment. The therapists' solutions to impasses in these cases can be broadly classified as reflecting either direct or indirect approaches to problems in the alliance. The *indirect approach*, associated with the structural and strategic models of family therapy, assumes that the therapist is an outside expert who is able to assess, both by observation of and by experience with the family, their preferred patterns of interaction. By actively testing and accurately understanding the therapist–family transactions, the therapist should be able to strategically join with family members so as to reduce friction and enhance cooperation. In order to "out-think" and sidestep a rupture in the alliance, the therapist flexibly alternates affiliation with family members to join with them as individuals while, at the same time, challenge the reality and system of relationships they have constructed and continue to enact.

The *direct approach*, associated with the interpersonal and symbolic–experiential traditions, assumes that placing even subtle difficulties in the therapeutic alliance on the table for discussion provides an opportunity for new learning and the restoration of positive therapeutic relationships. The following case illustration describes the indirect approach to managing the therapeutic alliance over a series of sessions in a brief family therapy context. The second case vignette describes an instance where the therapist's open, direct reflection about a breach in the therapist–couple process in the early part of couples therapy strengthens the alliance between therapist and couple.

The Indirect Approach With a Family

Presenting Problem and Client Description

Daniel, a 13-year-old boy with a learning disability, was referred for a psychiatric consultation by the medical center's neurology department following reports from the school that he was "spacing out" and failing his classes. The family, an urban Latino family consisting of Celia (age 35), Daniel, and Patricia (age 12), was seen for a family consultation after their neurologist found no evidence of a seizure disorder. In terms of family history, Daniel and Patricia's parents, Celia and Jorge (age 36), separated shortly after Patricia's birth. Celia and her children lived with her parents while she struggled to keep a full-time job as a housekeeper.

However, as time went on, Celia began to feel that her children were being "spoiled" by their grandparents and that Daniel was "not learning how to act responsibly." As a result, when Daniel was 10-years-old, Celia arranged to find her own apartment. Prior to this transition, Daniel had been seen in the medical center's child psychiatry clinic for individual therapy for behavioral problems thought to be related to his learning problem. The therapist at the time had recommended that the grandparents attend the sessions, but they adamantly refused because of their belief that the problem was their daughter, not them or their grandson. Although Celia and Jorge remained separated, he continued to see the children on a nearly daily basis, but he also refused to be involved in his son's psychiatric treatment.

The initial session provided information about the family's structure and organization. Celia described the story of her decision to "take back" her children as an act of protection, noting that she did not want them to grow up "handicapped" like her own younger sister (age 29), who continued to live with her parents and who neither worked nor went out much. Celia believed that her own mother had taken a special interest in her only male grandson and that her mother had treated him "as her own." Patricia described her older brother as spoiled: "He never picks up after himself and acts like a baby." The therapist pursued the theme of Daniel's "acting young," wondering aloud whether he had convinced his mother that he needed such continued attentive caretaking. Daniel was quiet, refusing to participate in the conversation. The therapist also inquired about their prior treatment experiences. The mother pointed out that the previous therapist had explained to her that she "just needed to stop treating Daniel like a little baby," and despite the outcome, she believed that she had indeed worked hard to not repeat the overprotective situation she saw in her parents' home.

Case Formulation

Working from a structural family therapy perspective, the therapist first assessed the family's patterns of hierarchy and affiliation. Daniel appeared to be a powerful presence in his family, and both mother and sister "waited on him hand and foot." The therapist hypothesized that some of his authority could be understood as deriving from his maternal grandmother's strong support as well as his mother's reluctance to challenge both this bond and her son's determined behavior. At the same time, mother and daughter seemed to act functionally as peers.

In order to support the mother's position as head of her family, the therapist chose to meet with the mother, Daniel, and Patricia. This decision reflected a desire to strengthen the bond between therapist and mother while minimizing resistance from the grandmother. At the same time, finding a way to support a mother who had been "disempowered" without displacing her, overdirecting her, or alienating Daniel posed a strategic dilemma for the therapist. Furthermore, given Daniel's noncommunicative stance in the first meeting and the therapist's initial difficulty in forming a relationship with him, the treatment had begun with an impasse that required careful attention.

Course of Treatment

In the next session, the therapist offered the family a new way of thinking about their situation. He noted that he was impressed by Daniel's great power and influence, and asked mother and daughter to make a crown out of construction paper for Prince Daniel. As they assiduously worked together on the crown, the therapist sat beside the young prince and began to discuss with him the prerogatives of royalty: He could order people around, expect others to pick up after him, and do as he wished. While shy at first, Daniel quickly warmed to the idea. Responding to Daniel's increasing comfort, the therapist urged him to speak with greater authority when addressing the women in his family and taught him how to use a scepter (a nearby umbrella) to accentuate his points by rapping loudly on a nearby table when mother and daughter were not sufficiently attentive. Meanwhile, as mother and daughter were completing the crown, the therapist whispered a suggestion to Daniel: that he was to reject the first crown and criticize it as being the wrong color.

Daniel criticized the crown with growing glee, and mother and daughter returned to make a new crown to order. As they applied themselves to the task, Patricia began to grumble: "He's getting what we make this time." Meanwhile, the mother worked hard in an effort to please her son. The therapist continued to coach Daniel in being a prince, even asking Daniel for pointers (since he was already so accomplished at the role). The therapist then constructed an imaginary throne, elevating Daniel by placing his chair on a table. When mother and daughter completed the second crown, the therapist offered them a raincoat to drape over Daniel's shoulders, found a piece of baroque music (by chance) on the clock radio in the treatment room, and asked them to conclude Daniel's coronation by placing the crown on his head.

However, once this new crown rested on his head, Daniel again complained, "It's not my size," and instructed them to make yet a third crown. This time, Patricia could not take her brother's behavior any longer and rebelled: "That's it, I've had enough!" She snatched the crown from her brother and settled it rakishly on her own head, while Mother sat down and watched the drama unfold. The therapist commented that Daniel had learned to be a prince early on and was reluctant to give up his privileged position. Patricia asked Daniel to move over, saying that she would like to be the Queen. Mother quietly recognized the familiarity of the situation, saying, "He's got to get off that throne." The therapist, beginning to shift his alliance toward the boy, suggested that Daniel should continue to act as Prince Daniel during the coming week; for example, when he kissed his mother goodbye or good night, he should hold out his hand (as royalty do) for his mother to kiss.

In the third session, Daniel reported that he had indeed succeeded in getting his mother to kiss his hand. However, Celia reported that Daniel had actually fed himself dinner one night, a behavior described as new and unanticipated. Patricia countered, telling a story about how Daniel had tricked her into ironing his pants one morning and that he "hadn't changed at all." Exasperated, her mother then took an appropriately authoritative position in relation to both children, asking them to stop bickering. In a soft voice, Patricia then asked the therapist if he knew the history of China. When the therapist declared his ignorance, she proceeded to tell him in considerable detail about how the Chinese peasants overthrew the greedy emperor—an obvious allusion to the prior session. Daniel smiled and shyly announced, "I'm the last emperor."

The therapist then met with Daniel alone, both to reconnect with him and to search for alternate ways the young teenager might feel powerful. They talked directly about his small stature, and Daniel described how he felt more comfortable being with younger kids because they looked up to him: "The big kids were all involved with drugs." The therapist validated his desire to feel accepted and safe. To the therapist's surprise, Daniel then went on to relate his many accomplishments in school. He served as a hallway monitor, handled the lighting in school plays ("powerful electricity"), and acted as the wood shop teacher's "right-hand man." Daniel then told about his skill in using power tools and described the intricate woodworking projects he had completed for various family members. He also proudly added that his father was a carpenter.

Shifting the focus to other areas of potential competence, the therapist then asked about Daniel's romantic interests. Daniel talked about one girl that he liked, and the therapist listened attentively to his worries and hopes. At that point, talking "man to man" with Daniel, the therapist wondered aloud whether someone who was so obviously accomplished, and yet who had also convinced his family that he was "so young," would be capable of attracting this particular girl. Daniel thought for a moment as the session closed, leaned over in a position reminiscent of Marlon Brando, and then lifted himself out of his chair and walked to the door with a confident, almost John Wayne-like gait.

In the fourth session, the mother began by describing how Daniel was "actually helping around the house." Patricia reluctantly confirmed her brother's improved behavior. The therapist complimented Daniel, and then talked with the mother about whether Patricia deserved to be honored for her role in helping both her mother and brother. After some discussion, Celia and the therapist determined that Patricia should receive an honorable discharge from her role as auxiliary parent. Mother was pleased to be able to formally recognize her daughter's assistance, and in the following session she presented Patricia with a gift acknowledging her helpful role. At the same time, Celia assured her daughter that she believed that she could now "handle things on her own" with Daniel.

Outcome and Prognosis

The ensuing four meetings, spaced over 2 months, were aimed at consolidating the family's changes. The therapist had little difficulty in crediting each family member for their respective shifts in roles, and he continued to support Celia for her ability to withstand the criticism of her own mother, who reacted strongly to the changing relationship with her "special" grandson. In order to strengthen the siblings as a subsystem, Daniel and Patricia were asked to find some way to thank their mother for her brave and caring convictions. In the meantime, Daniel's teacher reported that he was less distractible in class and that his schoolwork had significantly improved to the point where he was getting "all As and Bs."

In the final session, Patricia reported that she had learned in the therapy that "women tend to treat men like they're babies" and vowed that she was acting differently with her boyfriend: "We treat each other as equals." Her mother said that the therapist had succeeded in "helping her see for herself what needed to happen," rather than making the changes for her. Daniel's mood and behavior had also improved, and he reported greater self-confidence and social success. A follow-up phone call 6 months later confirmed that the changes described at termination had persisted and that "everyone was doing well."

Commentary

The sessions in this family case were approached in a planful way in that the therapist anticipated the resistance or "pushback" of specific family members and continually managed the alliance between himself and the family, his alliance with each family member, and the relationships between individual family members. The therapist's structural model consisted of joining, acknowledging each member's strengths, and then playfully challenging the family's organization, yet there was little overt, in-session discussion of the therapeutic alliance. Instead, his ability to strategically shift his alliances with the individual members and subsystems helped the family-level alliance remain strong even at points of therapeutic challenge and consolidation.

In contrast to the indirect strategy for managing the therapeutic alliance, the therapist using a direct approach to the therapeutic alliance also recognizes that the therapist and family will eventually become entangled in a mutual, noncreative process. However, the therapist brings these impasses directly to the surface for discussion. The assumption is that attention to and metacommunication about the therapist–family process will result in experiences of greater authenticity. In the direct approach, the reflective practitioner views the professional relationship as open to examination and tries to discover the limits of his or her competence through reflective conversation with the client. Expertise is therefore constructed and then reconstructed as part of a mutual process of exploration and accountability (Schon, 1983).

In considering the inevitable power of the therapeutic encounter, interpersonal analyst Levenson (1972) contends that therapists cannot help but be transformed by their patients. Furthermore, it is precisely in the therapist's recognition and lifting him- or herself out of these durable, stereotypical transactions that crucial, transforming moments in treatment occur. Believing that such experiences offer "new points of departure" for the couple, family, and therapist, Taffel (1993) observed that after years of activist, technique-centered family therapy, the field's newest frontier may be a heightened respect for the therapist's own internal emotional processes. He has suggested that "many family therapists, focused on intergenerational patterns or jujitsu-like therapeutic maneuvers, were never taught to keep alive a running internal dialogue" relating to their own thoughts, feelings, and experiences (Taffel, 1993, p. 54). According to Whitaker (1976), the disclosure of these feelings with the family can minimize the risk of the therapist's acting out due to countertransference. At the same time, the therapist's ability to articulate and share his or her experience with a couple or family can also lead to new opportunities for learning.

The Direct Approach With a Couple

Presenting Problem and Client Description

Sara (age 30) and Mark (age 36), both middle-class professionals, came to therapy because of marital conflict. Both had grown up in successful, achievement-oriented families on the East Coast and came to California together to pursue professional and educational opportunities. Since early in their marriage, they described themselves as "locked in a power struggle with each other," and they hoped therapy would provide a safe place where they could learn to communicate better. They admitted that they were "good at acting the happy couple," but that their problems together were demoralizing.

Impasse or Rupture

At the close of the third session, in which the therapist collected some historical data about Mark's family, Sara strongly urged the therapist to contact her individual therapist before the next session, indicating that she considered such coordination among her therapists to be essential. The following day, the couple's therapist received a phone message from Mark, reiterating his wife's expectation and adding that they preferred not to attend another session until the contact was made with her individual therapist. The therapist returned the call, assuring Sara that he would contact her individual therapist.

At the beginning of the following session, the couple began to discuss their week together, neglecting to return to the issue of therapist collaboration. Tensely battling each other for the floor, the therapist noticed his own rising level of irritation and redirected them to the previous week's conversations:

> Let's stop for a moment and look at what's happened here. Before we go on, I want to reassure you that I did speak with your therapist, which I found to be very helpful. However, I would also like to talk about what occurred between us this past week. To tell you the truth, I found myself with some mixed feelings about our recent exchanges.

The therapist then described how at first he had felt "pushed" by Sara, a feeling that was intensified by Mark's subsequent phone call. Sara showed surprise, noting that she believed that she and her husband were in complete agreement about the importance of contacting her therapist. Mark agreed that it was important, but stated that "it seemed far more important to her." Furthermore, he had felt uncomfortable turning the request into an ultimatum. The couple rationalized their differences by describing their agreement that Mark would handle the administrative tasks of the couples therapy, since she had her own individual therapist, but the couples therapist wasn't willing to accept this as a full explanation.

"So, how is it that you became your wife's agent?" asked the therapist. Sara responded with surprise.

"It wasn't a control thing," she countered.

"But the interesting thing is that *I* felt controlled by you," responded the therapist with a gentle tone. They then discussed whether Mark had similar feelings, which he admitted to having experienced frequently in their relationship. They cautiously agreed that this pattern was one of the very difficulties that had brought them to treatment in the first place.

The therapist added, "If we're to work together, I'll need to be able to address these kinds of issues directly with you both. By the same token, I invite you to do the same with me." Sara and Mark looked to each other, sharing a moment of recognition. They agreed that a frank discussion of problems in the therapeutic relationship was crucial. After all, in their own respective lines of work, "relationships were always the key."

Outcome and Prognosis

In the ensuing sessions, it became clear that resolving this early impasse in the therapeutic alliance had a felicitous effect on the process of treatment. Both Sara and Mark frequently referred back to their ability to "get through that business at the beginning of therapy" as a model for what they too could accomplish with each other by directly discussing breaches in their understanding rather than avoiding such discussions.

Commentary

In this case, the therapist risked exposing his feelings about a breach in the alliance, rather than avoiding discomfort and conflict. He modeled a commitment to authenticity and accountability in the alliance by intensifying focus on the therapeutic relationship, described his dilemma with regard to what he experienced as Sara's position and Mark's tacit support, made his assumptions explicit and thereby open to falsification, and invited feedback from both members of the couple on his interpretation of the data (Argyris & Schon, 1974). The couple responded positively to the therapist's *direct* intervention and eventually felt safe enough to open up new areas of disagreement with each other and work toward successful resolution.

Conclusion

Although forming and maintaining the therapeutic alliance in brief couples and family therapy is a critical aspect of the treatment process, this phenomenon has received little systematic attention. Regardless of the therapist's theoretical orientation, the therapeutic alliance is distinctive in that it involves multiple relationships, is informed by triangles, and must withstand and respond to the powerful influences exerted by the family system. Without question, the condensation of couples or family treatment into a briefer time frame requires greater leadership on the part of the therapist, as "making every session count" entails identifying achievable goals, monitoring the momentum and pace of treatment, and devising planful interventions while managing the therapeutic milieu.

Although couples and family therapists have addressed the therapeutic relationship from within their own frame of reference, adopting a broader, nondenominational perspective on this subject has distinct advantages. A common factor among all psychotherapies, the therapeutic alliance serves as a critical tool for clinical understanding and vehicle for therapeutic change. Although case illustrations can never hope to adequately capture the subtleties in the clients' interactions with each other and their therapists, they do highlight how focused attention on these therapeutic relationships can have a direct impact on both the process and outcome of brief treatment.

The evolution of the therapeutic alliance in couples and family therapy follows a developmental trajectory that characterizes many brief psychotherapies. In meeting the couple or family, the therapist validates both family members and their intimate relationships through joining. At this point, the therapist "must feel comfortable in accepting the paradoxical job of leading a system of which he is a member" (Minuchin & Fishman, 1981, p. 29). The multifaceted therapeutic alliance forms the basis for the therapist's understanding of and subsequent challenge to problem-maintaining patterns of interaction. Assuming that impasses in the alliance will invariably occur, the couples and family therapist can either indirectly or directly convert these difficulties into learning opportunities by avoiding redundant interactions with family members, offering direct feedback, providing corrective experiences, or modeling new behaviors. In doing so, the therapist remains engaged with the family until they can consolidate changes and are able to continue on their own.

Although clinical experience indicates that a positive relationship between therapist and family is crucial to therapeutic effectiveness, research looking at the therapeutic alliance in time-limited treatment for couples and family has been slower to develop than in the neighboring field of brief psychotherapy (Bourgeois, Sabourin, & Wright, 1990; Gurman, Kniskern, & Pinsof, 1986). The systematic study of brief couples and family therapy process, focusing on the possibilities and vicissitudes of the therapeutic alliance, will, we hope, shed light on the specific elements of these relationships that are predictive of successful treatment outcomes. Given the importance of the therapeutic relationship in clinical practice, there is little question that couples and family therapists—as well as those clients they treat—will benefit from a growing acceptance of the concept and continued exploration of the therapeutic alliance in their work.

References

Ackerman, N. (1966). *Treating the troubled family.* New York: Basic Books.

Anderson, C., & Stewart, S. (1983). *Mastering resistance: A practical guide to family therapy.* New York: Guilford Press.

Anderson, H. (1994, October). *Collaborative therapy: The co-construction of newness.* Workshop presented at the American Association for Marriage and Family Therapy, Chicago.

Anderson, H., & Goolishian, H. (1988). A view of human systems as linguistic systems: Some preliminary and evolving ideas about the implications for clinical theory. *Family Process, 27,* 371–393.

Anderson, T. (1987). The reflecting team: Dialogue and meta-dialogue in clinical work. *Family Process, 26,* 415–428.

Andolfi, M., & Angelo, C. (1988). Toward constructing the therapeutic system. *Journal of Marital and Family Therapy, 14,* 237–247.

Argyris, C., & Schon, D. (1974). *Theory in practice: Increasing professional effectiveness.* San Francisco: Jossey-Bass.

Bischoff, G., & Sprenkle, G. (1993). Dropping out of marital and family therapy: A critical review of the research. *Family Process, 32,* 353–375.

Bourgeois, L., Sabourin, S., & Wright, J. (1990). Predictive validity of therapeutic alliance in group marital therapy. *Journal of Consulting and Clinical Psychology, 58,* 608–613.

Bowen, M. (1976). Theory in the practice of psychotherapy. In P. Guerin (Ed.), *Family therapy: Theory in practice* (pp. 42–91). New York: Gardner.

Colapinto, J. (1991). Structural family therapy. In A. Gurman & D. Kniskern (Eds.), *Handbook of family therapy: Vol. II* (pp. 417–444). New York: Brunner/Mazel.

deShazer, S. (1985). The death of resistance. *Family Process, 23,* 79–93.

Falloon, I. (1991). Behavioral family therapy. In A. Gurman & D. Kniskern (Eds.), *Handbook of family therapy: Vol. II* (pp. 65–96). New York: Brunner/Mazel.

Gurman, A. (1981). Integrative marital therapy: Toward the development of an interpersonal approach. In S. Budman (Ed.), *Forms of brief therapy.* New York: Guilford Press.

Gurman, A., Kniskern, D., & Pinsof, W. (1986). Research on the process and outcome of marital and family therapy. In S. Garfield & A. Bergin (Eds.), *Handbook of psychotherapy and behavior change* (3rd ed., pp. 565–624). New York: Wiley.

Haley, J. (1976). *Problem-solving therapy.* San Francisco: Jossey-Bass.

Hodas, G. (1985). A systems approach on family therapy supervision. In R. Ziffer (Ed.), *Adjunctive techniques in family therapy* (pp. 209–245). New York: Grune & Stratton.

Kerr, M. (1981). Bowen theory and therapy. In A. Gurman & D. Kniskern (Eds.), *Handbook of family therapy: Vol. II* (pp. 226–267). New York: Brunner/Mazel.

Levenson, E. (1972). *The fallacy of understanding.* New York: Basic Books.

Minuchin, S., & Fishman, C. (1981). *Techniques of family therapy.* Cambridge, MA: Harvard University Press.

Minuchin, S., Lee, W., & Simon, G. (1996). *Mastering family therapy.* New York: Wiley.

Neill, J., & Kniskern, D. (Eds.). (1982). *From psyche to system: The evolving therapy of Carl Whitaker.* New York: Guilford Press.

Nichols, M., & Schwartz, R. (1991). *Family therapy: Concepts and methods* (2nd ed.). Boston: Allyn & Bacon.

Pinsof, W., & Catherall, D. (1986). The integrative psychotherapy alliance: Family, couple and individual therapy scales. *Journal of Marital and Family Therapy, 12,* 137–151.

Rait, D. (1995). The therapeutic alliance in couples and family therapy: Theory in practice. *In Session: Psychotherapy in Practice, 1,* 59–72.

Safran, J. (1993a). Breaches in the therapeutic alliance: An arena for negotiating authentic relatedness. *Psychotherapy, 30,* 11–24.

Safran, J. (1993b). The therapeutic alliance rupture as a transtheoretical phenomenon: Definitional and conceptual issues. *Journal of Psychotherapy Integration, 3,* 33–49.

Safran, J., Crocker, P., McMain, S., & Murray, P. (1990). The therapeutic alliance rupture as a therapy event for empirical investigation. *Psychotherapy: Research and Practice, 2,* 154–165.

Satir, V. (1967). *Conjoint family therapy.* Palo Alto, CA: Science & Behavior Books.

Schon, D. (1983). *The reflective practitioner.* New York: Basic Books.

Sexton, T., & Whiston, S. (1994). The status of the counseling relationship: An empirical review, theoretical implications, and research directions. *The Counseling Psychologist, 22,* 6–78.

Sullivan, H. (1953). *The interpersonal theory of psychiatry.* New York: Norton.

Taffel, R. (1993). In praise of countertransference. *Family Therapy Networker, 1,* 52–57.

Tomm, K. (1984). One perspective on the Milan appoach: Part II. Description of session format, theory and practice. *Journal of Marital and Family Therapy, 10,* 113–125.

Whitaker, C. (1976). The hindrance of theory in clinical work. In P. Guerin (Ed.), *Family therapy: Theory and practice.* New York: Gardner.

Whitaker, C. (1982). The psychotherapeutic impasse. In J. Neill & D. Kniskern (Eds.), *From psyche to system: The evolving therapy of Carl Whitaker* (pp. 38–44). New York: Guilford Press.

Whitaker, C., Felder, R., & Warentkin, J. (1965). Countertransference in the family treatment of schizophrenia. In I. Boszormenyi-Nagy & J. Framo (Eds.), *Intensive family therapy* (pp. 323–343). New York: Harper & Row.

White, M., & Epston, D. (1988). *Literate means to therapeutic ends.* Adelaide, Australia: Dulwich Centre Publications.

K. Roy MacKenzie

The Alliance in Time-Limited Group Psychotherapy

9

In this chapter we describe how the concept of the therapeutic alliance can be applied to the group context. Substantial modifications are required for this to occur. The group literature has centered on several dimensions of group interaction. In the individual literature, the alliance is generally thought of as a single global entity. In addition, writers of group descriptions have been concerned with the identification of stages of development in group process. The individual psychotherapy literature has not emphasized to the same extent this notion of increasing complexity over time as the therapy progresses. We describe a series of clinical intervention strategies that have been developed to address the combined constraints of the time limit and the group context as they affect the alliance.

One general finding in the alliance literature is that early identification of ruptures of the alliance will both improve and shorten therapy. These findings have immediate relevance for the design and implementation of clinical services where an increasing emphasis on the use of time-limited models of psychotherapy has occurred. This may, in part, be seen to be driven by pressures for cost-effective treatment. However, it is also in keeping with the large database indicating that a substantial majority of clients achieve at least symptomatic improvement with a few months of psychotherapy.

Considerable evidence also exists that the outcome for clients receiving psychotherapy in the group modality is essentially the same as that for an individual approach using the same theoretical model (Piper & Joyce, 1996). These results, not generally appreciated, suggest that there will be increasing emphasis on the use of time-limited group models. Although the group psychotherapy process–outcome literature is modest in comparison with the individual literature, empirical data support the general findings of literature on the alliance in the group context.

Applying the Concept of the Alliance to the Group Context

Measures of the therapeutic alliance in individual psychotherapy are conceptually based on the quality of the direct relationship between the client and the therapist. However, the context of group psychotherapy provides a more complex set of possibilities. The literature on group therapy has historically emphasized the principle of psychotherapy through the group process (MacKenzie, 1997; Yalom, 1995). This implies that the role of the group leader is necessarily diluted compared with the polarized role disparity present in individual therapy.

The technical strategies of the leader are directed at creating an interactional network through which therapeutic processes may work. This includes encouraging member-to-member discourse and often actively discouraging member-to-therapist interaction. Many leader interventions are directed to the whole group or to the interactions between members, rather than to the individual members. The majority of observations, reflections, interpretations, and information will originate from the members themselves. This multilevel interactional climate requires a different perspective on the concept of the alliance.

The individual group members will experience the group at four levels. First, there is the impact of the group as a whole. This has been described as a global reaction to the group system environment that often elicits responses from the individual members that reflect early attachment patterns. Second, the members may also find themselves to be part of a subgroup and experience differing reactions to "their" subgroup versus the other members' subgroups. Third, there is, of course, an abundance of opportunities for interaction between individual members; for example, an eight-member group provides 28 such possible directions of communication. Finally, the members will interact directly with the leader, or with the leadership dyad.

In addition, the individual members have two perspectives to consider. They can view and describe the group as a whole from the various group system levels outlined above. Or they can describe their own personal reactions to the group. At least one report suggests that there may be quite a difference in these perspectives. MacKenzie and Tschuschke (1993) studied two long-term psychodynamic groups and found a cluster of members who described their group as positive, supportive, and hard working; however, they themselves felt they were not understood by other members and, therefore, felt isolated and insecure in the group. This second perspective is closer to the usual definition of the alliance in that it deals with the individual member's personal reaction to the therapeutic setting. These levels of complexity and perspective all influence an understanding of the concept of alliance in the group setting.

Group Cohesion

The concept of group cohesion is the closest analogue to the therapeutic alliance, particularly to that version of the alliance captured by the more general term *therapeutic bond*. *Cohesion* is considered a global concept of how attractive or important the group is to the collection of its individual members. It is reflected in such terms as *group morale* or *esprit de corps*. Unfortunately such a nonspecific definition has led to a lack of precision in attempts to measure group cohesion. Some authors have argued that the idea of group bonds between individual members and the group leader is not the same as the concept of whole-group cohesion (Piper, Marrache, Lacroix, Richardsen, & Jones, 1983). Reviews of the group psychotherapy field (Bednar & Kaul, 1994; Drescher, Burlingame, & Fuhriman, 1985) and the small-group literature in relationship to management groups (Mudrack, 1989) agree that the definition of *cohesion* remains unresolved. Despite these problems, it seems to be a general human attribute to rather quickly evaluate groups in terms of some sense of "groupness," attraction, and vitality. Such terms can be applied to all small groups whether they be a sports team, an administrative committee, or a therapy group. The important point is that *cohesion* is a useful term for describing the whole group, not specifically the individual members.

Cohesion suggests that the members are committed to the goals and work of the group and that they experience a need to belong. They can identify with each other in their common task, and there is a sense of compatibility with the group activities. Generally, this also includes positive identification with the group leader (although this is not perhaps a necessary component). A group can be quite cohesive around an internal leader and polarized against the designated leader. The level of cohesion may be reflected in such phenomena as dropout rate, attendance, tardiness, low participation, or inhibited affect among other possible features. But all of these are indirect measures that may be influenced by factors other than cohesion. Generally, cohesive groups are seen as supportive with high levels of compatibility among the members. This is reflected in strong evidence of trust, spontaneity, and an eagerness to learn. At the same time, cohesive groups also show higher levels of challenging, confronting, and risk-taking behaviors. The overall result, therefore, is that the members of a cohesive group have access to a broad range of group experiences that are likely to be therapeutic.

The empirical literature indicates a correlation between cohesion and outcome (Bednar & Kaul, 1994; Fuhriman & Barlow, 1983) and preliminary evidence that, as in the individual literature, early measures of cohesion are correlated with outcome (Budman et al., 1989). Groups that are rated with higher mean cohesion scores tend to have better mean outcomes. Also group members who rate their group as more cohesive tend to have better outcomes than other members of that group. This dual perspective emphasizes that process–outcome studies of groups must report results both in terms of the individual members and for each group as an entity. It is not uncommon to find studies of multiple groups that report some outrider groups that have significantly higher or lower outcome than the overall average.

Group Therapeutic Factors

The literature on group therapy has also emphasized the importance of "group therapeutic factors." Corsini and Rosenberg (1955) provided the first major review of this literature, and the concept has formed a central organizing feature of major group psychotherapy textbooks (MacKenzie, 1990, 1997; Yalom, 1995). A modest empirical literature has offered some support for these concepts (Butler & Fuhriman, 1983; Dierick & Lietaer, 1990; Shaughnessy & Kivlighan, 1995).

These therapeutic factors may be thought of as mechanisms available within the group that are independent of the theoretical orientation of the leader. They are mutually reinforcing, so that the enactment of one will promote the emergence of others. There is also a reciprocal relationship between group cohesion and the presence of therapeutic factors. In a cohesive group, the therapeutic factors will flourish, and, vice versa, promoting the therapeutic factors will increase group cohesion.

A comprehensive review of the therapeutic factor literature is found in Crouch, Bloch, and Wanless (1994), who list the following 10 factors of which the first 5 are unique to group sessions:

1. Universality
2. Acceptance
3. Altruism
4. Learning From Interpersonal Action
5. Vicarious Learning
6. Guidance
7. Instillation of Hope
8. Insight (self-understanding)
9. Catharsis
10. Self-Disclosure

MacKenzie (1997) has described a subset of three ideas from the therapeutic factor literature under the heading of "supportive factors." They are termed supportive because they help the member to regain a sense of mastery. These factors are specifically effective in addressing the sense of demoralization and low self-esteem that is commonly found in clients presenting for psychotherapy. They are also unique to the group context and take a quite different form than in individual therapy.

1. *Universality.* Members quickly find that others in the group have had similar experiences. The resulting sense of commonality stimulates an appreciation of group membership. This is particularly relevant in early sessions in which the individual may have begun the group with strongly negative self-attitudes. The process of universality is a specific antidote to a sense of isolation from others. It reappears at times of group tension to serve as a reinforcement for a sense of group membership.
2. *Acceptance.* It is a powerful experience for a client who is experiencing distress and a sense of alienation from their normal life to be accepted into a group. This experience is quite different from the nature of acceptance in individual therapy, in which the role of the therapist is expected to include an attitude of basic concern. In a therapy group, acceptance is something that must be earned. Therefore the experience of acceptance provides a strong boost to self-esteem. It is rare for a client not to be accepted especially in early sessions. The therapist can promote and reinforce the

experience by ensuring that all clients participate in early sessions so that there are specific opportunities for a response from other members.

3. *Altruism.* Many clients report that it was helpful for them to experience an opportunity to be of help to another group member. They may have offered support, made a helpful suggestion, or shared a similar problem. This process of altruism is a factor that is unique to the group setting. It reinforces self-esteem and helps to create a sense of self-worth.

These three supportive factors will emerge spontaneously early in group interaction. Universality promotes a sense of linkage and acceptance. Helping others encourages others to help you. All of these promote a sense of hope that change might be possible. These are the mechanisms by which the early group develops a sense of cohesion. Although these factors are particularly crucial early in a group's life, they continue to be important throughout. The parallels to the therapeutic alliance are obvious, as well as the unique nature these phenomena take in the group context.

Measures of the Alliance in Group Psychotherapy

There are a number of measurement instruments available to measure aspects of the group process that appear to be related to the concept of the therapeutic alliance. However, the great majority have been used in only a small number of studies. Two promising measures that may be used by the clinician are described in the following sections: the Group Cohesiveness Scale (for use by observers or the therapist) and the Group Climate Questionnaire (for group members).

GROUP COHESIVENESS SCALE

In the Group Cohesiveness Scale (Budman et al., 1987), the authors describe *cohesion* in these words:

> Cohesion is what keeps members coming to group; but, it is also what keeps members giving to one another under circumstances where for periods of time there may not be many clear or direct rewards for the givers except vicarious learning and the knowledge that they are helping others. Cohesion may also allow the members to sustain an involvement with the group,

even in the face of strong or frightening emotionality, such as confrontation and hostility. (p. 80)

This is an observer rating scale that uses global ratings on a 10-point scale (−5 to +5) consisting of six clinically relevant dimensions:

1. Withdrawal and self-absorption vs. interest and involvement
2. Mistrust vs. trust
3. Disruption vs. cooperation
4. Abusiveness vs. expressed caring
5. Unfocused vs. focused
6. Fragmentation vs. cohesion

The use of the scale has been limited, although acceptable interrater reliability has been reported and correlation with outcome demonstrated (Budman et al., 1989). Whether this should be considered a single dimension scale or whether it has the traditional bonding and working components remains to be seen. The ease of use makes this a convenient scale for observers to complete.

GROUP CLIMATE QUESTIONNAIRE—SHORT FORM (GCQ–S)

The GCQ–S (MacKenzie, 1983) has been used in a number of recent studies. It is a brief 12-item group climate scale that captures the perceptions of the members about their group on three independent dimensions. Items consist of clear behavioral descriptions with minimal need for inferential interpretations. The language is simple and nontechnical (see Figure 9.1). Experience has indicated that the group climate can shift considerably from session to session. Regular measurements are therefore important. Simply calculating a mean score across all sessions of a group would obscure important and clinically relevant shifts in climate as the group develops.

The scale descriptions are as follows.

1. *Engaged.* A positive working atmosphere. The scale encompasses general items reflecting Rogerian dimensions (Item 1) and group cohesion (Item 4), as well as psychological working concepts of cognitive understanding (Item 2), challenging each other (Item 8), and self-disclosure (Item 11). This scale is closely related to the working alliance from the individual psychotherapy literature. It also captures aspects of group cohesion and the supportive therapeutic factors.

2. *Conflict.* An atmosphere of anger and tension. This scale pulls together items reflecting a more negative group environment

Name:_____ Group: _____ Date:_____

Group Climate Questionnaire (GCQ-S)

Instructions: Read each statement carefully and try to think of the GROUP AS A WHOLE. Using the Rating Scale as a guide, circle the number of each statement that best describes the group during today's session. Please mark only ONE answer for each statement.	RATING SCALE 0 not at all 1 a little bit 2 somewhat 3 moderately 4 quite a bit 5 a great deal 6 extremely
1. The members liked and cared about each other	0 1 2 3 4 5 6
2. The members tried to understand why they do the things they do, tried to reason it out	0 1 2 3 4 5 6
3. The members avoided looking at important issues going on between themselves	0 1 2 3 4 5 6
4. The members felt what was happening was important and there was a sense of participation	0 1 2 3 4 5 6
5. The members depended upon the group leader(s) for direction	0 1 2 3 4 5 6
6. There was friction and anger between the members	0 1 2 3 4 5 6
7. The members were distant and withdrawn from each other	0 1 2 3 4 5 6
8. The members challenged and confronted each other in their efforts to sort things out	0 1 2 3 4 5 6
9. The members appeared to do things the way they thought would be acceptable to the group	0 1 2 3 4 5 6
10. The members rejected and distrusted each other	0 1 2 3 4 5 6
11. The members revealed sensitive personal information or feelings	1 2 3 4 5 6 7
12. The members appeared tense and anxious	0 1 2 3 4 5 6

Group Climate Questionnaire. "The Clinical Application of a Group Climate Measure," by K. R. Mackenzie, 1983, in R. R. Dies and K. R. Mackenzie, *Advances in Group Psychotherapy: Integrating Research and Practice*, New York: International Universities Press. Copyright 1983 by International Universities Press. Reprinted with permission.

with anger (Item 6), distancing (Item 7), distrust (Item 10), and tension (Item 12).

3. *Avoiding.* Avoidance of personal responsibility for group work. While the items differ somewhat in content, they all reflect ways by which the individual member might avoid

constructive involvement. Items include avoiding important issues between members (Item 3), depending on the leader (Item 5), and following group norms (Item 9).

No substantial correlation has been reported between the factors Engaged and Conflict, suggesting that an engaged group may also have higher levels of conflict. The GCQ–S has been quite widely used, with over 40 reports in the literature. It is a short and simple instrument that is completed in a couple of minutes and can be easily used in a sequential fashion to track a group over time without undue interference with the process.

A Model of Group Development

There is general agreement that it is useful to follow the development of psychotherapy over time. This has generally been done using the dose–effect concept of assessing the response of various types of presenting problems over time. The individual psychotherapy alliance literature has generally focused on tracking a single measure of the alliance. In contrast, as shown by the instruments previously described, the group literature has consistently used multidimensional measures of group climate. The shifting patterns between dimensions have been used to identify stages of development (MacKenzie, Dies, Coche, Rutan, & Stone, 1987).

A recent literature review supports a basic developmental sequence consisting of four stages: engagement, differentiation, interpersonal work, and termination (MacKenzie, 1994). More complex models have been presented, but empirical validation is limited. This simple model is particularly relevant to time-limited group psychotherapy with closed group membership where an excellent arena is provided in which to track group developmental phenomena. The following synopsis of the group developmental stages is accompanied by a description of how these are reflected in group climate measures. Of course, the clinician is in a position to be identifying the same phenomena as the group progresses.

ENGAGEMENT STAGE

The foremost task of the beginning group is to engage the members in the group process. Until the members appreciate that they are actively part of the group, group therapy is difficult. There are two basic mechanisms underlying this process of engagement. The first of these is the search for common issues and interests. This process of universality makes the group safer because the members have some means of relating comfortably to each other. The process is driven primarily by a desire to find similarities. The second process for the engagement stage is a recognition that the group is a special place that has its own features that make it different from outside situations. This is in a technical sense a firming of the group external boundary. The use of limited self-disclosure is essential for this process. This first stage tends to be leader-oriented, as the members seek guidance and support in how they should participate in the group. The Engaged scale of the GCQ typically rises rapidly during this stage, while the Conflict scale is low and the Avoiding scale relatively high.

The tasks of engagement are considered to have been met when there is a firm sense of commitment from all members and when each member has, at least to a limited extent, participated in the discussion with some degree of important self-disclosure. This stage is generally accompanied by a rapidly rising sense of group cohesion and individual self-esteem.

DIFFERENTIATION STAGE

The positive and collaborative atmosphere of the first stage is followed by a shift into a more negative and confrontational tone. Evidence of disagreements and potential conflict emerge. The underlying pressure driving this shift is the need for members to assert themselves as unique individuals. This stage counterbalances the commonality theme "we are all the same" characteristic of the first stage. For this reason, the second stage is called the *differentiation stage* (rather than the term *conflict stage* found in much of the small-group dynamics literature). The essential task of this stage is to develop patterns within the group for resolving tension and conflict when it emerges. This stage is characterized by a sharp increase in the Conflict scale and a gradual lowering of the Avoiding scale. The Engaged scale usually suffers an early decline followed by a gradual rise as the tensions are addressed.

At the same time, during this stage each member is also beginning to address aspects of self that may be problematic and associated with negative, angry, or shameful feelings. The intensity of the more challenging atmosphere eventually results in an increase in self-definition as members begin to sense themselves as more complex beings in the group. This stage is often, perhaps always, accompanied by a challenge to the group leader, which may be understood as the need for the collective membership to differentiate itself from the control of the leader.

INTERACTIONAL WORK STAGE

The group is now equipped to begin addressing problematic issues for each member in a more vigorous manner. The onus for initiation of group work shifts increasingly toward the members. Now, it is expected that this interactional process will be used to address more specifically the issues that each member has brought into the group. The capacity to be both supportive and confronting provides an environment in which interpersonal patterns can be identified and challenged. For the individual member, a parallel process of challenging self and being open to a more introspective process is triggered. Here the Engaged scale tends to be in the higher range with fluctuations around tension points. The Conflict scale will also fluctuate, but no longer necessarily in tandem with the Engaged Scale. Similarly, the group may go through periods of increased Avoiding.

The personal nature of this work increases the level of closeness among the members. This provides further opportunity to look at the nature of relationships. A growing sense of intimacy, sometimes of a romantic nature, brings the threat of possible rejection by people who have become quite close. Issues of self-esteem and trust are often central to this process. This will lead the members to become increasingly aware of issues of independence versus overinvolvement. Features related to dependency and control are central to this task. These interactional features will be explored to various depths, depending on the goals of the group, the time available, and the interactional capacity of the members.

TERMINATION STAGE

The final task for the group involves addressing the termination process. Although this is listed as the fourth stage, in fact, termination may occur at an earlier point in the group's development. For example, a crisis intervention group will remain in an engagement atmosphere throughout its course. Addressing termination issues is particularly central in time-limited group psychotherapy where the entire group ends together. As the group approaches termination, the Engaged scale typically rises, whereas those of Conflict and Avoiding decrease during the last few sessions.

A number of important issues are brought into sharp focus in the process of dealing with ending the group. Members may feel that they have not received as much time in the group as they would have liked. This is often reflected in a tone of resentment and anger and accompanied by a sense of being rejected or abandoned. They must address the ending of relationships that, although brief, may have become quite important for them. This triggers a sense of loss, which frequently contains echoes of previous grief. In addition, members must now face the necessity of managing for themselves. Thus, termination brings with it many existential themes of responsibility for self and dealing with loss that are all central to the maturational task. The intensity of the termination process will be related directly to the amount of time the members have spent together and the degree of interpersonal exchange.

Longer term groups with a gradual turnover of members do not show these clear-cut stages of development. However, they do go through a similar process of acceptance, testing, and reconsolidation with the addition of new members. One advantage of this slow-open type of group is that a working culture can be maintained by the continuing members. Shifts in climate dimensions will follow the tensions of membership change and points of greater stress that accompany psychotherapeutic work. As noted above, it is common for the Engaged and Conflict scales to be simultaneously high at these times. As in the individual psychotherapy literature, much of the psychotherapeutic work of the group centers around understanding and resolving these tensions.

Clinical Intervention Strategies to Foster and Maintain the Alliance

The primary early task for the group psychotherapist is to develop and maintain a cohesive and increasingly working group atmosphere. Careful considerations of group objectives and composition, as well as the establishment of the frame of the therapeutic experience, are central to this task. This requires the leader to think continuously of how the whole group is progressing and to be sure all members are part of this process. Once a sense of "groupness" has been developed, more attention can be directed toward the issues that individual members need to be addressing. A series of sequential strategies have been developed to assist this process, creating a semimanualized approach. The majority of these strategies focus on the pretherapy and early therapy experiences and strive to create an early positive group culture. The development of a cohesive interactional group provides a vehicle that can be used to deliver many types of psychotherapy, ranging through behavioral, cognitive, interpersonal, and psychodynamic models.

PREGROUP STRATEGIES

Closed Time-Limited Groups

A recent major group text (MacKenzie, 1997) is structured around the concepts of the generic model of psychotherapy, the common factor literature, and group development as a metaperspective on the whole group. This approach encourages the use of closed time-limited groups in part because of the increased possibilities for addressing common group phenomena as they emerge in accordance with the group development model. The format allows intentional reinforcement of stage-appropriate themes and the resulting recruitment process among the full membership. Because each stage emphasizes a different aspect of interactional behavior, this approach allows a systematic coverage of issues that are important to the psychotherapy task.

Homogeneity in Group Composition

A degree of homogeneity promotes rapid group cohesion in the engagement stage. This allows the group to move into differentiation issues at a relatively early point. However, homogeneity may interfere with more confrontational activity as clients reinforce their mutual blind spots, for example, interpersonal passivity. Conversely, it may enhance group members' ability to see the defenses of others, as is common in groups for substance abuse disorders. Most groups that are formed on the basis of a diagnostic condition, such as depression, will, nevertheless, still have considerable variation in interactional style to counterbalance the common features of the illness.

Assessment for Focus Areas

As in the individual psychotherapy literature, the focus during the assessment process is on the identification of important issues to be addressed (Piper & McCallum, 1994). For group psychotherapy, it is useful to connect these issues to aspects of interpersonal functioning, because the group context automatically brings with it the requirement to address interactional phenomena. This is true for all groups, even those that are not interpersonal or psychodynamic in nature. It is necessary to address group participation and interaction even in more structured approaches to ensure maximum learning.

A brief interpersonal inventory of key relationships should include the nature of early family relationships, including interactions with parents, siblings, and key extended family members, as well as current and previous intimate partners, and closest friends. From this assessment process, it is usually possible to establish focus areas, such as key toxic or supportive relationships, and the importance of specific events, such as separations or deaths. Major themes in these relationships can be outlined using core dimensions from the interpersonal literature, for example, positive or negative affiliation; control and submission balance; and under- or overinvolvement in relationships. In this assessment process, group members must identify the reciprocal roles of both participants in each relationship.

Pretherapy Preparation

Because many clients have concerns about participating in groups, the group psychotherapy literature has emphasized for many years the importance of systematic pretherapy preparation (Kaul & Bednar, 1994). This has also been identified as a helpful tactic in individual therapy, but historically it has been done in a more casual manner. A usual pregroup handout might include ideas about how groups can be helpful and how to get the most out of them. It would also identify specific group expectations such as confidentiality, attendance, contact with the therapist between sessions, and not attending under the influence of alcohol or drugs. Extragroup socializing between members constitutes another important aspect of the frame of therapy. For groups that will be focusing on intragroup process phenomena, a clear statement about the potential harm of socializing is called for, as well as a request that any socializing that does occur be reported back to the group. In groups that focus on social skills training, there may be encouragement for members to do things together as part of the group strategy. The goal of pretherapy preparation is to promote early group cohesion and to forestall early dropouts. This is commonly done with a descriptive handout to be discussed with the individual client or in larger programs with a structured group presentation. An example is provided in MacKenzie (1997).

These assessment tasks are conducted preferably over at least two individual sessions: the first to gain a general diagnostic opinion and to begin problem identification and provide general information about group therapy, and the second to finish pretherapy orientation and establish more formal focus areas.

EARLY GROUP STRATEGIES

Encouragement of Interactional Process

From the very beginning of the first session, the therapist will reinforce communication between members more than that with the therapist. This assists in the early development of group cohesion. It also mobilizes a sense of being included and accepted that can be a power-ful antidote to thoughts of early termination. Often simply breaking eye contact is enough to divert the member away from the leader. The therapist might refer to the pretherapy material by saying, "As we dis-cussed in our meetings, it is really helpful for members to talk with each other about these issues. I wondered if you were responding to John when you said that. Maybe you could address it directly to him." Through the early sessions the therapist is focusing primarily on devel-oping constructive group dynamics, not on individual pathology. The early sessions are typically filled with preliminary self-disclosures that are important more for the process of beginning to know each other than for detailed exploration. However, this process serves as a pow-erful vehicle for developing a sense of group cohesion.

Reinforcement of the Supportive Therapeutic Factors

The supportive factors of universality, acceptance, and altruism almost always automatically emerge quite early in the group's life, usually early in the first session. The therapist is in a position to subtly but knowledgeably reinforce these during the first few sessions. They are the group mechanisms by which cohesion is formed. They can be underlined at any point in the group's life when tension or conflict poses a challenge to group integrity. The therapist can facilitate cohe-sion by reinforcing the supportive factors using low-tech interventions such as: and "It sounds like you have been having the same sort of problems as Mary" (universality); "It sounded like you were surprised that others thought your experiences were worth hearing about" (acceptance); and "What's it like to hear Jennifer say what you had to say was quite helpful for her?" (altruism).

Regular Debriefing Concerning the Group Process

It is useful for the therapist to regularly and directly inquire about how the members are reacting to the group environment. This is particu-larly important during and at the end of the first session, but is use-fully continued through several early sessions and at any point where higher levels of tension are evident. In the early sessions, any revela-tion of major events or of strong affect is usefully addressed immedi-ately in terms of its impact on the individual and the group. This might include information such as the death or loss of an intimate partner or family member, tears related to a sense of hopelessness, or states of heightened anxiety. The intent is not to work through the issues, but to make sure that the process of self-revelation is safe. For example, the therapist may say "That sounded like an awful experience for you.

What has it been like sharing it with the group?" Or "What Henry was talking about is something others might have been through. Can anyone share their experiences with him?" These sorts of interventions assist the creation of an interactive working group environment from the first few minutes of the first session onward.

A good general principle is to regularly debrief before the session ends following any powerful incident. This is true whether the event is basically positive, such as a sharing of grief themes, or more challenging, such as a disagreement or negative reaction between members. Calmly encouraging members to talk about the process of expressing such material provides a modeling of learning to address affect-laden material openly and directly. Groups have the capacity to elicit strong affective responses within their members that are frequently a clue to major underlying issues. Often these reactions are connected with critical or shameful self-concepts. The member may go home and ruminate on what the group members or the leader must think of them for talking about such issues. The opportunity to get a response from others usually results in a normalizing and sharing process that deepens the group experience. The therapist can be quite straightforward about this process: "It is really important that when anyone in the group talks about something quite sensitive they get a chance to hear how it sounds to others. Anna has just talked about some very troubling experiences. Who would like to respond to her?" Such debriefing interventions are designed to prevent sudden termination over an issue that, although the source of tension or anxiety, may be quite important and workable. Loss of group members, particularly under adverse circumstances, is frequently reflected in a drop of group morale and a negative experience for the individual.

Early Presentation of Focus Areas

A very useful technique is to specifically incorporate into the early group process the focus area discussions that have taken place with each member individually. A double sequence is quite helpful. In the first session, immediately after the initial round of introductions, the members can be encouraged to introduce themselves in more detail by talking about the pretherapy discussions and the issues that they believe they need to address during the group experience. This process is couched in relatively cognitive terms that are not too threatening. The goal is to have most issues placed on the table by the end of the first session. The process of identifying key issues can then be reinforced by circulating written focus area sheets at the end of the first session, which are prepared by the therapist on the basis of the mutual discussion in the assessment interviews. Members are asked to consider these sheets and bring them back to the second session with their comments. Are they a good representation of what was talked about? Have some things been missed? Are there additional issues to add? This double-focusing structure creates a situation in which the early group therapeutic factors of Universality and Acceptance are enacted around working themes beginning in the first session.

Some examples of issues that might be included on a focus area sheet follow (see numbered list). These are drawn from the members of an intensive time-limited antidepression psychotherapy group:

1. You find yourself experiencing a lot of emotion around your relationship with your father. This emerges with a strong sense of disappointment and anger and an underlying wish that it could be better even though you doubt that it can change much. However, you do see him as shifting somewhat in his desire to be closer, but this creates a difficult resentful response in you. Exploring these issues in the group might be quite helpful.

2. You describe your episode of depression as being associated with the breakdown in an intimate relationship with a woman. This seems to have occurred in circumstances where you have not been able to understand why it happened, and you wonder if it has something to do with how alert you are to what your partner is thinking. This pattern has occurred before, so it seems important to sort it out because it has led you to avoid further relationships. The group will be a good opportunity to investigate these issues.

3. The death of your grandmother last summer was a significant loss. It appeared, as you described the circumstances, that you had not really had an opportunity to mourn her passing. This seems important, since she was an important supportive figure throughout your life, as your parents were not available to you.

4. You state that it would be useful to address your tendency to be very self-critical. You have a sense that you quit easily and do not live up to some standard, and you wonder if this is another issue involving your relationship with your father. This pattern seems connected to issues around having a low sense of self-esteem and how you might protect yourself from these negative thoughts.

These early group strategies are designed to promote a rapid development of group cohesion with a working focus. Thus, the group members themselves become the agents for maintaining a working alliance. The therapist is able to assist by using the modest structural techniques noted previously and by continuously reinforcing intermember discussion. The natural early group need to become a member of the group and to experience the group as a safe and supporting environment is harnessed in the service of also promoting rapid immersion in key targeted focus areas.

MIDGROUP STRATEGIES

Promotion of the Shift Into the Differentiation Climate

The early sessions of a therapy group are usually characterized by a positive and accepting climate that is important in beginning to address a demoralized or self-critical state. As the group shifts into a more confrontational style, they risk undoing earlier work. The therapist is in a position to judge whether a particular group should simply manage this shift or address the personal issues involved.

In groups with a more cognitive–behavioral than process–learning focus (e.g., a group for panic disorders), the therapist may choose to dampen exploration of intermember or leader tensions in the service of the goals of the group. This may be handled by acknowledgment that group work can be difficult, but that it is important, just as one might do with similar situations in an administrative meeting.

If the group is designed for interpersonal learning, then the therapist may actively promote the differentiation process and even model it. "It sounds like there is some tension around how much direction I am providing for the group. I wonder if this is something that needs to be explored further. What has it been like for you over the last few sessions here with me?"

During this stage regular debriefing interventions are helpful to acknowledge the tension and see it as something that is important to the success of therapy, a sign of progress and not of difficulty.

> People have been addressing some pretty upsetting issues today. How has that been? You will probably find yourselves thinking about these matters over the week. How can you best do this? Would writing in your journal be helpful? Is there someone you can talk with who can understand? How would you like to continue this important work next session?

Monitoring Nature of Negative Feedback

As the group moves into more active interpersonal work, the meaning of the relationships established within the group is subject to greater scrutiny. This can be a powerful learning process, but the therapist needs to be aware of the potential for negative therapeutic events. These usually center on extended criticism or an attitude of nonacceptance or outright rejection. The therapist has a specific responsibility to ensure that no member is harmed by the experience and must be prepared to intervene at an early point if uncharitable or dismissing interactions occur. This may happen as part of the differentiation stage in which projective mechanisms may lead to the possibility of scapegoating. In one session, a man found himself blurting out that he thought the way a woman was talking showed just how much she just had to dominate the group. She responded resentfully that no one ever paid enough attention to the pain she was experiencing. The therapist moved in relatively soon to wonder what the other members thought about what was being discussed. Both of the central figures received support for being forthright in addressing such things, but they also were told that it looked like both of them were overreacting and might need to look at what other issues were going on. This led to a major period of deepening exploration for the two of them. The process also served as a model for other group members to begin questioning aspects of themselves that were held in a negative light.

This issue of negative interactions among group members is a parallel to recognizing negative countertransference reactions from the therapist in the individual alliance literature. The group context offers somewhat less control and more likelihood of this occurring, and therefore, the emphasis is on therapist vigilance that no enduring harm results. A particularly dangerous situation is where the therapist colludes with some members in a prolonged scapegoating process focused on one member.

Midpoint Review of Focus Areas

At the midpoint of the group (i.e., Session 8 of a 16-session group), the therapist makes a clear statement of the time line. The focus areas outlined at the beginning are reviewed with each member in the session. If these were provided in a printed form, that form may be recirculated to each member. It is assumed that the therapist will have been keeping these areas in mind throughout the group and encouraging reference to them, but this provides a structured opportunity for a formal review. During the second half of the group, there is a consistent reference to these areas and expectation of more intense, personally oriented work using the group for feedback, stimulation, and application. Time-limited groups spend their first half developing an interactional working atmosphere, then throughout the second half must begin to deal with termination. The continual focusing ensures the maintenance of an alliance that gives the group experience a sense of heightened relevance for the members.

The midgroup strategies are designed to maintain an active working focus while promoting the use of the group interactional environment. The efforts of the therapist to maintain a focus on important issues for each member is a challenging one because of the numbers of members involved. Much of this work, however, is managed among the members themselves, and efforts in the early group to develop an interactive working alliance will have major payoff at this point. A slippage in the sense of active engagement would be an important sign to address group resistance and refocus the work. This is, of course, to be expected because resistance reflects that difficult issues are being addressed.

TERMINATION STRATEGIES

Predicting Termination Stress

Many clients presenting for group psychotherapy have difficulties with attachment issues and may be particularly sensitive to loss situations. As the group approaches termination, such reactions may be quite powerfully activated. The therapist must be sure that these reactions do not go underground. One common phenomenon is for a member to consider leaving the group early, so as to avoid saying goodbye. It is useful, therefore, for the therapist to raise this possibility a few sessions from the end and explore such thoughts among the members. "Dealing with endings is often not easy to contemplate. Sometimes it might seem easier just to not come for the final sessions. But the group started together and it's important that we all end together. Who has had these sorts of thoughts?"

Systematic Focus on Termination Themes

The final four sessions of a group that has been meeting for several months need to be viewed primarily through the lens of termination (MacKenzie, 1996). Predictable themes will involve not getting enough treatment, facing loss, assuming responsibility for oneself, as well as the attendant anger or resentment that may accompany these. This provides an opportunity to address powerful existential issues of maturation: "Can you say some more about the anger you feel about the group not continuing, your feeling that you are not getting all you want from therapy?" Or "It sounds like it is important to say some more about how difficult it was for you when your mother died. Perhaps there is some grieving yet to be done around that very powerful human experience. It fits in some ways with also addressing how to master the fact that the group will also be ending soon." And "How is it going to be in two weeks when there is no group on Tuesday evenings? What will it be like to be on your own again?"

The therapist will usually need to be persistent in bringing the group back to these issues. These themes are always encountered as a cohesive group faces termination. By addressing them openly and promoting an exploration of the meaning they have for the members, the therapist is aligning with and promoting the final group task. This continues the evolution of the working alliance as it shifts in its focus between group developmental stages.

Structured Good-Byes in the Final Session

Many therapists find it useful to have a structured go-around of final statements of each member to each of the others. This ritual binds some of the anxiety, while still addressing termination as a real and final event. This can be outlined in the second-to-last session as a task for the final session. Members are encouraged to reflect seriously on their experience with each member in turn. This almost always results in powerful messages of affirmation and support for continuing the work begun in the group after it ends. It thus supports the continuation of an internalized working alliance despite the absence of the group.

Follow-Up Session

There are some advantages to scheduling an individual follow-up session 3 or 4 months after the group ends. Outcome data indicate that improvement usually continues for several months after therapy ends. A follow-up interview to "touch base" reinforces motivation to keep working on issues. It also provides the therapist with an opportunity to assess the need for further treatment if indicated.

The termination strategies are designed to maximize the core themes mobilized around termination. Many clients seeking psychotherapy are dealing in part with issues of loss or grief. The strategies are designed to shift but maintain a working alliance to the very end of the last session.

Summary

The concept of the therapeutic alliance can be usefully applied to the group context. However, the complexity of the group system requires some significant adjustments to deal with the additional levels of organization and perspective. The group process literature is still at a relatively early stage of development. However, there is support for the use of a small number of interactional dimensions that form complex patterns of how successful and unsuccessful groups develop over time.

This perspective is of direct value to the clinician in identifying negative indicators that will place stress on the alliance. A series of specific intervention strategies pertinent to each stage of the group is described. By tracking the group climate in this manner, the therapist is simultaneously providing important therapeutic opportunities for the individual members, as well as reinforcing a sense of the working alliance. This material is particularly geared toward application in closed time-limited psychotherapy groups.

References

Bednar, R. L., & Kaul, T. J. (1994). Experiential group research: Can the canon fire? In A. E. Bergin & S. L. Garfield (Eds.), *Handbook of psychotherapy and behavior change* (4th ed., pp. 631–663) New York: Wiley.

Budman, S. H., Demby, A., Feldstein, M., Redondo, J., Scherz, B., Bennett, M. J., Koppenaal, G., Daley, B. S., Hunter, M., & Ellis, J. (1987). Preliminary findings on a new instrument to measure cohesion in group psychotherapy. *International Journal of Group Psychotherapy, 37,* 75–94.

Budman, S. H., Soldz, S., Demby, A., Feldstein, M., Springer, T., & Davis, S. (1989). Cohesion, alliance and outcome in group psychotherapy. *Psychiatry, 52,* 339–350.

Butler, T., & Fuhriman, A. (1983). Curative factors in group therapy: A review of the recent literature. *Small Group Behavior, 14,* 131–142.

Corsini, R., & Rosenberg, B. (1955). Mechanisms of group psychotherapy: Processes and dynamics. *Journal of Abnormal and Social Psychology, 51,* 406–411.

Crouch, E. C., Bloch, S., & Wanless, J. (1994). Therapeutic factors: Interpersonal and intrapersonal mechanisms. In A. Fuhriman & G. M. Burlingame (Eds.), *Handbook of group psychotherapy: An empirical and clinical synthesis* (pp. 269–315). New York: Wiley.

Dierick, P., & Lietaer, G. (1990). Therapeutic factors in group psychotherapy and growth groups: An exploratory study on member and therapist perceptions. In G. Lietaer, J. Rombauts, & R. van Balen (Eds.), *Client-centered and experiential psychotherapy in the nineties* (pp. 1–23). Leuven, Belgium: Leuven University Press.

Drescher, S., Burlingame, G., & Fuhriman, A. (1985). Cohesion: An odyssey in empirical understanding. *Small Group Behavior, 16,* 3–30.

Fuhriman, A., & Barlow, S. J. (1983). Cohesion: Relationship in group therapy. In M. J. Lambert (Ed.), *Psychotherapy and patient relationships* (pp. 263–289). Homewood, IL: Dow-Jones-Irwin.

Kaul, T. J., Bednar, R. L. (1994). Pretaining and structure: Parallel lines yet to meet. In A. Fuhriman & G. M. Burlingame (Eds.), *Handbook of group psychotherapy: An empirical and clinical synthesis* (pp. 155–188). New York: Wiley.

Mackenzie, K. R. (1983). The clinical application of a group climate measure. In R. R. Dies & K. R. MacKenzie (Eds.), *Advances in group psychotherapy: Integrating research and practice* (pp. 101–116). New York: International Universities Press.

MacKenzie, K. R. (1990). *Introduction to time-limited group psychotherapy.* Washington, DC: American Psychiatric Press.

MacKenzie, K. R. (1994). Group development. In A. Fuhriman & G. M. Burlingame (Eds.), *Handbook of group psychotherapy: An empirical and clinical synthesis* (pp. 223–268). New York: Wiley.

MacKenzie, K. R. (1996). Time-limited group psychotherapy (Special section: Termination in group therapy). *International Journal of Group Psychotherapy, 46,* 41–60.

MacKenzie, K. R. (1997). *Time-managed group psychotherapy: Effective clinical applications.* Washington, DC: American Psychiatric Press.

MacKenzie, K. R., Dies, R. R., Coche, E., Rutan, J. S., & Stone, W. S. (1987). An analysis of AGPA institute groups. *International Journal of Group Psychotherapy, 37,* 55–74.

MacKenzie, K. R., & Tschuschke, V. (1993). Relatedness, group work, and outcome in long-term inpatient psychotherapy groups. *The Journal of Psychotherapy Practice and Research, 2,* 147–156.

Mudrack, P. E. (1989). Defining group cohesiveness: A legacy of confusion? *Small Group Behavior, 20,* 37–49.

Piper, W. E., & Joyce, A. S. (1996). A consideration of factors influencing the utilization of time-limited, short-term group therapy. *International Journal of Group Psychotherapy, 46,* 311–328.

Piper, W. E., Marrache, M., Lacroix, R., Richardsen, A. M., & Jones, B. D. (1983). Cohesion as a basic bond in groups. *Human Relations, 36,* 93–108.

Piper, W. E., & McCallum, M. (1994). Selection of patients for group interventions. In H. S. Bernard & K. R. MacKenzie (Eds.), *Basics of group psychotherapy* (1st ed., pp. 1–34). New York: Guilford Press.

Shaughnessy, P., & Kivlighan, D. M. (1995). Using group participants' perceptions of therapeutic factors to form client typologies. *Small Group Research, 26,* 250–268.

Yalom, I. D. (1995). *Theory and practice of group psychotherapy* (4th ed.). New York: Basic Books. (Original work published 1970)

ance in
herapy:
ıl Principles

10

array of both common
eptualization and man-
ce in short-term psy-
ımmarize some of the
reading of these chap-
ıerging from our own
he therapeutic alliance,
ıg some of the principles
ıination issues in short-

General Principles

Because of the constraints of short-term therapy, patient selection is particularly important. A number of contributors to this book (e.g., Binder, chapter 3; Newman, chapter 5; Watson & Greenberg, chapter 6) emphasize the importance of selecting patients who are at a relatively high level of interpersonal functioning. When time is limited, it is critical to be able to establish an adequate therapeutic alliance reasonably early. Thus, patients who are seriously impaired in their fundamental capacity to trust other people are more likely to benefit from a longer term treatment, in which the establishment of a therapeutic alliance can become the work of the therapy, rather than a precondition for treatment. MacKenzie (chapter 9) adds another important consideration from a group perspective in suggesting that patients should be selected in terms of homogeneity with respect to important dimensions (e.g., diagnostic conditions such as depression) in order to maximize group cohesiveness.

Facilitate the development of the bond aspect of the therapeutic alliance by conveying warmth, respect, and genuine interest. Although attention to the bond aspect of the therapeutic alliance is important in all forms of therapy, it is particularly important in brief therapies, which are likely to place strains upon the patient–therapist relationship because of the high level of activity and the relatively short time frame. Binder (chapter 3) emphasizes the importance of conveying respect and warm interest in patients and of treating them as "co-equal collaborators." Newman (chapter 5) suggests that cognitive therapists should strive to be "part Marcus Welby and part Sherlock Holmes" (i.e., combine an attitude of warm benevolence with one of systematic, critical thinking). Watson and Greenberg (chapter 6) emphasize that the establishment of safety and trust is critical in order to allow patients to engage in the task of turning attention inward to symbolize experience in new and safe ways.

Outline the therapeutic rationale (including tasks and goals) at the beginning of treatment. Explicitly educating patients about the therapeutic rationale is conventionally more common in the cognitive behavioral tradition than it is in other approaches. This is consistent with the psychoeducational dimension of this approach (Newman, chapter 5). Because the rapid establishment of a therapeutic alliance is a priority in short-term therapy, however, the explicit discussion of therapeutic tasks and goals at the outset can be particularly important (e.g., Been & Winston, chapter 2; Watson & Greenberg, chapter 6). In longer term therapies, the ongoing negotiation of therapeutic tasks and goals is a central part of the therapeutic process. Although this is true to some extent in short-term therapy, a clear lack of fit at the outset between the therapeutic rationale and the patient's sensibilities may be grounds for trying a different therapeutic modality. In some cases, a patient's skepticism about the therapeutic rationale may reflect a more general and fundamental skepticism that may make it difficult to establish a therapeutic alliance in a short period of time. In such cases, long-term treatment may be indicated.

Establish realistic goals. Whether the therapeutic goals are framed in terms of specific target problems (as is more common in the cognitive–behavioral approach) or in terms of more general capacities (e.g., the ability to self-observe), it is critical to establish limited and realistic goals (e.g., Newman, chapter 5; Watson & Greenberg, chapter 6). Coyne and Pepper (chapter 7) add that from a strategic perspective it can be useful to work toward specific, small changes in behavior in order to ultimately instigate change of a more general nature. Limiting one's therapeutic ambitions can be as difficult for therapists as it is for patients; the ability to do so can require a fundamental change in attitude for therapists who are more accustomed to practicing long-term therapy. Furthermore, even when limited and realistic goals have been agreed upon, it is highly likely that patients will experience some degree of disappointment and resentment when the reality of this limitation is experienced at termination (e.g., Been & Winston, chapter 2, and MacKenzie, chapter 9). It is thus critical for the therapist to be prepared to process whatever painful and negative feelings that emerge about termination in a nondefensive fashion.

As therapy proceeds, be prepared to educate or remind patients about the purpose or function of therapeutic tasks that do not make sense to them. Whether the task consists of speaking to an empty chair (as in Gestalt therapy), trying an experiment between sessions, or exploring the therapeutic relationship in the here and now, outlining or reminding the patient of the underlying rationale can play an important role in developing and maintaining a therapeutic alliance (e.g., Watson & Greenberg, chapter, 6; Been & Winston, chapter 2). This is particularly important when the relevance of the task to the patient's problem is not immediately apparent to him or her or when the task is anxiety provoking.

Establish and maintain a therapeutic focus. Different approaches tend to do this in different ways. Short-term dynamic approaches tend to emphasize the importance of case formulation. Binder (chapter 3), for example, emphasizes the importance of making proplan interpretations, that is, interpretations that are likely to disconfirm patients' pathogenic beliefs. Cognitive–behavioral approaches (e.g., Newman, chapter, 5) tend to emphasize the importance of working collaboratively with patients to establish therapeutic agendas. Watson and Greenberg (chapter 6) emphasize the importance of attending to the live, poignant aspects of patients' experience in order to help illuminate their inner tracks. Been and Winston (chapter 2) emphasize that although it is important to establish a focus, it is also important to be attuned to rapid shifts in the dynamic issue that is salient in a given session.

Maintain a balance between activity and receptivity. Because short-term therapies tend to be relatively active, it can be easy to misattune to the patient's fluctuating needs and experience, thereby jeopardizing the therapeutic alliance. On the other hand, failure to be sufficiently active with the patient can lead to a lack of therapeutic focus and a subsequent deterioration in the alliance. Been and Winston (chapter 2) emphasize that the consistent confrontation of defenses must be balanced with the reduction of pressure when the alliance is strained.

Watson and Greenberg (chapter 6) emphasize the importance of balancing the directiveness characteristic of Gestalt therapy and process–experiential work with adequate responsiveness to patients' moment-by-moment experiences.

Where possible, minimize the enactment of vicious cycles. Strategic therapists (e.g., Coyne & Pepper, chapter 7) suggest that therapists can establish an alliance by avoiding others' problem-maintaining solutions. Psychodynamically oriented therapists speak about the importance of minimizing transference and countertransference enactments. As Binder (chapter 3) points out, it is inevitable that therapists will be recruited into the countertransferential roles associated with the patient's salient maladaptive interpersonal patterns. In long-term therapy, therapists have more time within which to disembed themselves from these enactments. Short-term treatment places greater pressure on therapists to be alert to these patterns and to avoid them when possible. It is critical to recognize, however, that such enactments are inevitable, and that in fact, the belief that one can avoid them can make it more difficult to recognize them when they occur.

Alliance ruptures must be detected early on and addressed. Most contributors to this volume emphasize the importance of detecting and addressing problems in the therapeutic alliance. Binder (chapter 3) maintains that it is critical for the therapist to pick up on subtle patient communications about problems in the alliance and also on disguised allusions to the therapeutic relationship. Although he agrees with interpersonal and relational theorists who theorize that transference and countertransference enactments are an inevitable part of therapy, he believes that in short-term therapy, it is crucial for therapists to minimize the amount of time participating in these enactments and to establish the examination of these enactments when they occur as the first priority. Consistent with a relational perspective, he emphasizes the importance of recognizing the therapist's contribution to the rupture and the importance of acknowledging this contribution to the patient when appropriate. Been and Winston (chapter 2) maintain that it is critical for therapists to be sensitive to patients' communications about therapist errors and not to interpret patients' experience in such cases as fantasies about the therapist or as transference. Kohlenberg, Yeater, and Kohlenberg (chapter 4) maintain that problems in the therapeutic relationship may be functionally similar to problematic interpersonal patterns that are characteristic for the patient. Consistent with a central thrust of psychoanalytic thinking, they emphasize the valuable opportunity that alliance ruptures present for providing patients with a corrective interpersonal experience. Watson and Greenberg (chapter 6) suggest that therapists should be particularly alert to difficulties patients may have in engaging in various tasks and should be careful not to coerce them. They emphasize the value of therapeutic metacommunication, both for purposes of negotiating agreement about tasks and goals and for illuminating characteristic patient patterns that may be contributing to misunderstandings. Finally, MacKenzie (chapter 9) highlights the complexity of the group setting by pointing out the importance of exploring and negotiating conflict between group members, as well as between group members and the therapist. From his perspective, the emergence of conflict between group members is a characteristic of the differentiation stage of group development, and the management of group conflict is an important change process.

Be aware of the types of alliance ruptures characteristic of particular approaches. Different therapeutic approaches emphasize different therapeutic tasks and goals, which are likely to be associated with different characteristic strains upon the alliance. Newman (chapter 5) points out that patients in cognitive therapy may perceive the therapist as "Pollyannaish" or patronizing, rather than optimistic or energizing, and he emphasizes the importance of being sensitive to this possibility. He also suggests the importance of being alert to struggles over control that may be emerging in response to the active and prescriptive nature of the approach. Watson and Greenberg (chapter 6) maintain that patients in person-centered therapy may feel particularly frustrated at the nondirective aspect of the approach, especially in the context of time-limited therapy. Been and Winston (chapter 2) note that brief psychodynamic approaches that emphasize the repeated confrontation of defenses and consistent pressure to experience underlying affect put particular strains on the alliance. High levels of therapist activity, they note, are by their very nature intrusive. They emphasize the importance of repeatedly reminding patients about goals that have been agreed upon and of processing alliance ruptures when they emerge. In general, it seems important to be aware of and prepared to acknowledge patients' realistic perceptions of problematic features of the approach, while at the same time, being prepared to explore the idiosyncratic meaning of these features for patients (e.g., Binder, chapter 3; Kohlenberg, Yeater, & Kohlenberg, chapter 4).

Be aware of the multiple alliances within a system. From different perspectives, both MacKenzie (chapter 9) and Rait (chapter 8) emphasize the importance of recognizing the multiple alliances within systems. In groups, therapists need to be concerned both with their alliance to the group and the alliances among members of the group (group cohesion). MacKenzie gives priority to the promotion of group cohesiveness, through the use of interventions such as promoting dialogue between members of the group rather than with the therapist. Rait discusses different perspectives on the establishment of the alliance with couples and families. Some systemic therapists emphasize the importance of maintaining an equidistant position from members of the system and a stance of neutrality. Others emphasize the importance of joining with different parts of the system at different times in order to shift the functioning of the system. The second perspective views the alliance as dynamic and shifting in nature and as a potent mechanism of change in and of itself.

Prepare patients for termination and explore its meaning for them. Preparing for and dealing with the meaning of the time limit is a central feature of all short-term therapy approaches. Been and Winston (chapter 2) follow Mann in suggesting that the constraints of brief therapy heighten the universal conflicts surrounding the repetitive separation crises experienced throughout life. MacKenzie (chapter 9) devotes the last few sessions of time-limited group therapy to processing predictable themes emerging around termination, such as feelings of not getting enough from therapy, facing loss, assuming responsibility for the self, and attendant feelings of anger and resentment. Newman (chapter 5) describes two extreme patient styles of dealing with the time limit. One extreme involves failing to invest in the therapy and to form a solid alliance because of the fear of loss and abandonment. The other involves throwing oneself into the treatment and the therapeutic relationship and then responding with intense grief or resentment, which if not dealt with adequately can jeopardize the alliance and the treatment. Kohlenberg, Yeater, and Kohlenberg (chapter 4) emphasize the importance of exploring the idiosyncratic meaning of termination for patients and responding accordingly. They suggest, for example, that for one patient, processing the meaning of an unchangeable time limit may be therapeutic, whereas for another, extending the termination date in response to his or her request may be therapeutic.

Termination in short-term therapy can be thought of as the ultimate rupture of the therapeutic alliance. It is inevitable that patients will have intense, conflicting feelings around termination: feelings of gratitude mixed with feelings of loss, disappointment, and resentment. If the therapeutic alliance is solid enough, these feelings can be tolerated and accepted by the therapist and processed in a fashion that allows the patient to come to terms with the meaning of termination. This process can help patients come to accept both the validity of their needs for help and support and the reality of the limitations of the therapeutic frame, without invalidating their own needs or devaluing what the therapist can offer. If, however, therapists become threatened by patients' needs and intense feelings around termination, they are likely to respond defensively by attempting to reassure them about the value of therapy or by blaming them for not benefiting. This can take a severe toll upon the therapeutic relationship and interfere with the opportunity to make constructive use of the termination.

In previous articles, we have explicated a model, emerging from our ongoing research program, that captures the stages that are typically involved in resolving ruptures in the therapeutic alliance (Safran & Muran, 1995, 1996, in press; Safran, Crocker, McMain, & Murray, 1990; Safran, Muran, & Samstag, 1994). This model can easily be adapted to clarify some of the processes involved in resolving tensions in the therapeutic relationship that emerge around termination in short-term therapy as well. The model consists of four stages: attending to the rupture, exploration of the rupture experience, exploration of the avoidance, and self-assertion or expression of the underlying wish. Each of these stages consists of a combination of patient states and therapist interventions that facilitate the transition between states (see Figure 10.1).

Stage 1 begins with the patient state (P1) involving a verbalization or action that indicates the presence of a rupture in the alliance. There are two major subtypes of ruptures: confrontation and withdrawal. In confrontation ruptures, the patient directly expresses anger, resentment, or dissatisfaction with the therapist or some aspect of the therapy. For example, the patient says, "We only have four sessions left, and we're not getting anywhere" or " I need more direction from you." In withdrawal markers, the patient withdraws or partially disengages from the therapist, his or her own emotions, or some aspect of the therapeutic process. For example, a patient may give up as therapy approaches termination, and she feels that she has gotten what she hoped for. She may not say anything directly, but the therapist may have an intuitive sense that she has withdrawn her investment in the treatment.

Confrontation and withdrawal ruptures reflect different ways of coping with the dialectical tension between the needs for agency and relatedness. In confrontation ruptures, the patient negotiates the conflict by favoring the need for agency or self-definition over the need for relatedness. In withdrawal ruptures, he or she strives for relatedness at the cost of the need for agency or self-definition. Different patients are likely to experience or exhibit a predominance of one type of rupture marker over another, and this reflects different characteristic styles of coping or adaptation. Nevertheless, over the course of treatment, both types of markers may emerge with a specific patient, or a specific impasse may involve both confrontation and withdrawal features. Thus it is critical for therapists to be sensitive to the specific qualities of the rupture that are emerging in the moment, rather than to become locked into viewing patients as exclusively confrontation types or exclusively withdrawal types. It is also important to recognize that these ruptures mark that both patient and therapist are embed-

FIGURE 10.1

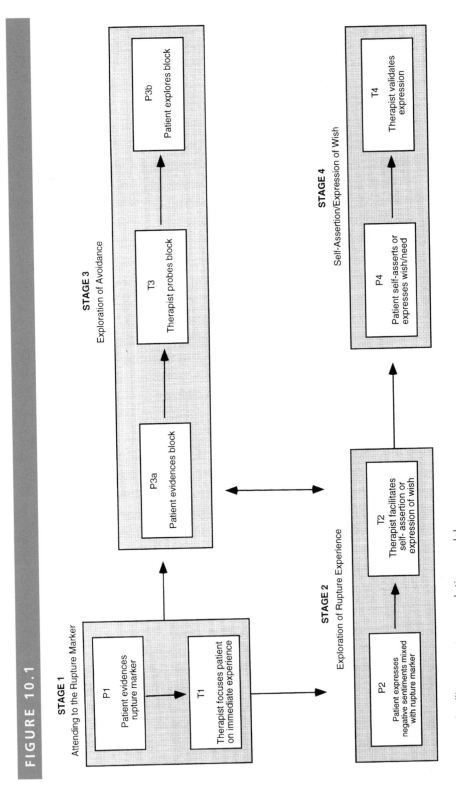

STAGE 1
Attending to the Rupture Marker

P1
Patient evidences rupture marker

T1
Therapist focuses patient on immediate experience

STAGE 2
Exploration of Rupture Experience

P2
Patient expresses negative sentiments mixed with rupture marker

T2
Therapist facilitates self- assertion or expression of wish

STAGE 3
Exploration of Avoidance

P3a
Patient evidences block

T3
Therapist probes block

P3b
Patient explores block

STAGE 4
Self-Assertion/Expression of Wish

P4
Patient self-asserts or expresses wish/need

T4
Therapist validates expression

Therapeutic alliance rupture resolution model.

ded or hooked in an enactment of a vicious cycle. Thus, it is critical for therapists to become mindful of their contributions to the cycle that is being enacted and to be open to exploring them at any point along the way.

Completing Stage 1, the first therapist intervention (T1) facilitates the exploration of the rupture by directing the patient's attention to the here and now of the therapeutic relationship or to his or her experience. Such a facilitative intervention reflects the therapist's openness and ability to unhook from a vicious cycle. Common examples are statements such as, "What are you experiencing?" or "I have a sense of you withdrawing from me" or "How are you feeling about what's going on between us right now?" Alternatively, the therapist may directly inquire how the patient is feeling about termination. This intervention leads to two parallel pathways of exploration. The first involves the exploration of thoughts and feelings around termination. For example, a desire to extend the treatment beyond the termination date or resentment and disappointment that more changes have not taken place. The second pathway involves the internal processes that block the exploration of feelings and thoughts about termination.

The first pathway can be subdivided into two successive stages (Stages 2 and 4). In the first of these (Stage 2), the patient begins to express thoughts and feelings about termination, but these are mixed with features of the initial rupture marker (either withdrawal or confrontation). In the case of withdrawal features, the patient begins to express negative sentiments or an underlying wish, and then qualifies the statement or takes it back. For example, "Sometimes I begin to feel a little upset with you because I haven't changed more, but I know you've done the best you can." Or "The thought occurred to me to ask for more sessions, but I think that would just be dependency." In the case of confrontation features, the patient expresses his or her feelings in a blaming and belittling way, rather than taking responsibility for them. This patient state should be followed by a therapist intervention (T2) that facilitates self-assertion or the expression of the underlying wish, through acknowledging his or her own contributions to the interaction, refocusing on the here and now of the therapeutic relationship, or the use of an awareness experiment. Examples of acknowledging one's own contribution are as follows: A patient accurately points out that the therapist had been trying to point out therapeutic gains to him rather than hearing about his disappointment, and the therapist acknowledges this. In another example, the therapist says, "You deserve to have somebody be there for you in a consistent fashion over time, and a right to be angry at me for abandoning you." In refocusing on the here and now of the therapeutic relationship, the therapist points out a tendency on the patient's part to diffuse the tension by speaking in general terms. In an awareness experiment, the therapist suggests that the patient should experiment with directly expressing the feelings that are being avoided and attend to whatever feelings are evoked. If the experiment is successful, the patient's evoked feelings will deepen his or her awareness and acknowledgement of the avoided experience. For example, the patient says, "Sometimes I feel a little upset when I stop to think that you won't be here for me, . . . but it's not a big deal." The therapist responds by saying, "Are you willing to experiment with saying 'I'm pissed off at you for abandoning me' just to see how it feels?" The patient tries the experiment, and subsequently begins to contact some of the anger and sadness he was having difficulty acknowledging.

The second pathway or Stage 3 involves the exploration of beliefs, expectations, and other internal processes that inhibit the acknowledgement and expression of feelings and needs associated with the rupture experience. There are two major subtypes of blocks (P3). The first subtype consists of thoughts, beliefs, and expectations about the other (the therapist) that block the exploration of the rupture experience pathway. For example, the patient who expects expressions of anger to evoke retaliation will have difficulty acknowledging and expressing angry feelings. The patient who believes that expressions of vulnerability and need will result in abandonment will have difficulty expressing such feelings. The second subtype consists of self-critical or self-doubting processes that function to block the acknowledgment or the exploration of the rupture experience pathway. For example, a patient who believes she is childish for feeling sad about the termination of therapy will not be able to explore her feelings of sadness. The patient who believes that she is immature for being angry about termination will have difficulty expressing those angry feelings to the therapist.

In a typical resolution process, the exploration of the rupture experience pathway proceeds to a certain point and then becomes blocked. This is indicated by the patient engaging in coping strategies, defensive verbalizations, and actions that function to avoid or manage the emotions associated with the rupture experience. Examples are changing the topic, speaking in a deadened voice tone, and speaking in general terms, rather than the here-and-now specifics of the therapeutic relationship. The most common facilitative response in such cases is to draw the patient's attention to the defensive or security operations and to probe for inner experience. For example, the therapist might metacommunicate by saying, "It feels to me like you attack and then soften the blow. Do you have any awareness of doing this?" This leads the patient to become aware of his attempts to soften the blow, and then the therapist can ask him to explore the reasons for doing so. Or the therapist might say, "I'm aware of you looking away when you say that. Are you aware of this?" The patient acknowledges that he is, and the therapist then asks him to explore what is going on.

As patients explore their avoidance and gain greater awareness of the processes interfering with their experience and more of a sense of agency or ownership of these processes, feelings associated with the rupture experience naturally begin to emerge more fully. Patients may move back to the rupture experience pathway spontaneously, or therapists may redirect attention to it once again. Typically, a resolution process involves an ongoing alternation between experiencing and avoidance pathways with the exploration of each pathway functioning to facilitate a deepening of the exploration of the other. It is critical during the exploration of both pathways that the therapist respond to whatever the patient expresses in a validating and accepting fashion. Accepting the patient's response during the exploration of the rupture pathway is critical because this challenges the patient's core organizing principles and provides a new, constructive interpersonal experience.

Expressions of patient hostility or anger are often responded to defensively by therapists or with counterhostility. The likelihood of this type of defensive response increases as termination approaches and therapists feel more vulnerable to the possibility of failing. At such time it can be difficult not to feel that one's treatment has been ungrateful, especially if one has invested oneself in the patient and there have been periods when it looked like progress was taking place. Compliant or avoidant responses to the rupture are often responded to with overbearing or domineering behavior. For example, the patient who responds to an interpretation in a compliant fashion may elicit further attempts on the therapist's part to control, dominate, or tell the patient what to do.

In such situations, it is critical for therapists to become aware of their countertransference feelings and to begin metacommunicating with the patient about the interaction rather than continuing to participate in a vicious cycle. For example, a patient nearing termination might question whether treatment has really been beneficial. The therapist responds by trying to demonstrate the ways in which change has occurred. In turn, the patient becomes more negative and pessimistic. In this situation, it is critical for therapists to begin realizing that they are embedded in a vicious cycle and to begin metacommunicating about what is taking place. For example, a therapist might say "We seem to be caught in a struggle in which you try to express your concerns and I try to talk you out of them." She can then go on to explore the patient's experience of the interaction. Or alternatively, she might say something like, "I have a sense that I am responding to your concerns by trying to reassure you, rather than allowing you to really explore and express your concerns more fully."

The final stage (Stage 4) of the resolution process entails the patient accessing primary feelings and asserting underlying wishes or needs directly to the therapist (P4). These may be feelings of anger or sadness. Feelings of sadness and disappointment are often mixed with feelings of gratitude. In some cases the patient may ask if it is possible to extend the treatment. If the therapist, in keeping with the time-limited frame, decides not to extend the treatment, it is still important to recognize the legitimacy of the patient's request.

Conclusion

The growing popularity of short-term psychotherapy has been one of the most prominent developments in the mental health field in recent years. Although there is considerable evidence for the effectiveness of different forms of short-term psychotherapy (Messer & Warren, 1995), it is important not to oversell their benefits. The National Institute of Mental Health (NIMH) Treatment of Depression Collaborative Research Program, for example, showed that at the 18-month follow-up period, only 30% of patients in short-term cognitive therapy and 26% of patients in short-term interpersonal therapy met stringent criteria for recovery (Elkin, 1994). The *Consumer Report* survey on consumer satisfaction with psychotherapy found a substantial advantage to long-term psychotherapy over short-term psychotherapy ("Mental health," 1995).

It is thus important not to regard short-term therapy with a type of simple-minded optimism, in which it appears to be the treatment of choice for all problems, or in which the complexity of human experience and the deep and intractable nature of many types of human suffering are denied. In fact, from our perspective, one of the most important factors in developing and maintaining a therapeutic alliance in short-term psychotherapy is recognizing the difficulty of the human change process and the impossibility of finding simple and definitive solutions to people's problems, while at the same time maintaining a realistically hopeful attitude about the possibility of meaningful change taking place within a short-term framework. In this light, one of the more intriguing findings emerging from research investigating factors associated with the effectiveness of individual therapists in the NIMH collaborative study on the treatment of depression is that therapists (all of whom were conducting short-term treatment) who believed that people take a long time to change were more helpful than those who believed that people could change more quickly (Blatt, Sanislow, Zuroff, & Pilkonis, 1996). Although this finding may appear counterintuitive, it is consistent with an important paradox of psychotherapy: that change is most likely to take place in the context of acceptance. This is particularly important to remember when working within a short-term framework, where the intensified pressure to achieve therapeutic objectives quickly can make it difficult for therapists to accept limitations—both their patients' and their own.

References

Blatt, S. J., Sanislow, C. A., Zuroff, D. C., & Pilkonis, P. A. (1996). Characteristics of effective therapists: Further analyses of data from the NIMH TDCRP. *Journal of Consulting and Clinical Psychology, 64,* 1276–1284.

Elkin, I. (1994). The NIMH Treatment of Depression Collaborative Research Program: Where we began and where we are. In A. E. Bergin & S. L. Garfield (Eds.), *Handbook of psychotherapy and behavior change* (4th ed., pp. 114–139). New York: Wiley.

Mental health: Does therapy work? (1995, November). *Consumer Reports,* 734–739.

Messer, S., & Warren, C. S. (1995). *Models of brief dynamic therapy.* New York: Guilford Press.

Safran, J. D., Crocker, P., McMain, S., & Murray, P. (1990). Therapeutic alliance rupture as a therapy event for empirical investigation. *Psychotherapy, 27,* 154–165.

Safran, J. D., & Muran, J. C. (1995). Resolving therapeutic alliance ruptures: Diversity and integration. *In-Session: Psychotherapy in Practice, 1,* 81–92.

Safran, J. D., & Muran, J. C. (1996). The resolution of ruptures in the therapeutic alliance. *Journal of Consulting and Clinical Psychology, 64,* 447–458.

Safran, J. D., & Muran, J. C. (in press). *Negotiating the therapeutic alliance: A relational treatment manual.* New York: Guilford Press.

Safran, J. D., Muran, J. C., & Samstag, L. (1994). Resolving therapeutic alliance ruptures: A task analytic investigation. In A. O. Horvath & L. S. Greenberg (Eds.), *The working alliance: Theory, research and practice* (pp. 225–255). New York: Wiley.

Index

A

Abandonment issues, in short-term cognitive therapy, 115–116
Acceptance, as group therapeutic factor, 197–198
Accurate empathy, 104–105
Ackerman, N., 178
Al-Darmaki, E., 136
Alexander, F., 4, 10
Allusions, disguised, 50
Altruism, as group therapeutic factor, 198
Arbitrary reinforcement, 72–73
Avoidance, in group therapy, 200–201

B

Beck, A. T., 95, 96
Beck Depression Inventory, 117
Behaviorism, 64, 66
  radical, 66–68
Behavior therapy, 66
Binder, J. L., 220
Bloch, S., 197
Bond, therapeutic, 6–7, 195, 218
Booster sessions, 109–111
Bordin, E. S., 6, 7, 9, 15, 43, 123
Bowen, M., 176, 177
Brief psychotherapy. *See also under specific therapies*
  drive–conflict models of, 16–20
  and functional analytic psychotherapy, 85–88
  therapeutic alliance in, 9–10
Brief Therapy Center, 147–148, 155
Buber, Martin, x, 127
Budman, S. H., 198–199
Burke, K., 153
Burns, D., 118

C

Causes, in radical behaviorism, 69
CCRT. *See* Core conflictual relationship theme
Clients' expressive stance measure, 131
Clinically relevant behaviors (CRBs), 65, 69–74, 78, 80, 81, 82, 85–87
  client improvements, occurring in sessions, 69
  client interpretations of behavior, 69–70
  client problems, occurring in sessions, 69
  evoking, 71–72
  providing interpretations of variables affecting, 73–74
  reinforcing effects of therapist behavior in relation to, 73
  reinforcing improvements in, 72–73
  watching for, 70–71
CMP (cyclical maladaptive pattern), 42
Coaching, by therapist, 98, 177–178
Cognitive-behavior therapy, 66
Cognitive therapy, short-term, 95–119
  abandonment issues in, 115–116
  autonomy/control issues in, 113
  booster sessions in, 109–111
  conceptualization of therapeutic relationship in, 97–103
  conveying positive regard/hope in, 107
  establishment of alliance in, 104–106
  maintenance of therapeutic alliance in, 106–111
  as model, 101–103
  overwhelming patient with activity/optimism in, 111–112
  and patient's beliefs about relationships, 99–101
  "readiness" of patients in, 113–114

recordkeeping in, 108–109
roles of therapist and patient in, 98–99
ruptures of therapeutic alliance in, 111–119
tapering schedules in, 110
therapist's responsibility in, 107–108
Cognitive Therapy Rating Scale, 111
Cohesion, group, 195–196, 198–199, 204–207
Collaborative empiricism, 97
Conceptualization of therapeutic alliance, 7–9
in functional analytic psychotherapy, 74–75
in psychodynamic therapies, 43–46
in short-term cognitive therapy, 97–103
in time-limited group psychotherapy, 194–195
Conflict, in group therapy, 199–200
Contextualism, 67
Control issues, 219–220
in brief strategic therapy, 162–164
in process–experiential therapy, 138–140
in short-term cognitive therapy, 113
Core conflictual relationship theme (CCRT), 40–41, 50, 56–57
Countertransference, 34–35, 44, 67
Couples/family therapy, brief, 171–189
case examples of therapeutic alliance in, 180–188
difficulties with therapeutic alliance in, 179–180
direct approach, with couple, 186–188
indirect approach, with family, 181–186
multiple alliances in, 173–175
position of therapist in, 177–179
system influence in, 176–177
triangles in, 175–176
Coyne, J. C., 152, 156
CRBs. *See* Clinically relevant behaviors
Crouch, E. C., 197
Current-figure–past-figure–therapist linkages, 25
Cyclical maladaptive pattern (CMP), 42

D
Davanloo, H., 15, 17, 19–23, 25–29, 33–35
Davanloo model. *See* Short-Term Dynamic Psychotherapy
Debriefings, in group therapy, 207–208
"Denial-numbing," 54
Depression, 160–161
de Shazer, S., 149
Deutsche, F., 10
Disguised allusions, 50
Drive–conflict models of psychotherapy
technique in, 16–19
working alliance in, 19–20

DTR. *See* Dysfunctional Thought Record
Dyads, 175
Dysfunctional Thought Record (DTR), 117–118

E
Edbril, S. D., 101
Efron, D., 155
Ego-psychological tradition, 4
Empathy
interpersonal, 49
simple vs. accurate, 104–105
Engagement, in group therapy, 199, 201–202
Establishment of therapeutic alliance
in brief psychodynamic therapies, 48–49
in time-limited group psychotherapy, 204–213
Experiential therapies. *See* Humanisitic/experiential therapies, short-term

F
Family systems, 176
Family therapy. *See* Couples/family therapy, brief
FAP. *See* Functional analytic psychotherapy
Feedback
in brief strategic therapy, 165
in short-term cognitive therapy, 111
in time-limited group psychotherapy, 210–211
Feeling Good (D. Burns), 118
Ferenczi, S., 3–4, 10
Financial constraints, 97
Fisch, Richard, 148, 161, 163
Fishman, C., 171, 173
Focus, therapeutic, 219
in brief strategic therapy, 154–155
in process–experiential therapy, 132–136
in time-limited group psychotherapy, 205–206, 208–212
Follow-up sessions, 213
Freud, S., 3, 9, 28
Functional analysis, 67
Functional analytic psychotherapy (FAP), 65–89
analysis of therapeutic alliance from perspective of, 77–78
clinically relevant client behaviors in, 69–70
conceptualization of therapeutic alliance in, 74–75
definition of, 65
and empirically based treatments, 82–84
five rules of, 70–74
focus of, 66
importance of therapeutic alliance in, 79–82
principles of, 68
and radical behaviorism, 66–68
and time-limited psychotherapy, 84–87

G

Gaston, L., 15
GCQ–S. *See* Group Climate Questionnaire—
    Short Form
Gestalt therapy, 126–128, 138, 139
Goals, therapeutic, 6, 218–219
    in brief strategic therapy, 152, 155
    limiting, 140
    reminders of, in brief psychotherapy, 21–22
Greenberg, Jay, 51
Greenberg, L. S., 131, 132–133
Greenson, R., 5, 19
Group Climate Questionnaire—Short Form
    (GCQ–S), 199–204
Group Cohesiveness Scale, 198–199
Group psychotherapy, time-limited,
    193–214
    conceptualization of therapeutic alliance
        in, 194–195
    creation/maintenance of therapeutic
        alliance in, 204–213
    developmental sequence in, 201–204
    differentiation stage in, 202
    early group strategies, 206–210
    engagement stage in, 201–202
    and group cohesion, 195–196
    group therapeutic factors in, 196–198
    interactional work stage in, 203
    measurement of therapeutic alliance in,
        198–201
    midgroup strategies, 210–212
    pregroup strategies, 205–206
    termination stage in, 203–204
    termination strategies, 212–213
Group therapeutic factors, 196–198

H

Haley, J., 171, 175
Henry, W. P., 44
Horowitz, Mardi, 39
Humanisitic/experiential therapies, short-
    term, 123–141
    Gestalt therapy, 126–127
    person-centered therapy, 124–126
    process–experiential therapy, 128–140

I

Interpersonal empathy, 49

J

Jackson, Don, 148
Joining, therapeutic, 174

K

Kiesler, D. J., 49
Kivlighan, D., 136
Kohlenberg, R. J., 65, 70–74, 79–80, 87

L

Levenson, Edgar, 55
Luborsky, Lester, 39

M

MacKenzie, K. R., 197–198
Maintenance of therapeutic alliance
    in brief psychoanalytic psychotherapies,
        20–31
    in brief psychodynamic therapies, 50–51
    in short-term cognitive therapy, 106–111
    in time-limited group psychotherapy,
        204–213
Malan, D. H., 15, 17
Mann, J., 23
Mental Research Institute (MRI), 147–149,
    155
Mentoring, by therapists, 98
Messer, S. B., 39
Metacommunication, 57–58, 139, 185,
    226–228
Milan systemic approach, 177
Minuchin, S., 171, 173, 178
Monitoring, in brief psychotherapy
    of patient's potential to defeat treatment,
        27–31
    of therapeutic omnipotence/patient
        compliance, 26–27
    of working alliance, 25–26
MRI. *See* Mental Research Institute
Multiple alliances
    awareness of, 221–222
    in brief couples/family therapy, 173–175
Muran, J. C., 51, 52, 76–77

N

Nacht, S., 161
Narrative therapy, 178–179
Natural reinforcement, 72
Negative feelings, 125
Negative transference, 3
NIMH Treatment of Depression Collaborative
    Research Program, 228–229

O

Object relations, 4
One-down position, 148, 162–164
Open-ended questions, 102

P

Patient compliance, 26–27
Patient selection, 217–218
Person-centered therapy, 124–126, 138
PFM. *See* Plan formulation method
Pizer, S. A., 9
Plan formulation method (PFM) therapy, 39,
    41–42, 44–50, 50, 52, 54, 55

Positive transference, 3
Problem-maintaining solutions, 151–152, 154, 160–162, 220
Process–experiential therapy, 128–140
  agreement on tasks in, 136–138
  directiveness vs. responsiveness in, 138–140
  establishment of focus in, 132–136
  limitation of goals of, 140
  safe working environment for, 130–132
Psychoanalytic psychotherapies, brief, 15–36
  drive–conflict models of vs. standard psychoanalysis, 16–20
  monitoring effects of working alliance in, 25–26
  parameters affecting working alliance in, 20–31
  patient's potential to defeat treatment in, 27–31
  reminder of time constraints in, 23–25
  repetitive clarification in, 21–22
  repetitive framing in, 22–23
  therapeutic misalliances/ruptures in, 31–35
  therapeutic omnipotence/patient compliance in, 26–27
Psychodynamic therapies, time-limited, 39–59, 81–83
  brevity and therapeutic alliance in, 46–48
  conceptualizations of therapeutic alliance in, 43–46
  establishment of therapeutic alliance in, 48–49
  maintenance of therapeutic alliance in, 50–51
  ruptures of therapeutic alliance in, 51–58
Psychopathology, 40, 42

R
Racamier, P. C., 161
Radical behaviorism, 66–68
Rank, O., 10
Rationale, therapeutic, 218
"Readiness" of patients, in short-term cognitive therapy, 113–114
Real relationship, 5, 75
Reframing, 152–153, 156–157, 165
Reinforcement, arbitrary vs. natural, 72–73
Relationship conditions, 123–124
Relationships, patient's beliefs about, in short-term cognitive therapy, 99–101
Rice, L. N., 130–131
Rogers, C. R., 6, 124–126
Role models, therapists as, 98–99
Ruptures in therapeutic alliance, 8–9, 76–77, 220–221, 223–228
  in brief couples/family therapy, 179–180
  in brief psychoanalytic psychotherapies, 31–35
  confrontation, 223–228
  in psychodynamic therapies, 51–58
  resolution, 223–228
  in short-term cognitive therapy, 111–119
  withdrawal, 223–228

S
Safe working environment, in process–experiential therapy, 130–132
Safran, J. D., 51, 52, 76–77, 179
SAS. *See* Sociotropy-Autonomy Scale
Satir, V., 177
S–E dynamic therapy. See Supportive–expressive psychoanalytic treatment
Short-Term Dynamic Psychotherapy (Davanloo model), 16, 17, 19–23, 25–29, 31, 34–35
Short-term psychotherapy. *See* Brief psychotherapy
Sifneos, P. E., 15, 19–20, 21, 33, 34
Sifneos model of brief therapy, 16, 19–20
Simple empathy, 104–105
Skinner, B. F., 67
Social skills training, 206
Sociotropy-Autonomy Scale (SAS), 105–106
Solution-focused therapy, 149
SRS brief therapy, 41, 44–48, 50, 51, 54, 56
Sterba, R., 4
Stern, S., 101
Stimulus generalization, 80–81
Stolorow, R., 8
Strategic therapy, brief, 147–167
  avoiding others' problem-maintaining solutions in, 160–162
  basic assumptions of, 151–154
  conduct of, 154–159
  and imbalance in client–therapist relationship, 162–164
  irony/paradox in, 164–166
  therapeutic alliance in, 148–151, 159–166
Structured role relationships, 40
Strupp, H. H., 39, 43–45, 77
Strupp, Hans, 39
Sullivan, Harry Stack, 148
Supportive–expressive psychoanalytic treatment (S–E dynamic therapy), 39–41, 43, 45, 47–48, 51, 54, 56
Systems, family, 176

T
Tapering schedules, 110
Tasks, therapeutic, 6
  agreement on, in process–experiential therapy, 136–138
  assignment of, in brief strategic therapy, 163–165

T–C–P (therapist–current-figure–past-figure) linkages, 17
Termination
    preparing patients for, 222–223
    of time-limited group psychotherapy, 203–204, 212–213
Therapeutic alliance, 217–229. *See also under specific headings, e.g.*, Conceptualization of therapeutic alliance
    and activity/receptivity balance, 219–220
    and avoidance of problem-maintaining solutions, 220
    in brief psychotherapy, 9–10
    dimensions of, 15
    in drive–conflict models of brief psychotherapy, 19–20
    and establishment of goals, 218–219
    facilitating bond aspect of, 218
    and focus, 219
    historical views on, 3–7, 63–64
    multiple alliances, 221–222
    and outlining of therapeutic rationale, 218
    and patient selection, 217–218
    and preparation for termination, 222–223
    ruptures in, 220–221, 223–228
    and task clarification, 219
    therapeutic relationship vs. in short-term cognitive therapy, 104
Therapeutic bond, 6–7, 195, 218
Therapeutic joining, 174
Therapeutic omnipotence, 26–27
Therapist–current-figure–past-figure (T–C–P) linkages, 17
Time constraints
    in psychodynamic therapies, 46–48
    reminders of, in brief psychotherapy, 23–25

Time-limited dynamic psychotherapy (TLDP), 39, 40, 42, 44–47, 49–52, 55–58
Time limits, 10
TLDP. *See* Time-limited dynamic psychotherapy
Transference, 3, 5, 19–20, 25–29, 31–35, 44, 80–81
Treatment of Depression Collaborative Research Program, 85
Triangles in couples/family therapy, brief, 175–176
Tsai, M., 65, 70–74, 79–80, 87

U
Universality, as group therapeutic factor, 197

V
Veenendaal, K., 155
Vocal quality, 130–131

W
Wagstaff, A., 130–131
Wanless, J., 197
Warren, C. S., 39
Watson, J. C., 131, 132–133
Watzlawick, P. W., 161
Weakland, J. H., 147, 161, 167
Weiss, Joseph, 39
Whitaker, C., 177–178, 179
Withdrawals, patient, 223
Working alliance, 5, 19–20, 75. *See also* Therapeutic alliance
Working Alliance Inventory, 132
Working conditions, 123–124
Working models, 40

Z
Zetzel, E., 4

About the Editors

Jeremy D. Safran is Professor of Psychology at the New School for Social Research in New York City and Senior Research Scientist at Beth Israel Medical Center in New York City. He was previously Director of Clinical Psychology at the New School. Dr. Safran is author of *Widening the Scope of Cognitive Therapy*, coauthor of *Emotion in Psychotherapy* (with Leslie Greenberg), of *Interpersonal Process in Cognitive Therapy* (with Zindel Segal), and of the forthcoming *Negotiating the Therapeutic Alliance: A Relational Treatment Manual* (with J. Christopher Muran). He is also coeditor of *Emotion, Psychotherapy and Change* (with Leslie Greenberg). He has published extensively on the therapeutic relationship and on psychotherapy process and is on the editorial boards of four professional journals. He also maintains a private practice in New York City.

J. Christopher Muran is Chief Psychologist and Director of the Brief Psychotherapy Research Program at Beth Israel Medical Center in New York City, where he maintains a private practice. He is also on faculty at Albert Einstein College of Medicine in New York City. He completed a postdoctoral fellowship in Cognitive-Behavior Therapy at the Clarke Institute of Psychiatry, University of Toronto, Ontario, Canada, and psychoanalytic training in the New York University Postdoctoral Program. Dr. Muran was the recipient of the 1997 Early Career Award from the Society for Psychotherapy Research and is an advisory editor for its journal. He has published extensively on psychotherapy process, specifically on self-changes and the therapeutic relationship. He is coauthor of the forthcoming *Negotiating the Therapeutic Alliance: A Relational Treatment Manual* (with Jeremy D. Safran).